Wanderings

Anthropology of Contemporary Issues

A Series Edited by Roger Sanjek

A full list of titles in the series appears at the end of this book.

Wanderings

Sudanese Migrants and Exiles in North America

ROGAIA MUSTAFA ABUSHARAF

CORNELL UNIVERSITY PRESS

Ithaca & London

First published 2002 by Cornell University Press
First printing, Cornell paperbacks, 2002.

Printed in the United States of America

   Library of Congress Cataloging-in-Publication Data
Abusharaf, Rogaia Mustafa.
   Wanderings: Sudanese migrants and exiles in North America / Rogaia Mustafa
Abusharaf.
      p. cm. — (The anthropology of contemporary issues)
Includes bibliographical references and index.
   ISBN 0-8014-4018-1 (cloth : alk. paper) — ISBN 0-8014-8779-X (pbk. :
alk. paper)
   1. Sudanese—Unites States. 2. Sudanese—Canada. 3.
Sudan—Emigration and immigration—Case studies. 4. United
States—Emigration and immigration—Case studies. 5. Canada—Emigration
and immigration—Case studies. I. Title. II. Series.
   E184.S77 A28 2002
   305.892'762407—dc21

                                                      2002002915

Cornell University Press strives to use environmentally responsible suppliers and materials to the fullest extent possible in the publishing of its books. Such materials include vegetable-based, low-VOC inks and acid-free papers that are recycled, totally chlorine-free, or partly composed of non-wood fibers. For further information, visit our website at www.cornellpress.cornell.edu.

Cloth printing   10 9 8 7 6 5 4 3 2 1
Paperback printing   10 9 8 7 6 5 4 3 2 1

Contents

Author's Note

To protect the privacy of informants, in this ethnography I have changed all personal names, drawing from a pool of common Sudanese names. All quotations from letters, newspaper articles, and interviews—except for those with some southern Sudanese migrants and refugees—were translated by me from Arabic.

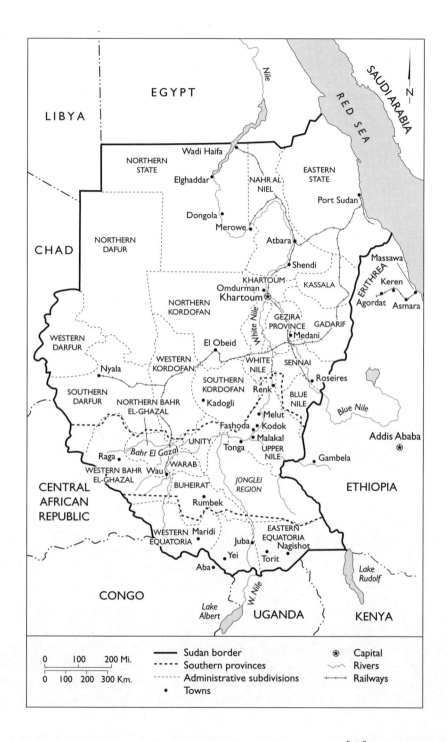

LIBYA

EGYPT

SAUDI ARABIA

RED SEA

Nile

CHAD

NORTHERN STATE

Wadi Haifa

Elghaddar

NAHR AL NIEL

EASTERN STATE

Port Sudan

Dongola

Merowe

Atbara

Shendi

NORTHERN DAFUR

NORTHERN KORDOFAN

KHARTOUM

Omdurman

Khartoum

KASSALA

ERITHREA

Massawa

Keren

Agordat

Asmara

GEZIRA PROVINCE

GADARIF

White Nile

WESTERN DARFUR

Nyala

WESTERN KORDOFAN

El Obeid

Medani

WHITE NILE

SENNAI

SOUTHERN DARFUR

SOUTHERN KORDOFAN

Renk

Roseires

BLUE NILE

Blue Nile

NORTHERN BAHR EL-GHAZAL

Kadogli

Melut

Fashoda

Kodok

Malakal

Addis Ababa

Raga

Bahr El Gazal

UNITY

Tonga

UPPER NILE

Gambela

WESTERN BAHR EL-GHAZAL

Wau

WARAB

BUHEIRAT

JONGLEI REGION

ETHIOPIA

CENTRAL AFRICAN REPUBLIC

Rumbek

WESTERN EQUATORIA

Maridi

EASTERN EQUATORIA

Juba

Nagishot

Lake Rudolf

Yei

Torit

Aba

CONGO

Lake Albert

W. Nile

UGANDA

KENYA

0 100 200 Mi.	—— Sudan border
0 100 200 300 Km.	- - - Southern provinces
	····· Administrative subdivisions
• Towns	

⊛ Capital

〰 Rivers

┼┼┼ Railways

[vii]

Acknowledgments

In writing this book I have incurred many debts. I had the honor of working with Roger Sanjek, editor of "The Anthropology of Contemporary Issues" series, who read this manuscript attentively and offered countless constructive suggestions. I wish to express my gratitude for his enthusiasm and support. I owe a great debt to Hugh Blumenfeld, a poet, who read the manuscript and gave me excellent suggestions and editorial comments, and to Bruce Acker for a superb job of copyediting the book. Thanks are due to James Faris, my mentor and best advocate. Many thanks also go to Cornell acquisitions editor Fran Benson, who has been a delight to work with. Her enthusiasm and unfailing intelligence are greatly appreciated. Two anonymous reviewers for Cornell University Press gave me helpful comments, for which I am also greatly appreciative.

I am extremely grateful to my father, Mustafa Abusharaf, who introduced me to the early Sudanese Bahhara community in Brooklyn, New York, and helped me locate the archives of Sati Majid, the first Sudanese to set foot on U.S. soil. I would like to acknowledge the invaluable assistance of Abd El-Hamid Mohamed Ahmed, Mohamed Ibrahim Abu Salim, and the staff of the National Record Office in Khartoum, the Sudan.

Other people in the United States, Canada, and the Sudan offered inestimable help and at different stages came to my aid: I want to acknowledge Mohamed Hussein, Eltayeb Elsalawi, Ahmed Albashir El Amin, Malik Balla, Fadil Hashimi, Mansour Hassan, Bernard Magubane, Scott Cook, Amir Zahir, Amir Mousa, Bakri Abdel Majid, Hassan Salih, Victoria Betali, Mohamed Baker, Muaz Atta Alsid, Adila Abusharaf, Moiz Eljamri Abu Noura, Obanik Hino, Mohsin Farid, Mona Hussein, Hala Hussein, Reginald Appleyard, El-Fatih Erwa, Dennison Nash, Amin Abd El-Samad, Farid Hassan, Father Filsouth Faraj, Kamal Eissa, Awad Baballah, Peter Agree, Senator Christopher Dodd, Richard Vengroff, Rosalind Shaw, Sharon Stanton Russell, Donald Spivey, Rose Lovelace, Fatima Osman, Angela Raven-Roberts, Dick and Carol Steuart, and Peter Ta-drous. Last but not least I would like to thank the people of Sudan, and the Sudanese migrant communities whose hospitality allowed me to write about the most private aspects of their lives.

I have benefited from discussions with students, friends, and colleagues during presentations I gave at Tufts, Brown, Georgetown, MIT, and the University of California at Berkeley-Stanford African Studies workshop. Portions of this book previously appeared in *Arab Studies Quarterly* and *International Migration*. I am thankful for permissions to reprint from the International Organization of Migration in Geneva, Switzerland. Last but not least, I would like to acknowledge the unwavering support of my extended family, at home and in exile, to whom this book is dedicated.

R.M.A.

An Airport Scene
Khartoum, the Sudan—January 17, 1997

It has been a long, tiring day, a day of saying many good-byes to neighbors and friends whom I had not seen for years. They have come from Omdurman and Khartoum bringing me gifts of spices, sandalwood incense, dried dates, and Sudanese ornaments made of pottery, ivory, and beads. Many apologize for not bringing more, for, as I know, the situation is very difficult for most of them. Having finally said goodbye to my father, I head to Khartoum Airport to catch the plane for Frankfurt en route to Boston. Hassan, the car driver, Kamal Eissa, a friend, and Fatima Mahgoub Osman, my mother, accompany me. We talk about how quickly the days have passed and how quickly my visit to the Sudan has come to a close. I promise I will do my best to come back next year for a longer stay. As I enter the terminal, the airport carrier approaches me.

"What airline?"

"Lufthansa."

He loads my bags in his cart and off he goes. Several young Sudanese men stand close by, some in their traditional long-robed Sudanese dress (*jallalib*) and hats (*twagi*), others in safari suits. As the carrier leaves, they too approach.

"*Ya okhot aan iznik* (Excuse us, Sister)."

I stop.

One asks if I might do them a favor. I ask what it might be, and he begins to explain that they are looking for someone to mail application forms for the Diversity Visa Lottery Program—a chance to come to the United States. A second man explains that they would send them through regular mail but these forms are often ripped up and confiscated by postal workers.

"They are told to do so," another adds.

I agree to their request. The joy and appreciation of these young men is immense.

"If we get the green card, we will repay your favor," the first one says jokingly.

I say goodbye and wish them luck.

Now, as I say goodbye to my mother, I think that no matter how eloquent I might be, I would never be able to convey to those young men—so eager to leave—the anguish and emptiness I feel as I am leaving. For when I left the Sudan thirteen years ago for America, the country was still under democratic rule and my departure was voluntary, strictly for the pursuit of a graduate education. Now, the situation is vastly different. The sense of urgency for people to leave is overwhelming. In the eyes of these young men, and hundreds of thousands like them who wish to leave, anything is better than staying in the Sudan.

I head toward the boarding gate. My mother and others wave to me as I catch a last glimpse of them. I feel homesick already. I am still thinking of the people who desperately want to leave: of the crowds in front of the American Embassy in downtown Khartoum on Ali Abd El-Latif Avenue hoping for a chance to get an appointment to apply. Many wait for days, months, and years for the opportunity to be granted an entry visa into the United States. Many others, like the young men I met, apply for the lottery visa, but only a few of them are lucky enough to be selected for a permanent residency permit in the United States.

Coming to the United States is a perennial dream for would-be emigrants everywhere, but for many Sudanese today, it is a dream they will sacrifice everything to fulfill.

Wanderings

Introduction

Departing

It was, gentlemen, after a long absence, seven years to be exact, during which time I was studying in Europe—that I returned to my people. I learnt much and much passed me by—but that is another story. The important thing is that I returned with a great yearning for my people in that village at the bend of the Nile. For seven years I had longed for them, had dreamed of them, and it was an extraordinary moment when I at last found myself standing amongst them. They rejoiced at having me back and made a great fuss, and it was not long before I felt as though a piece of ice were melting inside of me, as though I were some frozen substance on which the sun had shone—that life warmth of the tribe which I had lost for a time in a land "whose fishes die of the cold." My ears had become used to their voices; my eyes grown accustomed to their forms. Because of having thought so much about them during my absence, something rather like fog rose up between them and me the first instant I saw them. But the fog cleared and I awoke, on the second day of my arrival, in my familiar bed in the room whose walls had witnessed the trivial incidents of my life in childhood and the onset of adolescence. I listened intently to the wind: that indeed was a sound well known to me, a sound which in our village possessed a merry whispering—the sound of the wind passing through palm trees is different from when it passes through fields of corn. I heard the cooing of the turtledove, and I looked through the window at the palm tree standing in a courtyard of our house and I knew that all was still well with life. I looked at its strong straight trunk, at its roots that strike down into the ground, at the green branches hanging down loosely over its top, and I experienced a feeling of assurance. I felt not like a storm-swept feather but like that palm tree, a being with a background, with roots, with a purpose.

—Tayeb Salih, *Season of Migration to the North*, 1979

This book describes a new "season of migration to the north," to borrow Sudanese novelist Tayeb Salih's title. It documents the lives and migratory experiences in North America of a people whose homeland has inspired some of the most influential works in the discipline of anthropology. There is no doubt that it is through the initiative of Edward Evans-Pritchard, James Faris, and Talal Asad that the Sudan became an archetypal area for ethnographic projects. For example, based on his earlier expedition to Darfunj, Zandeland, and then to Nuerland, Evans-Pritchard's work raised critical issues regarding the relation of colonial ethnographers to their politically oppressed subjects and regarding the effect of their work on the production of ethnographic knowledge. Asad's work on the structure of the nomadic society of the Kababish Arabs became a classic of social anthropology because it provided a sophisticated analysis of how power is exercised in stateless, segmented societies. Faris's insights into the personal art of the Nuba—how they use their bodies and bodily art to express social relations—has been widely cited in studies on the intersection of politics and aesthetics. Regardless of the widely varying epistemological and political convictions of each, together these ethnographers, along with several others, have put the Sudan on the map of anthropological inquiry (e.g., Adams 1984; Al-Shahi 1986; Asad 1970; Boddy 1989; Cunnison 1966; Evans-Pritchard 1940, 1956, 1974, 1976; Faris 1972, 1989; Harries-Jones 1972; Holy 1991; A. Ibrahim 1994; James 1979; Kenyon 1991; Lienhardt 1961, 1967; MacMichael 1912, Mohamed 1980; Nadel 1947; and Seligman 1932).

The Sudan, which is the largest country in Africa, remains generally obscure to most people in North America. Yet its place in world history is of prime importance. Not only was the Sudan cradle to ancient civilizations, including the Nubian and the Meroetic, the heretofore ignored diaspora of its peoples in modern times has put its mark on the history and culture of the New World.

The Sudanese presence in the Western Hemisphere dates to 1863, when the Black Sudanese Muslim Conscript Battalion crossed the Atlantic en route to Veracruz, Mexico, in response to Emperor Napoleon's request for troops in his war against Mexico. As Richard Hill and Peter Hogg describe *The Black Corps D'Elite,*

Secretly, on the night of 7–8 January 1863, an under-strength battalion of 446 officers and men with one civilian interpreter sailed from Alexandria, Egypt in a French troopship for service with the French expeditionary force in Mexico. They were being dispatched by the ruler of Egypt at the urgent request of Emperor Napoleon III to replace French troops who were dying of yellow fever in unacceptable numbers in France's ill-fated 1863–1867 campaign to establish an imperial presence in Mexico. Most of the Sudanese troops had

been forcibly acquired by the Egyptian government, which avoided the stigma
of slavery by emancipating them at enlistment and holding them as military
conscripts for the rest of their working lives. (1995, ix)

These Sudanese who "fought so gallantly in Mexico were in a sense pawns
in a Euro-American imperial conflict. But they were not demeaned by it.
Their story not only highlights some of the differing perceptions that prevailed about the institution of slavery—Egyptian, French, American—it
also shows how the men themselves transcended their narrow lot" (Hill and
Hogg 1995, 3).

Members of the battalion who survived the war were received by
Napoleon as "guests of the Emperor" in Paris on their voyage back to
Egypt. Many were promoted to higher ranks in Alexandria, where the majority remained for the rest of their lives. However, some of their descendants, themselves army officers, returned to the Sudan and settled in Hai El
Doubatt (Army Officers' Neighborhood) in El Morada, Omdurman (see
also Saikinga 2000).

In the first decades of the twentieth century, Sati Majid, a Dongolawi,
converted 45,000 African Americans to Islam and had major early influence
on the country's African American Muslim movement. Then during World
War II, Dongolawi sailors recruited in Brooklyn earned honors in the U.S.
Navy as wartime servicemen. In the late 1950s Ahmed Abdul-Malik, the
brilliant bass, cello, and oud player, worked with jazz legends Thelonius
Monk, John Coltrane, and Randy Weston, and made his own recordings, including *Jazz Sahara* (Riverside Records 1958) and *East Meets West* (RCA
Victor 1959) (see Cook and Morton 1992). More recent Sudanese immigrants include, Manut Bol, the seven-foot, seven-inch National Basketball
Association center, and Alek Wek, the Dinka woman who has become an acclaimed fashion model.

Previous studies on Sudanese international migration have been concerned only with migration to Egypt and the oil-rich Arab countries (i.e.,
Kuwait, Saudi Arabia, United Arab Emirates, Libya, Qatar, and Iraq). This
book focuses on the more recent phenomenon of Sudanese migration to
North America. It attempts to penetrate the contextual web of politics, history, and religion to explore these new migration patterns that are associated with, and emanate from, the social organization of Sudanese peoples. I
explore questions such as: Who migrates? Why do members of different
groups migrate? And how do they lead their lives after their settlement in
the new society? I will argue that this new migration is a unique phenomenon. For unlike border crossing to Kenya, Uganda, or Zaire, which is dominated by war-ravaged southern Sudanese, or to the Persian Gulf states,
which are dominated by Arabic-speaking Muslim northerners, North

[3]

American migration represents a cross-section of Sudanese society from almost every ethnicity, region, and religion. These migrants are young and old, Christians and Muslims, voluntary migrants and exiles. For the first time in the history of Sudanese population mobility, we witness a movement that is as diverse as the country itself.

My theoretical approach for understanding these questions is drawn from a combination of macrostructural and microindividual perspectives. The first set of theories treats migration as a process generated by large-scale structural inequalities around the world and within nation-states (e.g., Amin 1974, 1995; Berger 1975; Castles and Kosack 1973; Massey 1987; and Zolberg 1989). These theories help position Sudanese migration in its appropriate geopolitical and ethnohistorical context. By illuminating the larger context, the book attempts to give some insight into a movement of people migrating—or fleeing—under different circumstances and encountering new challenges as they navigate their way across what are to them uncharted waters in North America.

The microindividual perspective, on the other hand, is useful for examining the particular socioeconomic and demographic attributes of the migrants and exiles (see Gold 1992; Heisler 1992; Lee 1966; Nigem 1986; Ogden 1984; Richey 1976; Todaro 1976). Guided by my conviction that individual agency is critical in the migration process, I have paid attention to attributes like age, gender, religion, ethnicity, and class and listened to the migration stories of hundreds of Sudanese. This examination not only sheds light on the human capital of the migratory process but also probes in depth the question of why some people move while others under similar circumstances stay put.

The Sending Society: Polity and Identity

In his seminal book *Resources of Hope*, Raymond Williams writes:

Every human society has its own shape, its own purpose, and its own meanings. Every human society expresses these in institutions and in arts and learning. The making of a society is the finding of common meanings and directions and its growth is an active debate and amendment under the pressures of experiences, contact, and discovery, writing themselves into the land. (1989, 4)

The Sudanese land and its location at the crossroads of Africa have influenced the course of its politics and history, and the Sudanese people have ardently developed multilayered identities across it. The characteristics of the land have influenced the life and social organization of its inhabitants, defining in a dramatic way the socioeconomic and political organization of the people, even when they are separated from it.

In 1993, an estimated 25 million Sudanese lived in a total area of 2.5 million square kilometers: the largest country in Africa and the Middle East. As a result of the geographical and historical heritage of the land, the Sudan straddles Africa and the Middle East, thus consolidating its place in history as a meeting point of Arab and sub-Saharan worlds.

Although characterized by a high degree of heterogeneity in ethnic identification and cultural outlook, the people of the Sudan are often classified into binary social categories on the basis of geography (north versus south), ethnicity (Arabs versus Africans), and religion (Muslims versus Christians). Nevertheless, the impressive array of ethnolinguistic and religious groups that inhabits this vast territory—including the Hadandwa, Mahas, Nuer, Danagla, Dinka, Shiluk, Nuba, Rubatab, Rikabia, Shayqia, Murle, Kababish, Manasir, Azande, Jaleen, Bori, Shuli, Joar, Anwak, Latuka, Beja, and others too numerous to list—do not necessarily fall into this opposition.

Despite this remarkable variation, many people hasten to demarcate a line between the north and the south. One reason is that the northern Sudan is, to a great extent, Arabized in cultural traits, identity, and political alignment. Historians of the Sudan attribute the twin processes of Arabization and Islamization to immigrants coming to the Sudan from the Arabian Peninsula, Egypt, and the Maghreb. A complex mix of conquest, migration, religious conversion, and miscegenation define the identity of the northern Sudanese as Arab. According to Ali Mazrui, two parallel processes of social transformation swept the country in the course of Arab expansionism: "one linguistic and cultural, by which the people of the land acquired Arabic as their language and certain Islamic cultural conceptions and became connected with the Arab tribal system; and the other racial, by which the incoming Arab stock was absorbed in varying degrees, so that today a modicum of Arab blood flows in their veins" (1973, 47).

As Mudathir Abdel Rahim points out, Arab immigrants' intermarriage with local populations facilitated the incorporation of the immigrants and the spread of their culture and religion in Sudanese society. This process subsequently gave them greater powers and political participation (1973, 31). Arabic is the lingua franca and Sunni Islam the religion professed by 70 percent of the Sudanese people. Arabic is also spoken by a Christian minority, the Copts.

Prior to Sudan's colonization by the British in 1898, two major types of migration had occurred. The first was the settlement of Sudanese men who traveled to Mecca for religious purposes but decided to remain after performing the pilgrimage rite—the Hajj. Although very little is known about this type of migration (known as *mujawara*, which marks a permanent set-

[5]

tlement in the Muslim holy lands), Sudanese migrants are believed to have
been permitted full citizenship in Saudi Arabia (Osman et al. 1996). The
second type of early migration was by the Nubians of the far north Nile Valley to Egypt, which will be discussed in some detail below. Apart from these
two examples, substantial out-migrations from the Sudan were few (G.
Eissa 1986; A.A. Eltayeb 1985; Galal el Din 1988; Mahmoud 1983; and
Osman et al. 1996), and Sudanese have tended to remain within their national borders. According to a document prepared by the Arab League Educational and Cultural Organization in 1960, the Sudan was at the bottom
of the list of Arab labor-exporting countries (Eltayeb 1985).

Since independence in 1956, however, political turmoil has been a permanent aspect of Sudanese sociopolitical life (Khalid 1989). The country
has experienced both civilian and military government since 1956. Parlia-
mentary governments were forced out by coups, and military dictatorships
have ruled for nearly thirty-one of the forty-five years from 1956 to 2001.
Since 1969, when the government of Gaafar Nemeiri seized power in a military coup, the policies of this and successive governments prompted large-
scale migrations. Since the 1970s the country has witnessed deteriorating
economic conditions precipitated by political decline and disruption from
the on-again, off-again civil war between the north and the south (Ali 1985;
Bechtold 1992; Deng 1995; Roy 1989; Voll 1992).

The military regime that seized control of government on June 30, 1989,
with its strong links to the National Islamic Front, overthrew the last
elected government of Sadiq El Mahdi, announced that the army had "put
an end to the chaos prevailing in the country," and dissolved all political institutions (Voll 1990, 153). The regime's strict application of Islamic law was
undertaken under the ideological slogan "defending the faith, rectifying
morality, and ending corruption." Moreover, other measures seen as limiting individual liberties were implemented: all articles of state law which
suppress civil rights, including freedom of speech, freedom of assembly and
trade unions, and the right to strike, have been rewritten into the criminal
code and the code of criminal procedure.

As a result of war, political and economic collapse, and the adoption of Islamic sharia law, massive movements of the Sudanese populace have taken
place to the extent that the country has recently become the largest exporter of migrants in Northeast Africa (Drumtra 1999; Galal el Din 1988).
Jeff Drumtra of the United States Committee for Refugees asserts that 4
million southern Sudanese are internally displaced and 350,000 are
refugees in the neighboring African countries of Kenya and Ethiopia. Furthermore, according to Drumtra, "Sudan's death toll is larger than the fatal-
ities suffered in current and recent conflicts in Bosnia, Kosovo, Afghanistan,
Chechnya, Somalia, and Algeria combined. Twice as many Sudanese have

died in the past 15 years than all the war-related deaths suffered by Americans in the more than 200-year history of the United States" (1999, 1). This death toll is made up principally of southerners. In Egypt, the size of the Sudanese refugee community, consisting of both northern and southern Sudanese, is estimated at five million. These migrants are recognized by the international community as meeting the definition of a refugee, which is:

> any person who is outside his or her country of nationality and is unable or unwilling to return to that country because of persecution or a well-founded fear of persecution. Claims of persecution may be based on race, religion, nationality, and membership in a particular social group or political opinion. (U.S. Immigration and Naturalization Service 1991, 96)

Sudanese are also now migrating farther than ever before, with many thousands finding their way to the United States and Canada. The numbers of Sudanese represented the greatest proportionate rise in United States immigration in the early 1990s (U.S. Immigration and Naturalization Service 1995). Although southerners most often flee as refugees, the number of northern voluntary migrants has also dramatically increased.

As a result of political instability and military control, the economy of the Sudan has deteriorated drastically. A 1996 survey characterized the economy as having slow growth, with a deteriorating balance of payments, escalating national debt, and declining purchasing power of the Sudanese currency. This national debt was estimated at thirteen billion dollars. Islamization of the economy has prohibited the use of interest in banking systems and thus limited foreign investment and international financial and commercial transactions (Sudan Economic Survey 1996). This has contributed to the contraction of the Sudanese economy, since very few new projects are undertaken and many existing firms have difficulty importing raw materials and spare parts, which has had a negative impact on development projects. These policies have not only led to inflation but have also prompted many to emigrate to the United States and Canada either as refugees, asylum seekers, or economic migrants.

Studying Contemporary Sudanese Migration

In order to investigate migration as seen through the eyes of Sudanese migrants and exiles, I employed several research methods, including interviews, life-history collection, participant observation, and review of textual material. I undertook a multisited ethnography, an "account that has different, complexly connected real-world sites of investigation" (Marcus 1998, 86).

In the United States and Canada, the bulk of my fieldwork was conducted between 1992 and 1998. Initially, I was preoccupied with obtaining an overall understanding of the community. An anonymous survey questionnaire method was employed to unravel the social characteristics of individual migrants and to clarify the demographic picture. I distributed this questionnaire on the basis of a nonrandom sampling procedure to 300 Sudanese in New York, Toronto, Washington, New Hampshire, Arizona, Connecticut, Virginia, California, and Michigan. At the time this research was conducted, there were no complete directories of migrants or lists of names to draw from. As this was the first study on Sudanese migration, the primary questions were satisfactorily answered through the nonrandom sampling procedure. Important socioeconomic and demographic characteristics were identified. In categories where responses were insufficient to draw conclusions (e.g., Copts and women), additional personal and nonanonymous attempts were made to solicit responses. Unfortunately, the lack of accurate data for the population in the Sudan at large inhibited precise comparisons of these results, and definitive generalizations could not be made concerning the whole universe of Sudanese migrant populations.

Of the 300 Sudanese migrants in North America surveyed, 57 percent were between the ages of thirty and thirty-nine, 24 percent were between twenty and twenty-nine, and 19 percent were forty and over. Of the respondents, 82 percent were male; and 92 percent were from the northern provinces and 8 percent were from the south. In addition, 92 percent were Muslim and 8 percent were Christian. No followers of traditional African religions were encountered. Only a few migrants indicated that they had initially come to the United States and Canada during the early 1960s (primarily for education) and then returned to the Sudan before deciding to emigrate. Only 8 percent of the sample arrived in the 1960s and 1970s, whereas a total of 50 percent arrived after 1980, many during 1989, and 39 percent arrived after 1990. Official immigration sources, including INS reports and the Canadian Refugee Board, corroborate the years of arrival given by key informants and respondents.

The 300 respondents gave many reasons for migrating. Those who stated that they moved for political reasons (civil war or expulsion from the oil-rich Arab countries during the Gulf War) represent 21 percent; economic reasons, 20 percent; for education or social mobility, 39 percent; and 21 percent reported other reasons, including winning the U.S. Diversity Visa Lottery. The claim that most southerners migrating to North America are refugees is borne out by the ethnographic data, which show that although only 21 percent of Muslim northerners indicated political reasons for moving, 82 percent of southerners reported war as a primary reason for coming to North America.

Migrating Sudanese, whether from the north or the south, were primarily from the most highly educated segment of their home society. College graduates comprised 78 percent of the sample; a further 20 percent had completed some high school education; and 7 percent had vocational training certificates. Yet the majority, as we shall see, have had to settle for low-skill and low-paying jobs in North America.

In making their plans to emigrate, 41 percent indicated that kin and social networks were the primary sources of support; 23 percent indicated that they migrated on their own; and 33 percent received assistance from the Sudanese government for graduate training (this assistance included a stipend, full coverage of graduate training, and travel and scholarship expenses). A further 15 percent indicated that U.S. and Canadian institutions had facilitated their migration, including refugee-sponsoring organizations and scholarship programs (Abusharaf 1997a, 1997b). Through international refugee organizations, most of these Sudanese refugees have been resettled in the United States and Canada. These organizations include, among others, the U.S. Catholic Conference, the Swiss Red Cross, United Nations High Commissioner for Refugees (UNHCR), the International Rescue Committee, and Christian Outreach.

The Sudanese in the survey tended to reside in large metropolitan areas, including 31 percent in New York City, 17 percent in Washington, D.C., 11 percent in Toronto, 8 percent in Boston, 9 percent in Los Angeles, and 5 percent live in Dallas. The remaining 20 percent were distributed across the United States in Minnesota, Arizona, Connecticut, and New Hampshire.

How They Enter

New York's Kennedy Airport and Washington's Dulles Airport have been the main ports of entry for Sudanese. Many Sudanese who enter the United States and Canada legally each year are refugees. According to the Immigration and Naturalization Service Yearbook (1999), the Sudan had been the twelfth top refugee-sending country since 1990 after Yugoslavia, Bosnia-Herzegovina, Croatia, Russia, Vietnam, Cuba, Somalia, Iraq, Congo, Iran, and Liberia. U.S. government officials estimate that of the 1,114 African refugees who were granted resettlement rights in the United States between 1997 and 2000, 60 percent are Sudanese.

Between 1991 and 1997, the total number of Sudanese refugee arrivals to the United States was 4,158. By 2000, the annual rate alone was estimated by the U.S. Department of State at 3,800 (Sudanet 2000).

Asylum seeking is the second avenue for resettlement in the United States and Canada, and by 1999 the INS reported that the number of Sudanese asylum seekers had reached 4,781. In fact, Canadian and U.S. policies on refugee and asylum status were identified by many Sudanese as a factor in why they came. A great number of Sudanese who are staying illegally (on expired student or tourist visas), moreover, sought Temporary Protection Status (TPS) after U.S. Attorney General Janet Reno issued a statement that included the Sudan among countries whose migrants qualify for TPS. This designation of the Sudan by the Department of Justice stated that nationals of the Sudan (and aliens having no nationality who last habitually resided in Sudan) who have been continuously living in the United States since November 1997 may apply for this status. Nearly 4,000 Sudanese whose decision to leave their homeland was motivated by political reasons thus found an opportunity to remain in the United States.

Apart from these avenues, entering the United States is extremely difficult, especially since the closing of the American and Canadian consulates in Khartoum. This difficulty is likely to persist, especially following the September 11, 2001, terrorist attacks in New York City and Washington, D.C., and with the Sudan being presented as a likely target of President Bush's war on terrorism. Four principal avenues remain open to Sudanese seeking entry into the United States. Hundreds of Sudanese enter the United States through the annual Diversity Visa Lottery Program. In 1999, of 2,030 Sudanese who were granted permanent residence visas, 642 were listed as lottery winners (U.S. Immigration and Naturalization Service 1999). Others enter as tourists but remain after the expiration of their visa term. Sudanese may also enter as students. I interviewed large numbers in this category who maintained that staying permanently in the United States was not their initial plan. Still others cross the border to Canada where they start asylum claims. Overall, 9,559 Sudanese managed to change their invalid visa status to permanent residence between 1987 and 1997 (U.S. Immigration and Naturalization Service 1999).

Most of these secured permanent residence through employment in jobs certified by the U.S. Labor Department as having insufficient numbers of U.S. citizens to fill them. Others legalized their status through marriage. I received conflicting views on the subject of marriage. Some informants told me that "there is an understanding between the couples who marry for the green card that the marriage will end." Others said that they "were sincere and happened to be lucky to get married to an American-born," and that they "live happily even after getting the green card."

In 1996 and 1998, I also carried out ethnographic research in Greater Khartoum (Khartoum, Khartoum North, and Omdurman, the three towns comprising the capital of the Sudan). There I conducted in-depth interviews with many people, including would-be migrants aspiring to come to the United States and Canada. Considering both ends of the migration continuum yielded excellent insight into Sudanese experiences back home and here in North America. It also helped in gaining knowledge about how migration affects those who stay behind and those who still want to move.

In the course of my research, I have come to agree with Paul Atkinson's argument that at the heart of the ethnographic enterprise lies a tension between observer and observed. He maintains that "[whether] or not 'strangeness' is thrust on the observer through an encounter with the exotic, or is achieved through imaginative bracketing of the familiar and the mundane, the confrontation of the self with the other is fundamental" (1990, 157). Throughout my efforts to research the Sudanese community, my own identity as a Sudanese reduced this tension between observer and observed and furnished many avenues for ethnographic understanding. As a Sudanese, I was able to participate in many aspects of life in the migrant community and back home in ways that a non-Sudanese evidently could not. Religious events, social gatherings, and political meetings all were open to me. Furthermore, when I wished, I was able to study people and proceedings without calling attention to myself as an observer and potentially altering them. Many casual conversations with other Sudanese friends regarding problems encountered after migration or dreams of migrating to the United States also proved productive and enabled my understanding of the intricacy of the Sudanese migratory phenomenon. In my experience, Sudanese in North America and at home in the Sudan were exceptionally helpful. They spared no effort in advising me about places I should go and people in the community who could provide information. Through them I cultivated my own networks and circles of people who provided data for this book.

Scope of the Book

In part I, I describe the first wave of Sudanese migration to North America. Chapter 1 tells the story of Sati Majid, a Muslim missionary who in 1904 was the first documented Sudanese migrant to the United States. His involvement in the Islamic Movement among African Americans in the early twentieth century reveals his historical importance. Then, some eleven years after Sati Majid's departure in 1929, a migration of Sudanese seamen, known as *Bahhara,* began when they joined the American Navy just prior to and during World War II. Chapter 2 documents this unique migration by focusing on individual accounts of how and why they arrived at a time when Sudanese migration to the United States otherwise was unknown. This chapter also demonstrates that, unlike later Sudanese migrants and refugees, the Bahhara constituted a cohesive ethnic, religious, and occupational community. Temporary migration from the Sudan to the United States and Canada took place following Sudanese independence in 1956 and resumed again in 1960 with the arrival of students and diplomats. The concluding section of chapter 2 touches on this resumption as a prelude to the influx of those escaping political unrest, economic hardship, religious oppression, and a perceived lack of choice in migratory destinations after 1989.

Part II is concerned with migration from the Sudan following the advent of the military regime of Omer Elbashir in 1989 (still in power as of December 2001). Unlike the Bahhara or the student migrants, the overwhelming majority of Sudanese arrivals in the United States and Canada since 1989 have been refugees, asylum seekers, visa lottery winners, or tourist-visa overstayers and students (some of whom end up with Temporary Protection Status). The primacy of ethnic and religious factors in shaping these migratory movements cannot be overstated. Chapter 3 is dedicated to the experiences of the southern Sudanese community. The chapter provides a historical contextualization and probes the internal as well as the international displacement that many southerners experienced before their arrival. Members of this community in the United States and Canada readily identify ethnic conflicts and war, politics, and religious oppression as the main determinants of their migration.

Chapter 4 focuses on the post–Gulf War immigration to the United States and Canada. In response to their Islamic government's support of the 1990 Iraqi invasion of Kuwait, Sudanese migrants in oil-rich Arab countries, particularly Kuwait, lost their jobs and were forced to leave. Like nationals of other governments that supported Iraq, Sudanese were punished for sins of their state in the post–Gulf War era. The closing of the Persian Gulf states as a migratory destination thus redirected the migratory flow to the United States and Canada. Large numbers of Sudanese, mostly northerners, now view their migration as an outcome of Desert Storm and the liberation of Kuwait from Saddam Hussein's foray.

Powerful internal circumstances have also forced numbers of Sudanese to depart their country reluctantly. From the vantage point of the northern Sudanese Christian Copts, described in chapter 5, Islamization, militarism, and their relegation to the status of second-class citizens compelled them to leave. My interviews with Coptic migrants and with Copts still in the Sudan revealed that their departure has had devastating effects.

A new phenomenon in the 1990s was the migration of Sudanese women by themselves. As political conditions at home and abroad have intersected to shape long-held traditions, there has been a feminization of international migration from the Sudan, as chapter 6 explains. Like their male counterparts, both northern and southern Sudanese women emigrate for a number of political and economic reasons. One substantial motivation has been the Law of Public Order, by which the government has restricted women's mobility and behavior (S. I. Eissa 2000).

Part III describes Sudanese life in exile through personal testimonies of young and old, Muslim and Christian, male and female, and refugees and voluntary migrants. These stories depict the tribulations of *"the ghorba,"* or life away from home. The *ghorba* is an Arabic word similar to *diaspora*, or "stateless power in a transnational moment," as Tölölyan defines it (1996, 3).

Migration often proves to be a dream followed by discouraging reality. Sudanese come to the United States and Canada with expectations of economic plenitude, and although some have managed to better themselves through small businesses or by obtaining higher education after arrival, the majority experience downward mobility. Chapter 7 shows the trials of proletarianization and deskilling as the talent migrants bring with them is systematically marginalized and rendered inconsequential. The deployment of previously white-collar Sudanese in unskilled occupations not only disaffects these migrants but constitutes a human resource now lost for the Sudan.

Chapter 8 examines the ways in which Sudanese adapt as they try to take their place in the multicultural societies of North America. As their stories begin to unfold, migration is clearly more than a geographical voyage; it is a passage to self-discovery and soul-searching as old identities are reinforced and new ones are constructed. The negotiation of their identity, first and foremost, as Sudanese (rather than, say, Nuer or Nubian) is an important process that migrants and refugees confront in powerful ways, particularly through their collective involvement in home-country concerns.

Chapter 9 describes Sudanese political life in North America, including immigrant organizations and various forms of transnational political activism. We see that collective forms of representation strengthen national identity because these organizations are comprised of Sudanese irrespective of religion, ethnicity, or gender. Previously guarded emblems of difference and exclusivity erode significantly during the course of migration, compelling Sudanese to look for commonality among themselves and to celebrate this through a cooperative engagement.

In the epilogue, I raise the issue of nationalism, which lies at the heart of this new Sudanese migratory phenomenon. I ask: Will these exiles who discover greater open-mindedness regarding their identity as Sudanese rather than as members of particular ethnic groups become more capable of forging a unified nation at home after—through necessity—becoming a nation in absentia?

[13]

PART I

INAUGURAL MIGRATION TO
NORTH AMERICA

[1]

The First to Arrive: Sati Majid, 1904–29

If people never left their place of birth, never sought refuge nor scrambled for
opportunity in other lands, what a different world we would live in and what a
different history we would celebrate!

Lambros Comitas, 1992

In 1904, a man disembarked on United States soil from a French passen-
ger ship en route from England. At six feet, he would have risen above the
heads of most of his fellow European passengers. Also striking and unmis-
takable would have been the three vertical scars he bore on each cheek, the
ethnic marker for men from the Dongola region of Sudan. In the blurred
photograph from his travel papers, the only known photograph of him that
remains, he looks into the camera with the determination and confidence of
a man on no ordinary journey. He was, after all, the first documented Sudanese to set foot on American soil.

Sati Majid was born in Elghaddar Village in the Nubian Province of Old
Dongola, a descendant of a prominent family of judges and clerics. A pas-
senger coupon issued by the Compagnie Francaise de Navigation of the
Fabre Line shows that he arrived in the United States at the port of New
Orleans, Louisiana. From there, he traveled to New York, where he spent
the next twenty-five years preaching Islam until his departure in 1929. The
arrival of this zealous Sudanese missionary at the turn of the twentieth century altered the course of history on two continents, with effects that persist
today.

What prompted a Dongolawi villager to travel to the United States? How did he manage to undertake this journey? What did he hope to accomplish upon his arrival? To be sure, for a villager from Elghaddar to travel to the United States was nothing but far-fetched, and anything but propitious. Majid's incredible journey is both located within and extends beyond the larger context of Sudanese migratory movements. A brief recounting of nineteenth-century Nubian migration puts the arrival of Majid and the subsequent arrival of the Bahhara, the Dongolawi sailors who came to the United States to settle after World War II, in their proper perspective.

Unlike people from other Sudanese provinces, Nubians have historically engaged in migration. Majid and his fellow villagers were descendants of Nubians who have from time immemorial occupied the land adjacent to the Nile River from the Aswan area in southern Egypt southward into the Sudan. They are known to have mastered the skills and crafts of swimming, fishing, sailboat building, and navigating the tranquil, placid Nile. Physical proximity to the Nile facilitated travel northward to Egypt—and beyond.

The Homeland

Nubian is a collective reference for the Mahas, Fadija, and Kenuz peoples, all of whom share a common cultural and linguistic genealogy; they recognize a shared origin; and their dwellings, clothing, and life-styles are closely related. For example, their related languages represent a part of the Eastern Sudanic group of the Nilo-Saharan family (Fernea 1961). Like the rest of Sudanese Muslims, the Nubians profess Sunni Islam and follow Maliki rites and precepts (Weeks 1984).

The Nubian region, where villages consist of close-knit communities revolving around extended kinship ties, has long been recognized as the only part of the Sudan with an established northward migratory system. These migrations to Egypt are believed to have occurred as early as the seventeenth century. As Peter Geiser writes:

> The Nubians, at least as far back as the seventeenth century and probably earlier, are known to have engaged in urban labor migration. It has been reported that over the past three hundred years Nubian males voluntarily went to Sudanese and Egyptian cities, worked there for small wages, and returned to Nubia when they had accumulated some savings. They were reported during this period to have worked as servants, in main, and to have been faithful in the discharge of their duties. The usual amount of time during which they remained in the cities was said to have been about two years. (1973, 188)

[18]

The Nubian migration to Egypt in the nineteenth century occurred when Egyptian landlords began hiring them as tenant farmers (El Tayeb 1985). It has been argued that the relatively low ratio of males to females as a constant characteristic of demographics in Nubian regions since 1882 has been due to some extent to the migration of Nubian males to the large urban centers in the Sudan and Egypt. Although a number of socioeconomic factors associated with scarcity of land, poverty, population growth, and environmental degradation have been seen as factors encouraging these migrations, many Nubians consider the building of the first Aswan Dam in 1898 to have been the most significant factor influencing their decision to emigrate. Another migration and resettlement of several thousand Nubians took place in the twentieth century after the massive flooding of the Nile, which spurred the building of the latest dam at Aswan in the 1960s. Nubians are also known to have sought employment on Egyptian and foreign ships. Some Kenuzi men spent a lifetime in maritime service abroad (Fernea 1961, 138).

Ethnographers have argued that despite a long-established pattern of migration, Nubian people managed to preserve their ethnolinguistic and cultural landscape in their new settlements in Egypt and elsewhere in the Sudan (Dafaallah 1975; Fernea 1961; Geiser 1973, 1986; Kennedy 1970). For example, Nubian ceremonial life, including marriage rituals, circumcision rites, and saint commemorations, not only persisted over the years but also formed a distinctive Nubian cultural configuration. This unique culture, according to Robert Fernea, "has helped this people at all times to retain a sense of who they are" (1961, 125). The significance of this type of Sudanese migration lies in the maintenance of cultural integrity and in the fact that the region was the only part of the country that fostered out-migration (G. Eissa 1986, 144).

Sources

Majid's story can be pieced together in several sources from Khartoum to Brooklyn. Most important were two archival documents pertaining to Majid's missionary work in the United States. Both were gathered by historian Abdelhamid Mohamed Ahmed and were made available to me by the National Record Office in Khartoum, the Sudan, and by Ahmed himself. They include Majid's memoirs, some of which were published in *Elbalagh*, an Egyptian newspaper, in the 1930s, as well as all of his extant correspondence. Majid's letters give invaluable insights into his character, his motivations, and his complex interactions with the communities in the United States, Egypt, and the Sudan of which he was a part. These sources reveal much about Majid's work as missionary and preacher, shed light on the difficulties of preaching Islam in early twentieth-century America, and highlight Majid's historical importance in the meteoric rise of Islam in the African American community.

I learned more about Majid's missionary work from a member of the Sudanese Graduate Conference who attended a series of lectures that Majid delivered on his return to the Sudan in the late 1930s. Interviews with members of the remaining Bahara community in New York who knew of Majid and his work through African American and Yemeni people in Brooklyn illuminated the man on a more personal level.

Beginnings

As a youngster, Majid was known as an avid leaner, a fervid pupil who learned the Quran by heart when he attended the *khalwa* (religious school) led by Wad Waddidi in the neighboring village of Roomey. When he was asked by some acquaintances to describe his experience in Roomey, he responded, "In Roomey, we did not have anything, except for *Bulbul* [hot sand], *balila* [chickpeas] and *oloumi* [religious learning]."

Majid's odyssey began to unfold when he boarded a boat that sailed northward to Egypt sometime around 1895. His goal was to attend the Azhar Seminary, one of the world's oldest institutions of theological learning. Although Majid did not complete his schooling there, his knowledge of Islamic philosophy, cosmology, and ethics was wide-ranging. At the end of the 1890s or thereabouts he ventured on yet another remarkable journey when he decided to board a merchant marine ship heading for Britain.

There are two explanations as to why Majid decided to leave Egypt. According to historian Mohamed Abdelrahim (1952, cited in Ahmed 1978), when Majid was still in Egypt he was exceedingly disturbed by the news of an anti-Muslim campaign led by an Italian missionary in New York. This missionary (whose name is not mentioned in these documents) was believed to have published numerous articles and talked at many gatherings about Islam—likening it to a hideous crocodile and describing it as a frightful, truculent, cannibalistic religion (ibid., 328). This propaganda fueled Majid's passion to defend the faith and prompted his decision to travel to New York. Alternatively, Majid's departure from Egypt can be explained by his determination from the start to preach Islam in foreign lands. As he spoke no English, he decided to go to England to learn the language from its source so as to be able to preach among non-Arabic speaking populations. This latter reason seems more plausible, because some of Majid's correspondence indicates that his sole purpose was to preach.

Upon his arrival in England, two men, a fellow Dongolawi and a Yemeni, welcomed him. The three set out to form a religious movement, of which Majid was leader and helmsman, engaging in preaching and lecturing all over the British Isles. Majid addressed listeners in Arabic while his two companions translated into English. Of the three men, Majid was the most intrepid and articulate public speaker, with a hollow, reverberating voice. Furthermore, Majid was skilled in advancing his arguments through citations from the Quran and the *Hadith*, the sayings of the Prophet Mohamed. Four years later, Majid and his companions deliberated over which of them was most willing and able to undertake the task of Islamic preaching in the United States. Majid took it upon himself to embark on the journey, indifferent to the difficulty of the project he hoped to launch.

The stay in England proved a shrewd strategy for the young missionary. By the time Majid left for the United States, his rhetorical skill and command of the English language were considerable. Within a very short time, he became one of the most influential proponents of Islam in North America. His life in New York would be an epic story of missionary zeal: he proselytized fearlessly and organized his converts into associations for worship and the conduct of daily life. His duties as a religious leader there lasted for a quarter century.

Arrival in America

Majid arrived on America's shore carrying with him a small suitcase and a big dream: to spread his religious message among those "whose hearts are favorably disposed to receiving it." When he arrived in New York, he met five men from the Turkish Embassy who helped him settle in the small Yemeni community in Brooklyn, with which he developed a strong bond. These men, one of whom was an imam, were extremely enthusiastic about Majid's vision and his intentions to spread Islam in the United States.

Clifford Geertz once offered the metaphorical view that "religion may be a stone thrown into the world, but it must be a palpable stone and someone must throw it" (1971, 3). Majid was clearly a man with a powerful arm and unerring aim. Majid's work was historically important because it marked one of the first attempts to legitimize and institutionalize Islam as part of the American religious configuration. One of Majid's paramount tasks in America, as he saw it, was to confront the prevalent misunderstanding of Islam and Muslim peoples. He would write later:

> I have lived in the land of freedom and justice over twenty-five years, during which I witnessed unjustified animosity toward Islam. I responded to these

damaging views constantly. At first I started responding to these views by writing articles on Islam, but I came to realize that writing articles in defense of Islam is not enough. I started my work by preaching about the tolerance and loving nature of Islam. I encountered stubborn and fierce resistance. But by the virtue and grace of Allah, and the acceptance of Uncle Sam, no one could change my mind from pursuing my dream. I felt that my soul would not rest until I showed people the true Islam. At that point no one could stop me or could hinder my efforts. The numbers of people whom I was able to convert to Islam grew considerably. (from *Elbalagh* 1935)

Also of prime historical importance was Majid's choice of audience for his message. Substantial evidence points to the fact that Majid gave his undivided attention to the African American community. His appeal to great numbers of African Americans testifies to his ability to explain religious philosophy as well as to address the important social and political issues regarding their position.

Historically, part of the immense spiritual power that Christianity holds for African Americans is its emphasis on an afterlife, which redeems a life of suffering and oppression. Therefore, one of the most remarkable successes of Majid's ministry was the conversion of an African American nun named Mary Williams. In an article in *Elbalagh,* he reflected on the importance of this event:

The conversion of Mary Williams was extremely encouraging and motivating. Although significant obstacles exist when we try to introduce new ideas, we were not dissuaded by these difficulties. Islam threatens many people. They describe it as a barbaric religion that is oppressive to women and treats them like chattel, like a commodity to be bought and sold. My engagement with these views is very important to our work. I want the true nature of the just Islam to be revealed and embraced.

Majid often engaged in ecumenical dialogue to stress why Islam was, in his view, a judicious option for African Americans. In communicating this message, Majid had two main preoccupations. The first was to convey the tenets of Islam and its universality. He did so by tackling prevalent misconceptions and explaining the egalitarian and humanitarian concerns of the religion. He highlighted these exchanges in his memoirs:

I participated in multireligious debates in New York. I was given the opportunity to speak after an Italian minister once. His talk centered on the degradation and defamation of Islam and its culture. I began my response by asking this minister: where did Jesus come from? Did he come from the East or from Europe? He answered me by saying he came from the East. Then I proceeded to tell him, why then are you trying to degrade the East, the cultures and peoples of the East. Didn't the East produce your God and the God of your forefathers? At the end of this debate I nearly lost my life. Somebody stabbed me on my way out of the crowded auditorium. I insisted that charges against this person be dropped. I forgave him for what he had done to me.

Majid's second preoccupation was to demonstrate Islam's particular relevance to African Americans, who continued to suffer social and economic discrimination. This emphasis gave Majid's argument much of its persuasive power. Concentrating on the social and political nature of Islam, he highlighted the centrality of the concept of *umma*, the "purposeful entity" or community of faith and justice that makes people aware of the here-and-now aspect of this religion. Majid's letters explain that he emphasized the idea of community as concept and common identity to all followers of Islam regardless of race, language, ethnicity, or complexion. Equally significant was his elaboration of Islam as a faith in which all marks of difference entailing a privilege and exclusivity are dissolved (see Abul Fadl 1991). Majid's worldly concerns were channeled through the *Hadith*, in which the Prophet Mohamed urged individuals to fight injustice. Majid's teachings stressed social and individual responsibility toward family and neighbors, which extended outward to encompass the fellowship of humanity at large. The call for justice became the overriding discourse in Majid's conversion project, the worldly and temporal component of his religion. The message that everyone is entitled to a good life on earth found enthusiastic support among Majid's converts and followers.

Throughout his ministry, Majid pointed to what he saw as flagrant violations of the rights of African Americans in the United States. From his point of view, Islam as both religion and moral system would be a practical check against injustice in America. He often recited the Prophet's saying, "In the eyes of God there is no difference between black and white, Arab and non-Arab, male or female, except by their piety." Islam, alone, Majid preached, would help people fulfill their spiritual and worldly needs, because it affected every aspect of one's existence.

Majid's genius lay in how he attuned his message to the rhythms of race in the African American community. His work in the United States fell within the context of *dawa* (literally "invitation"), or missionary efforts (Poston 1991). Among Majid's African American converts, Islam's significance constituted an imaginary return to roots extirpated by displacement and slavery. For these African Americans, the invitation to rejoin an "imagined community"—to use Benedict Anderson's (1991) phrase—made them part of a "powerful story about continuities between a present and past of African people in the Americas" (Scott 1991, 267).

The symbolism of Majid's identity as dark-skinned African Nubian may well have been a favorable ingredient in his accomplishments. The introduction of Islam as a "diasporan spirituality" certainly permitted African Americans to connect to their ancestral continent (see Murphy 1994). Many, no doubt, were moved by an invitation extended by an African "to come back home," so to speak. This invitation to undertake a spiritual return to Africa took yet another significant form embodied in the adoption of Muslim names. In his book *Islam in the African-American Experience*, Richard Turner has argued that the issue of identity is "the interpretive thread that runs through the historical narrative of Islam in Black America" and that "a Black person preserved his or her Muslim name to maintain or reclaim African cultural roots or to negate the power and meaning of the European name" (1997, 2).

The names that Majid provided for his devotees are of great importance in understanding how he helped transform identities. A Muslim name was more than a symbolic return to African roots; it was a rejection of all European-imposed categories and forms of identification (Turner 1986, 1997). New names were a metacommentary on one's view of self, history, and the world and one's place in it. Thus, these newly achieved religious identities were central to the political and social transformations that the lone Sudanese cleric assisted. According to Turner, "for blacks, both slave and free, slave names were an emblem of the cultural pain of Africans" (1997, 45). Renaming among African American converts, therefore, became a powerful pronouncement on the nature of the individual and society, "an ideological fulcrum which has enabled this community to achieve independence from the dominant culture" (1997, 3).

As Majid mastered knowledge of the issues facing the African American community, he communicated with leaders who shared his concerns. On December 17, 1928, he received a letter from an African American, one Elijah Muhammad, which bears an air of familiarity and warmth:

Respectable Father, Sheikh of Islam of America
Reverend Sati Majid
Honorable Sir,
    It's your children of the Muslim faith writing you these few lines to inform you that we are doing very well at the time present. Our membership is still increasing. Also you will find enclosed the letter which we were supposed to send you and tonight we are mailing you twelve letters which we were to make out and send to you thanking you for the many kind words that you spoke to us when you were in our presence. We also pray for your success in your long journey. I will close by saying God be with you.
Yours truly,
Elijah Muhammad

Although some sources suggest that Elijah Muhammad, founder of the "Black Muslim" Nation of Islam, converted to Islam in 1931, Karl Evanzz indicates in his book *The Messenger: The Rise and Fall of Elijah Muhammad* (1999), that he had already converted many to Islam by 1928. Thus, it is not unlikely that it was Elijah Muhammad who corresponded with Majid in the letter above.

One of the important distinctions that Majid acquired was the title of imam, a term bestowed upon those whose work, piousness, and sanctity are recognized by the communities within which they work. Recently, the topic of how the American context has contributed to the professionalization of the imam and the creation of a professional Islamic clergy has received attention (Abusharaf 1997a, 1998b; Haddad and Lummis 1987). Majid was among the first imams whose roles were thus professionalized, taking on dimensions not present in Sudanese society. He received remuneration from several organizations financially maintained by annual membership, including the Muslim Union, the Islamic Charitable Group, the Red Crescent of America, and the Islamic Missionary Society.

In addition to missionary and ministerial obligations, Majid played several secular roles during his stay in the United States. As an imam, he saw himself not only as a teacher and preacher, but also as a representative of Muslim peoples everywhere. This role is reflected in several letters Majid sent to the British consulate in New York, the Immigration Board, and other governmental authorities. One cause that occupied Majid for some time was the situation of Yemeni sailors working aboard British ships. Upon their arrival in New York, several lost their jobs and were contending with hardship and poverty. The following letter to the counsel general of Great Britain in New York City, dated August 4, 1921, illustrates how he viewed his duty:

I am Sati Majid, leader of Muslims in the state of New York. I beg to inform your Excellency, that here in the City of New York are a great number of sailors from the City of Aden, Arabia that is under British authority. These men were serving during the World War as sailors on board of British ships. A good number of their comrades who were their compatriots perished during the war either by German submarines, or by other destructive means by the enemies of Great Britain. The said surviving sailors were employed for the service of the British ships by English officers at the said city of Aden. Now these men who are British subjects, and who served England honestly and faithfully are without employment, and suffering from distress and poverty, as those who employ sailors for English steamers give preference in obtaining employment to those who are under their commission.

May I further inform your excellency, that I wrote on behalf of the said sailors to Mr. John Rockefeller, requesting him to kindly give them employment, and he replied that he had no work for them.

At present these people are kept from starvation by Sheikh Yahia, who has already sent a good sum of money helping them and cannot continue to help any longer. I, therefore, in the name of humanity and renowned British justice, beg of you to take this matter into your kind consideration, and to graciously help them in obtaining employment on British steamers and you would thereby serve God and humanity. Thank you in advance for any kind service you may offer.

Majid's call for help did not pass unmarked. Two days after his letter was sent, the British counsel general responded.

I beg to acknowledge receipt of your letter of the 4th instant, in which you draw my attention to the fact that there are a great many sailors from the city of Aden who are in distress in this city. In reply I must assure you that the distressing situation of many seamen has received my very careful attention and I have given relief in every case where the regulations permit me to do so. It is, however, unfortunately impossible for me to extend assistance to seamen who do not apply for relief within a period of three months after leaving a British ship, and I fear that the seamen to whom you refer do not come within the category of those who I am empowered to repatriate. I am doing everything I can to have these seamen shipped away, but the opportunities for so doing do not frequently present themselves at the present time. Many of the seamen now in distress left British ships at a time when they thought that they could obtain employment on shore or elsewhere under more favorable circumstances and now that this employment has ceased owing to the commercial depression it does not appear to me altogether reasonable for them to expect the British Government to assist them in a situation which is entirely due to their own action.

I assure you, however, that as far as the regulations permit, I shall do everything possible for these men, but in the meantime I can only suggest that they apply to local charitable organizations.

As a result of his concern over the lot of his people, the imam amassed a sizable following, consisting mainly of African Americans who dubbed him reverend, imam, supreme director, father, and sheikh of Islam. His attempts to institutionalize Islam expanded beyond the frontiers of New York as he organized his newly converted Muslims by founding community associations, charitable groups, and places of worship.

The Noble Drew Ali Controversy: Claims and Counterclaims

The success of Noble Drew Ali, who was born Timothy Drew in North Carolina in 1886, represented a dramatic turn of events for Majid. Drew Ali established his first Moorish Science Temple in America in Newark in 1913, and temples in other cities followed. Drew Ali's new movement was inspired by a philosophy of redeeming identity for the African communities in the Americas. According to Evanzz, Noble Drew Ali's combination of Black nationalism and religion proved as popular as Garveyism, and within ten years there were chapters of the Moorish Science Temple of America in the cities of the northeast and the Midwest (1999, 65). Yet unlike Marcus Garvey, Drew Ali taught that Blacks had both African and Asiatic origins, and therefore he did not espouse, as did Garvey, a return to Africa as an ideology. In his book *Black Gods of the Metropolis*, Arthur Fauset argues that Noble Drew Ali was obsessed with the idea that "salvation of the Negro people lay in the discovery by them of their national origin, i.e. they must know whence they came, and refuse longer to be called Negroes, black folk, colored people, or Ethiopians. They must henceforth call themselves Asiatics, to use the generic term, or, more specifically, Moors or Moorish Americans" (1944, 41). According to Fauset although Noble Drew Ali had little formal education, "a certain magnetic charm, a sincerity of purpose, and a real determination to lead his people out of the difficulties of racial prejudice and discrimination brought him followers" (1944, 42).

One of Drew Ali's claims was that he was the last prophet of Islam, and that the book which he had authored and titled "The Holy Koran" was the true book of Islam (Haddad and Smith 1993). Drew Ali, like Majid found a warm reception in the African American community. His Moorish temples were soon established in Detroit and Pittsburgh, where Majid's missionary work had also expanded.

Majid and Drew Ali had a similar objective in mind: to reclaim the identity of African Americans through religious conversion, a move viewed by both men as critical for affirming Black pride and autonomy. However, in Majid's correspondence with other Muslim clerics, it is obvious that he found Noble Drew Ali's claim to prophecy to be outrageous.

The Drew Ali movement challenged Majid to seek counsel from all over the Islamic world, and his extensive correspondence on the Drew controversy extended to clerics in Pakistan, Iraq, Sudan, Egypt, Jerusalem, Afghanistan, Saudi Arabia, Turkey, and other Muslim countries. The following letter was widely distributed to Muslim clerics:

What is your say concerning the man called Noble Drew Ali, who claims to be the last prophet whom Jesus (peace be upon him) had mentioned. This man has authored a book and given it the title The Holy Koran. His book includes a claim that he is the last prophet after our Prophet Mohamed (peace be upon him), that the Islam which people preached before his advent is not the true faith. That he received his education at the City of Fez in Morocco and that he met with Muslim clerics in Egypt, Hijaz, and Iraq. He has told everyone that Islamic clerics acknowledge his prophecy and divinity. Please advise. We are in a great hurry to hear your opinion on this matter. May Allah empower you in the service of all believers.

Majid believed Ali was a threat to his missionary work among African Americans. He wrote: "I have challenged Drew Ali every step of the way, urging him to retreat from his lie and fabrication of verses and sayings that are not from the Quran which was revealed to the Prophet Mohamed. I challenged him by stressing the authenticity of the Quran. Drew Ali refused to yield and to acknowledge the outrageousness of his claims." Majid continued to combat Drew Ali, finally deciding to go to Egypt to obtain a *fatwa,* or a binding legal opinion, from the highest authority in the Azhar Seminary. He felt that this *fatwa* would enable him to convince adherents of the Moorish Science Temple of the absurdity of its leader's claims. In an interview in *Elbalagh* (1935) after arriving in Egypt, Majid explained:

> I came to Egypt to settle very critical problems regarding my mission in America. I am very sorry to say that in spite of the length of my stay, these issues are far from settled. I hope that I can accomplish what I came to Egypt for, so that I can return to America immediately. These problems concern two sects, which are attracting some people now. The first one is about a man called Noble Drew Ali, who claims that he is the last prophet of Allah. He is distributing his book, which he calls the Holy Koran, and now 350 people have this book. The other one relates to the Qidania movement, which is also not based on true Islamic principles. . . . These two sects are trying to undermine the work we are doing, and they are confusing people. . . .

In another article in *Elbalagh*, Majid related: "I wrote to Noble Drew Ali, and urged him to retreat. He refused. The so-called Holy Koran is in the hands of three hundred and fifty people now, but when you ask him basic questions about Islam, he fails to answer. I confronted him by saying that his book is a lie, reciting the Quranic verse: 'The word of the Lord hath been completed in Truth and in Justice; none can change His Words: Verily He is the all-hearing and the all-knowing.'"

Muslim clerics around the world, including some of the Azhar theologians, showed their enthusiastic support of Majid's efforts to defeat Drew Ali's claims. However, the Azhar's most important figure, Mustafa Elmaraghi, refrained, describing Majid as "unqualified for missionary work in great countries like the United States." Mohamed Abdelhamid Ahmed (1995) has speculated that there might have been professional jealousy on the part of Elmaraghi because the Azhar Seminary did not have its own mission in the United States. Majid's correspondence suggests that the growing professionalization of his position as imam in the United States also may have been an issue. Obtaining the *fatwa* from Azhar clerics who questioned his credentials proved arduous, but he persisted. As he wrote one "virtuous sheikh" at the seminary:

> I am presenting your Excellency with this memo in order to verify a few issues. First, I am a representative of the Muslims of North America. I work on their behalf to solve all matters relating to their lives. Second, as for your question about how I make my living, I want you to know that from the day I set foot on the land of freedom in 1904 until my departure in 1929, I did not beg anyone for help. We have Islamic associations to guide our affairs and help us in conducting our work. We have established the Islamic Union, the Islamic Muslim Charity, The Islamic Missionary Society, and the Red Crescent. All of these groups are independent bodies. The Islamic Union attempts to unionize Muslims and to organize them regardless of color, language, or origin. The Islamic Muslim Charity aims to serve Muslims and to establish mosques, purchase burial grounds, and assist the poor, the forlorn orphans, and widows. The Red Crescent assists Muslims all over the world. . . .
>
> But now I am turning to you for help because I want to confront the enemies of Islam. God will reward you for your good deed. Please arrange to send *Nur El Islam* magazine so that it can be distributed to American and other people who are interested in learning about the beauty and tolerance of Islam. Please take note of the importance of my work in the American land, which is like a prepared soil, fertile and vast and accepting of new ideas. You will empower the newly converted by sending these magazines. It will indeed be an excellent way to publish enlightened views of Islam in the American press. If you allow me, my hope is to seek affiliation for these organizations with the Azhar, the supreme source of Islamic knowledge, where Muslims come from all over the globe. I hope that you will find this request acceptable. Finally, I ask Allah to empower you and to allow Islam to triumph with your work.

Several events in Egypt converged to obstruct Majid's return to the United States. He experienced unexpected delays in obtaining the *fatwa* from the Azhar authority. The resulting prolonged stay in Egypt led to financial burdens. Members of his African American Muslim community tried to come to his aid. In a letter dated February 3, 1930, his followers wrote:

> Father Sati Majid,
> Supreme Director of African Muslim Welfare Society,
>   We write you this letter calling your attention to draft number 120238–L 20–12–0 of June 13, 1929 which amount of money we forwarded to you

[29]

through the East End Savings and Trust Company to you at the National Bank
of Cairo, Egypt. According to your letter of April 24, 1929 you asked us to
send you some money necessary and we sent you what we had and today we
receive a letter from the East End Savings and Trust Company informing us
that they have a letter from the National Bank of Cairo, Egypt stating that you
have not called at the Bank for it and the said bank is waiting for our instructions as to what to do. Please at your earliest convenience call at the National
Bank of Cairo or inform us what to do so we can notify the East Savings and
Trust Company.

We await your reply and remain,
Your children

Apparently, either the American assistance was not sufficient, or there
were barriers to obtaining the money that his supporters attempted to
send. Another letter Majid sent to Bahador Ahmed Alaa Eldin of Pakistan
in 1930 shows his determination to return to his work in the United States:

I lived for thirty years in the United States preaching Islam. I have managed to
convert forty-five thousand people. When I lived there, there were also Indi-
ans and Afghan preachers who worked hard to establish Muslim places of worship and associations. I came back to the Sudan to visit my family. I brought
with me documents about my activities, so that I could get support for building a mosque in New York. I have been advised to approach Muslims Counsel.
Here, I am asking for financial assistance to enable me to cover travel expenses
to the United States. I have left all my work and the people who assist my efforts there. I am truly in need for help to return. May Allah empower your efforts in the service of Muslims.

In addition to financial trouble, Majid is believed to have been denied a
reentry visa to the United States. Ahmed (1995) argues that negative accusations by the Azhar cleric Mustafa Elmaraghi may have precipitated a U.S.
refusal to allow Majid to resume his work.

Majid continued to reside in Egypt for a few years while he endeavored
to return to America. Significantly, his ties to the community he left behind
were not severed by this turn of events. A letter to him dated November 9,
1935, verifies this.

Dear father,
I write to you about my health and about the black American community.
We wrote to you several months ago in response to your letter. In our letter we
requested the translated books from Arabic to English. We have the feeling
that you are extremely busy. Here we are very concerned with the Italian-
Ethiopian conflict. We hope that Ethiopia will not suffer at the hands of the

Italians. God-willing one day we will be able to go back to Africa. We have been overcome with joy to hear the defeat of the colonialists in many parts of Africa. I want you to rest assured that we are hard working trying to promote the word of Islam.

Father, please send us your picture. Also do not forget to change all the English names of people who converted to Islam. I sent you a long list with the names. I beg God to enable us to hear from you again.

Your son, Elias Mohamed

Majid responded:

Dear Sons,

You mentioned that Ali Hassan is preaching Islam after my departure. I advise you to give him your support and attention, till I come back by Allah's grace. Please be kind and generous towards him. He worked with us to help Muslims who immigrated to America. Regarding the names of people who converted, I changed them to Muslim names and decided to present them to religious clerics. Here Sheikh Abdelrahman Diab is constantly praising you and begging God to help you triumph in your work. I have enclosed the names within this letter. I am hoping that you can start registering those along with the old English ones. When you do that, make sure to write the names before and after conversion to Islam. I am working very hard, day and night to finish my work so that I can resume my work with you.

In spite of his efforts, Majid never returned to the United States. Instead, he was forced eventually to return to the Sudan, as reported by a Sudanese newspaper which began to publish articles about the zealous Sudanese Muslim missionary in New York. These articles stimulated university graduates to invite Majid to lecture at the graduate club (*nadi elkhirijeen*) in Omdurman, the Sudan. Majid was introduced by the club secretary as a pioneer who had migrated to the New World but also preached to African Americans in New York. A journalist, whom I interviewed, was among the audience.

As I recall, Majid was talking about how Americans reacted to his mission of preaching Islam. He said Black Americans were much impressed by the principles of Islam and they developed a keen interest to find out, learn, and embrace all aspects of this religion. What they found more convincing and appealing to them is the principle, the ideal of social equality. It was Islam that considers us as slaves of God, the Creator of the Universe, and respects man whether Black or White. We are all brothers in front of God. The high ranks in Islam are given to those who devote their life to the happiness of others. . . . In answering questions about the Black American experience in converting to Islam, Majid conceded that it was a long process that required patience and conviction. He also was said to have related: "the last time I had concluded the prayers as a recognized imam, there was quite a large number of Black Americans, and I think that is why they drew the attention of the church and subsequently the Christian missionaries." Given his inability to return to the U.S., Majid urged the audience to make donations to send translated copies of the Quran to his followers in New York and a committee was believed to have undertaken this task at that time.

Until his death, Majid worked assiduously for the benefit and welfare of others. In the Sudan he encountered a group of migrants from Dongola in the capital city, Khartoum—a diaspora within his own country of persons who spoke his local dialect and formed a community. Drawing on his American experience, Majid played a pivotal role in the founding of Hai Eldangala, an ethnic Danagla neighborhood in Khartoum North. After a long exchange of letters with the British Civil Secretary, Majid was successful in securing land for their settlement. Majid passed away in his village of Elghaddar in 1963, leaving behind an illustrious reputation in the Sudan.

[2]

The Bahhara
An Immigrant Community

In North America there was a vision of a limitless future, made more gleaming by the constraint, dissatisfaction and turmoil left behind. It was a promise genuinely promising.

Toni Morrison, *Playing in the Dark*, 1992

Eighty years after the Sudanese conscript battalion served in Mexico, and a decade after Sati Majid returned to Egypt, a distinct, small Sudanese migration began in response to the American demand for seamen (*bahhara* in Arabic) during World War II. Merchant marines working on various international naval vessels arrived at American ports and were recruited into the U.S. Navy. Under similar circumstances, still more Bahhara were recruited in the 1950s during the Korean War. The stories of these Bahhara in this chapter are personal narratives told to me in the 1990s. The character of this ethnic community reveals a resilience that helped keep alive organizing principles of language, customs, beliefs, and kinship ties from their homeland, a *genre de vie* that historically has enabled Sudanese Nubians to reinforce their identities wherever they go.

Unlike the culturally and politically differentiated Sudanese migrants to North America in more recent years, the ethnically distinctive Bahhara encountered unique, welcoming political circumstances in the United States. Joining the American navy during World War II and the Korean War, the Sudanese were eligible for American citizenship as wartime servicemen. Moreover, they enjoyed relatively decent standards of living and an opportunity in the American navy to broaden their technical skills and range of

[33]

opportunities. The Bahhara servicemen were officially naturalized as citizens after the Department of Defense verified their war service. The ruling statute provided "any non-citizen owing no allegiance to the nation, who undertakes the risks and burdens of military service, should be awarded the opportunity to acquire citizenship at an earlier date and upon more favorable terms than other aliens" (Rudnick 1971, 429). For some Bahhara, war experiences resulted in physical injury or loss of life. During the Normandy invasion, for instance, several Sudanese casualties occurred.

This opportunity for naturalization, as many Bahhara explained to me, was the primary motive for settling in the United States. As early as the 1940s, a Sudanese-American community in Brooklyn was formed by these Bahhara wartime veterans.

Individual Experiences of the Bahhara

Khairi

Khairi was among the first Bahhara to settle in the United States. I interviewed him in Brooklyn at the age of eighty in 1993, several years before his death in 1996. He had arrived in the United States in 1943 on a boat that was later purchased by the British and converted into a military hospital.

After the acquisition of this steamship by the British, we were given the choice of staying permanently in the United States or leaving. Recruitment of officers at that point was going on. I did not want to end my work or go back to the Sudan. Some of the Bahhara chose to leave. Others like myself preferred to seek new life and new opportunities in this country. The people from our region always traveled. . . . Particularly it was extremely easy for us to secure new careers as members of the American navy. We got high salaries and health benefits, and for us it was indeed the opportunity of a lifetime. I served in the navy during World War II and remained in the service for more than five years. During peacetime, after the war, the major missions I worked in took place between the United States and Russia. But working during the war in the navy enabled me to obtain American citizenship without any trammel or hindrance.

Those of us who stayed in the U.S. maintained very strong ties with each other, even with those who did not reside in Brooklyn, where the majority remained. . . . We founded the seeds of a Sudanese migrant community. We also attended one of the oldest mosques known as Masjid Daoud. We all came from Dongola, spoke the same dialect. After we came we managed to exist as an ethnic community. However, it is an important point to stress that it took quite a long period of time before other migrants started to arrive. . . .

Although living in Brooklyn was easy and prosperous, it was not without problems. Americans were not accepting of other migrants. This attitude toward foreigners manifested itself in several disputes and racial discrimination. I still recall certain incidents that I faced: one time the clerk in a movie theater refused to sell tickets, but finally when he did and I went in, many Whites changed their seats because they were upset about a Black person sitting beside them. Although living here had its advantages, I wish I could go back to my homeland. Despite these long years I am only here physically. I had been and always will be in the Sudan in my hopes and my thoughts.

Khairi's adaptation experience to his new life was founded on his ethnic, occupational, and religious affiliation. His narrative shows that, notwithstanding the racial incidents they faced in America, the Bahhara made substantial efforts to establish a foothold in New York. In so doing, they relied on Nubian cultural traditions of communality and reciprocal obligations. His story also demonstrates the sense of security and confidence that the Bahhara enjoyed as wartime veterans, and as American citizens. Finally, his account reveals a profound diasporic consciousness, his desire to return to the Sudan, and his loyalty to the village of his birth. After Khairi passed away in Brooklyn, his Bahhara friends told me that although he was eligible for formal military burial, his will stated that he wished to be buried in Dongola.

Babikir

Babikir, age seventy-two in 1993, also comes from Dongola. He arrived in 1942 under the same circumstances as his fellow migrant Khairi.

I worked on a Greek steamer that was affiliated with what was called the British War Ministry. After my arrival we were given the option to join the American navy, because the Americans were recruiting people and there was an urgent need for people to work for them. I decided to stay because I came as a single man. Actually most of us were not married and life looked more promising. Because of the opportunity given to us we decided to stay. Some of our fellow Bahhara went back to Sudan after staying here for years in spite of obtaining citizenship. To this day these Bahhara are granted monthly pensions from the American embassy in the Sudan. Now they are living comfortably, they have property and good incomes.

All of the Bahhara who settled here in America shared a common ethnic background. We are all Danagla [i.e., from Dongola]. That is why it was only logical for us to limit our relations with other communities in Brooklyn, except with Egyptians. Given our history with Egypt, we formed an organization that was known then as Ithad Wadi el Nil, but after Sudan's independence we had our separate *jamiiaa* [group] organization known as the Sudanese-American Society. We had a good reputation and all Sudanese who started to come used to come to us for help and advice. We had extensive ties in the professional sense with ninety-nine nationalities affiliated in both the National and World Union for navy officers. . . . Our relationship with Black Americans was exceptionally good. In fact, through Blacks in the union we met other Blacks in New York who told us of a Sudanese man who was presumed to be the first Sudanese North American migrant in the entire history.

Babikir vividly reveals how Majid was still remembered a decade or more later by his devotees in the African American community.

Majid, as he was known, is believed to have left in 1930s. For Black Americans, Majid was an example of a true, virtuous, kind individual, with a wide horizon of tolerance and hospitality. These attributes had persuaded many Blacks to convert to Islam at the hands of Sati Majid. Other Blacks mentioned to us that Majid was highly respected in the Harlem community, to the extent that he was convinced to stay and to be the imam of their mosque. However, what had happened later on to Majid still vexes many that related his history and elevated him to a prophet-like status. Many of the Harlem community apparently attribute Sati Majid's unpredictable departure to the Christian missionaries who would not leave him alone. It was said that he was required to obtain a certificate from Al Azhar College for Islamic Studies in Cairo in order to be able to preach. He left to Egypt, and in fact was recognized by Al Azhar; but when it was time for him to return to the U.S., he was denied an entry visa. In this way he was forced to return to the Sudan. Others maintained that Majid had been deceived by the missionaries, and he was offered a ticket to go back to visit his homeland, as he had spent long years without having the opportunity to go back. I don't know what exactly happened. People always felt very sad when they remembered him. Majid went back to the Sudan and he was not allowed to return to the U.S. In any case, this was the end of Sati Majid's efforts to preach Islam.

Osman

Osman, seventy-three years old, recalls arriving on December 6, 1941, one day before the Japanese bombed Pearl Harbor. He had been working for the Egyptian navy, but after his arrival in Manhattan from Alexandria, his Egyptian steamer was purchased by the Red Cross and converted to a hospital ship. Many of his fellow Egyptian and Sudanese Bahhara found their way back to Alexandria, but Osman settled in New York.

I joined the American navy. In due course I acquired American citizenship. However, those who did not join were not allowed to stay. In fact after the end of the mission, we were only allowed twenty-nine days to decide whether to accept offers here or to go back where we came from. I worked for the American navy for a long time and participated in the Normandy invasion in France, where we fought against the Germans until their defeat. A lot of soldiers were killed fighting in that war, including a few Sudanese Bahhara. I came back to Brooklyn and founded with other migrants the Sudanese American Society. I went back to the Sudan in 1950 for the first time since I settled in the U.S. It was a big surprise for Mahgoub and Azhari, the Sudanese independence leaders, when they came to the U.S to find us. They knew nothing about us. All of us had a big reception in their honor, held in New York to welcome them and celebrate their outstanding efforts for the independence of the country.

Hamid

Hamid, age seventy-five in 1993, also a migrant from Dongola, arrived in the United States just before the Korean War. Like the earlier migrants, he served in the navy and was granted naturalization.

The steps of the Sudanese Bahhara toward the United States and other places had not been recorded. In our province, some chaps had run the risk and migrated. Our people, being near the Nile, always managed to get work as sailors by the Steamers' Department in Khartoum North. At that time the ferries and steamers used to sail toward different parts, including the southern town Juba. The people of Dongola have strong ties with Egypt. Many of the sailors from Dongola worked in the Egyptian steamers which sailed toward Britain. They persuaded their relatives in the Sudan to join force with them, and that took place a long time ago, even during the World War I in 1914–18. I came to the United States on a Swedish ship just before the end of the Korean conflict. My main port was in Sweden, and at that time the Sudanese Bahhara were dispersed all over the world: some were in Egypt, Sudan, Norway, Sweden, etc. When I arrived, sailors were in high demand by the U.S., as it was during wartime. After my arrival, I decided to join the U.S. Navy, since recruitment campaigns had succeeded to recruit large numbers of people. Once I decided to join the navy during the Korean conflict, I immediately became a citizen. I went back to the Sudan and remained there for ten years before I decided to return to America in 1968. I have not visited the Sudan since. Some of the other Bahhara who were injured were granted disability benefits; some of them went back to the Sudan, and some of those who were here since World War II in our community have died. Our employment history was limited to our service in the navy. We never really pursued other occupations. All of us, whether here or those who returned to the Sudan, live comfortably on our pensions. We enjoy being with other Sudanese, and it is customary for us to host parties, social events, and receptions for newcomers, as well as for Sudanese politicians and diplomats, and in fact we had very good relations with them. The unfortunate thing, however, is that most of the recent arrivals residing in New York refuse to join our group *jamiiaa*. They call it Jamiiat el Danagla, or Dongola group, in spite of our efforts to expand it to include all Sudanese regardless of their ethnic origin.

Salih

Salih arrived in New York before the Korean War and served as a marine during that conflict. At age seventy, he still lives in Brooklyn with his wife Maimoona and his four daughters. After a career in the merchant marine, Salih is fluent in Arabic, English, French, and Spanish, in addition to Dongolawi. Salih narrated his life story and his arrival in New York:

I came here many years after Khairi. But of course, I have a very good relationship with all the Bahhara. I served during the Korean War, and as you know I became an American citizen. I was injured during the war and right now in addition to my pension, I receive disability benefits. My war experience was dramatic, of course. We spent days in rescue boats in the Indian Ocean. After I settled here I got married to my first wife and I have a son by her. Our marriage ended in divorce and I decided to go back to Dongola to take a wife. I got married and I have four girls, two in high school and two in middle school. I try to work very hard to make sure that my daughters remember who they are. Yes they are Americans—three are born here—but they are also Sudanese and Dongolawis. Now my daughters speak our dialect fluently at home. English is only used when they are not at home. I also worry about things that are not acceptable for us, like dating, but I am confident that my daughters are not easily influenced by these practices. I take them to Dongola every year for the entire summer vacation. So they have a life in Dongola that is equally wonderful. They have close friends and relatives who teach them a lot about our way of life and culture. They go to Islamic schools in Brooklyn, and they observe their religion closely; they fast and never miss a prayer. As far as my experience here is concerned, I think that we are not in trouble like the Sudanese who come here for asylum and have to wait for years before they know whether their applications are accepted. Also I noticed that most of the *shabab* [young Sudanese] here are not aware of what they are up against. Here you need to work very hard to secure an income; especially if you do not have papers, you are vulnerable to deportation and psychological pressure. That is why they struggle just to make ends meet, whichever way they can. Having worked in the American navy, I did not have to worry about where my next meal is coming from.

For us, we have our *jamiiaa*, the Sudanese American Society, which is only open for citizens or green-card holders. Members pay subscriptions to be used later as a help fund for people in need. For example, we sponsor religious and nonreligious celebrations and we pay for funeral services from this fund. Some of the Bahhara own an apartment complex in Brooklyn, and they have decent incomes from it. We also managed to secure a burial ground now. We have the mosque. Although for a long time its constituency was Sudanese and other Blacks, now it is Yemeni, but we still worship there. I always think of myself as a person with two homes. As an American, I did what an American should do. I risked my life in the war. As a Sudanese, I maintain my ties as do the rest of the Bahhara. Both places are very dear to us.

Salih's account stresses how transnational linkages between New York and Dongola are created as the Bahhara maintain familial and social ties that straddle their two homes, confirming Roger Rouse's assertion that they experience "a combination of old dispositions too deeply inculcated to be shed and new ones adopted in reaction to the fresh environment" (Rouse 1992, 42). The account also highlights the role of the family in keeping alive the subjective experience of one's ethnic and cultural heritage. As Michel Laguerre argues, "the family provides a niche within which cultural continuity can be adapted to the exigencies of the new environment. Through the medium of the family, which influences the behaviors of its members through the mechanism of socialization, immigrants are able to retain some of their cultural heritage and develop awareness of their ethnic legacy" (1984, 66).

The Bahhara Community

This group of Sudanese immigrants to the United States consisted of a community whose number never exceeded fifty men. They originated from the same part of the country, Dongola, and thus shared a common origin, dialect, culture, and religion. These attributes contributed to their adjustment in North America as a cohesive, if tiny, community. Given their common occupational background as Bahhara, demographic characteristics as single young males at the time of their arrival, and the historical experience as World War II or Korean War servicemen, they formed a well-knit group that managed to reinvent home in their Brooklyn diaspora. Through a systematic bolstering of the linguistic and ethnic traditions, this community has been able to survive across five decades.

The Bahhara's experience has distinctive features not shared by more recent Sudanese arrivals. As sailors, when they docked in New York, they brought occupational skills in great demand. Moreover, their migration was voluntary, not a result of political or economic distress or compulsion. The Bahhara were, overall, well situated to take advantage of an opening in the opportunity structure of the United States. This distinctive migratory context made their lives significantly easier than those of their successors.

[39]

As navy enlistees, the Bahhara enjoyed many chances for improving their lives and for learning the ways of the new society. They thus avoided the dramatic downward class mobility that would face the Sudanese migrants in the 1990s. Because the military's promotional system is based on merit, many Bahhara won career advancement that would have been hard to procure in civilian life. Their opportunities to achieve social and economic success impacted affirmatively on their subsequent adjustment. For example, the Bahhara's relatively high incomes enabled them to own property both here and in the Sudan. Salih and others own an apartment complex of a hundred units in Brooklyn Heights; Babikir is known as a charitable, generous person who contributes to many causes and projects in the Sudan. One of Babikir's most generous donations was to the construction of a mosque in Amarat, a suburb of Khartoum, where he owns property.

Yet, despite the Bahhara's successful adjustment, they have not been totally transformed by their new society. Their Nubian culture also crossed the ocean and survived in a variety of ways. These include close kin and ethnic group endogamy and perpetuation of Islamic congregational worship. Ethnicity, a defining feature of their Nubian identity, is clearly rooted in their marriage patterns and their religious experience. Moreover, as Tölölyan has argued of diasporan communities, the Bahhara "actively maintain a collective memory that is a foundational element of their distinct identity" (1996, 13). Despite sixty years of residence in the United States and U.S. citizenship, their cultural identity has persisted.

Although the Bahhara arrived as single males, many remained committed to entering socially acceptable marriages within the Danagla community in the Sudan. Marriage there is generally arranged between two families; a union made without parental approval is very rare. Marriages are also by and large endogamous within ethnic groups, and young singles are expected to marry people of Nubian descent. As Babikir explained, "We all moved here when we were young and unmarried. Some of us never married. Very few married in this country; one had got married to an Egyptian from Brooklyn, but we heard that these marriages to Americans did not last. Most of us went back to Dongola to get married." While conducting the interviews, I was told that the son of one early immigrant was getting married to a Sudanese and his daughter was marrying the son of a fellow Bahhar. Both wedding ceremonies, moreover, would be held in the Sudan. As Abu Labban concluded for other Arab North Americans, "the incidence of endogamous marriages are important factors in the perpetuation and renewal of ethnic loyalties" (1969, 35). For the Bahhara community, patterns of intermarriage across religious and ethnic boundaries were almost unknown through the 1990s.

Religious Experience

In his examination of religion as a cultural system, Clifford Geertz argues that "for the anthropologist, the importance of religion lies in its capacity to serve for an individual or for a group as a source of general, yet distinctive, conceptions of the world, the self and the relation between them"; he also notes that "religious concepts spread beyond their specifically metaphysical contexts to provide a framework of general ideas in terms which a wide range of experience—intellectual, emotional, moral—can be given meaningful form" (1973, 123). Both arguments are important in unearthing meanings of Bahhara religious life. How have the Bahhara carried on their religious faith and traditions in the context of a predominantly Christian America? What elements of their religious performance reflect a structural continuation from their old lives?

Because of their quick access to the benefits of citizenship, as well as their relatively high incomes, the Bahhara encountered fewer social problems than did many other immigrants in the United States. However, experience of sociocultural and religious isolation prompted them to congregate with each other and with other Muslims.

The Bahhara, then, not only preserved their culture through endogamous marriages but sought religious and social identification with the collectivity of Muslims. This motivated them to join the mosque that was previously known as Masjid Daoud (now the Islamic Mission of America). It was founded by Sheikh Daoud Ahmed Faisal, who emigrated in 1913 from Martinique (Toomey 1951). From its original location at 128th Street and Lenox Avenue in Harlem, the masjid was moved to Brooklyn Heights in 1935. To explore the religious experience of the Bahhara, I visited the masjid on Fridays during the congregational prayer (*jumaa*) in 1996–97. This mosque is situated in a residential Brooklyn neighborhood near Atlantic Avenue, where the bulk of Muslim immigrant-owned businesses are located. The Bahhara, who have been worshipping for decades at the mosque, represent a distinct community within it by virtue of their ethnicity and historical experience. This congregation has been and continues to be the medium through which the Bahhara have practiced their identity as Muslims; for them, it has been a religious and cultural "home away from home" (Abusharaf 1998b).

This mosque also attracted substantial numbers of other Muslim and Arab migrants during weekly Friday prayer as well as the annual holidays of *Eid Elfitr* (The Small Feast) and *Eid El Adha* (The Big Feast), both significant religious occasions for Muslims. By performing prayers in the mosque, Muslims' social existence in North American society is fulfilled at the individual religious level as well as at the community level. As Mona Abul Fadl points out, "communal prayer—*salat el jammaa*—remains more than an act

Masjid Daoud, now State Street Mosque, Brooklyn, New York was the Bahhara's place of worship for fifty years.

of devotion in a formal place of worship: it is an act that transcends the individual and crosses the bounds of space and time, thus nourishing and fortifying the sense of community and identity" (1991, 27).

Oscar Handlin has suggested that for immigrants to the United States, "the more thorough the separation from the other aspects of the old life, the greater was the hold of religion that alone survived the transfer. Struggling against heavy odds to save something of the old ways, the immigrants directed into their faith the whole weight of their longing to be connected with the past" (1973, 105–6). More than most immigrants in North America before the 1960s, the Bahhara struggled to remake their past in unfamiliar surroundings. They found ritual observances a compelling place to regain some of the life they had experienced at home, as Osman and other Bahhara indicated to me. The symbolism of the mosque—a space where Islamic ideals were valued—was clear in Salih's account of its attraction for the Bahhara. As he epitomized its meaning to his compatriots: "Through some Black American friends, we were introduced to Haj Daoud. Haj Daoud was extremely fond of Sudanese because he knew of Majid. His mosque helped us in the ghorba, and helped us get to know other Muslim people."

[42]

An Established Community

The Bahhara have celebrated visits to the United States by Sudanese officials, strengthening their network locally and maintaining their sense of continuity with their homeland. This network played a significant role in the initial migrant adjustment for the first wave of immigrants, as well as for the Sudanese students and members of the professional elite who started to arrive in the late 1950s. The early Bahhara immigrants extended assistance to the new arrivals, and some explained that friends and relatives in the Sudan even told people coming to the United States to contact them and they would help find a place to stay and advise the new arrivals about American society.

By the 1990s many Sudanese Bahhara had died. Others had repatriated to the Sudan, and still others had relocated to warmer regions of the United States. In 1999, only three Bahhara still lived in Brooklyn.

The Bahhara's occupational mobility, ethnic homogeneity, and unique migratory experience combined to create favorable views about their decision to stay in the United States. This experience stands in stark contrast to that of the newer refugees and migrants whose stories will be told in the pages that follow.

Temporary Migrants after 1956

The temporary movement of Sudanese to North America after independence in 1956 consisted primarily of students who came for graduate education, diplomats, and other embassy and consulate employees posted for brief periods. However, it would also become a prelude to the large influx of Sudanese arriving after 1989. One of the very first people I interviewed, in 1992, Abdel Rahim, then sixty-four years old, told me that he arrived in New York in 1963 with the Sudanese delegation to an international art exhibit being held in New York. Abdel Rahim, a master carpenter, was responsible for setting up the Sudanese section, and after the event ended, he decided to stay. Now Abdel Rahim is a successful entrepreneur who owns an apartment complex and holds the leadership of the Sudanese immigrant association (*jalia*) in New York City. Still, his story is probably unique. Most Sudanese migrants who arrived in the United States between 1956 and 1989 and stayed on were "temporary arrivals," a nonimmigrant classification shared with smaller numbers of Sudanese government officials, tourists, and exchange visitors. A 1993 examination of the Sudanese embassy records indicated, moreover, that most who arrived after 1960 attended top educational institutions, which enhanced their later careers and mobility. By 1982 thousands of Sudanese had obtained graduate degrees in the United States and Canada: a few hundred of these were enrolled under the sponsorship of the Sudanese government. According to government policy, the Sudanese who went abroad for advanced studies were required to sign a contract to return and work at least ten years in Sudanese institutions. Those who failed had to refund the amount that the government spent on them. The majority of those who signed such contracts did in fact return to the Sudan after completing their education and only a few of them decided to remain in North America.

Statistics collected by Osman Hassan Ahmed, a Sudanese cultural attaché in Washington, D.C., indicate that between the early 1960s and 1982, the total number of Sudanese graduate students in American and Canadian universities reached 1,382 (O. H. Ahmed 1983). In some cases, former students adjusted their F–1 visa to a permanent residence visa or "green card" status. This group of Sudanese immigrants consisted mainly of degreed professionals: lawyers, teachers, doctors, and bureaucrats. In the several cases I encountered of these Sudanese who remained after completion of education or training, the key "pull" factors were the prospect of higher incomes, availability of research facilities, favorable living conditions, and aspirations for upward social mobility. However, several from this group also cited political repression, economic deterioration, and lack of academic freedom in the Sudan as determinants in their decisions to remain in the United States. Since this group of Sudanese migrants had acquired relatively high levels of academic and professional skills, their adaptation and integration within North American society was facilitated by their qualifications.

Khadija is a good example. Born in 1958 in Shendi in northern Sudan, she came to the United States in 1984 at age twenty-six solely to pursue her education. She had completed a bachelor's degree in the Sudan and as a teaching assistant at a Sudanese university was sponsored to pursue graduate education here. Now she is a senior scientist, owns a house, and has no intention of returning to the Sudan. "I have more power, more impact, and more responsibilities. For me it is very convenient to be here; you work hard and you get what you want." Her husband Atta, who accompanied her, began working at an American university.

Aziz, forty-seven years old in 1993 and from Atbara, a town in northern Sudan, arrived in 1980 to attend school in Wisconsin. After completing his graduate degree in engineering, he moved to Minnesota. "My main reasons for my decision to stay are the prospects of professional advancement, access to resources, and better research facilities. I felt at this point I could not go back to the Sudan."

The Sudanese economy in the 1970s was characterized by low levels of growth, falling per capita income, rising foreign debt, high unemployment and underemployment, and low productivity (Ali 1985). Those Sudanese who choose to move to North America well understand these conditions.

[44]

Per capita income in the Sudan even lagged behind other developing countries, where per capita income increased from $140 in 1965 to $270 in the early 1980s, while those in the developed world rose from $8,800 to $14,400. Furthermore, by the late 1980s, per capita income in the developing countries had slipped back to the levels of the late 1970s (Appleyard 1991, 15).

Sudanese even assert that a low-paid job in the United States is more financially rewarding than the highest-paid occupations in the Sudan, especially considering the deteriorating value of the Sudanese currency. Many indicated that their incomes here put them in a better position to meet social obligations back home by sending money to kin.

It was these feelings of frustration over life in the Sudan, combined with perceptions of opportunity in the United States, that motivated most of the handful of migrants who arrived between 1956 and 1989 to remain. Such spatial flows from one region of the world to another can best be seen as a function of people's constant search for opportunities and prospects for a better life and of their assessments of limitations and constraints in their societies of origin (Balan 1988; DuToit 1990; S. I. Eissa 1996; El Tayeb 1985; Guha 1977). The inability of the Sudan to provide opportunities for educational and occupational advancement led large numbers to go elsewhere. More recent conflicts have only intensified the pressure to move. And with the rise of the most recent military government after 1989, policy changes have curtailed opportunities for students and professionals in the Sudan to travel overseas, regardless of their promises to return. This effectively put an end to the type of Sudanese migration, although small in number, that prevailed between 1956–1989. It also provoked the more diverse and large-scale movements since, to which we turn next.

PART II

POST-1989 MIGRATION: FOUR EXPERIENCES

[3]

Southern Sudanese: A Community in Exile

For a long time, I believed that the men of Africa would not fight each other. Alas, black blood is being spilled, black men are spilling it, and it will be spilled for a long time to come.

Franz Fanon, in conversation with Jean-Paul Sartre

The horrific media images of the war-ravaged, ailing, starving people of the southern Sudanese provinces of Bahr El Ghazal, Equatoria, and Upper Nile bear witness to the longest ongoing civil war in the world. They also conceal the nobility and pride of a people whose rich culture, means of livelihood, and cosmology have seized the imagination of generations of travelers, artists, and photographers from all over the world. Anthropologists too have supplied well-wrought descriptions of the peoples and cultures of the southern Sudan. Classic ethnographic works by Sir Edward Evans-Pritchard, Godfrey Lienhardt, Charles Seligman, Simon Simonse, Pierre de Schlippe, and Francis Deng offer a convincing affirmation of the cultural complexity of the region. The scene, however, has been shattered by a civil war between the north and the south that has raged since 1955. Today, in the words of Roger Winter of the United States Committee for Refugees, "the people of Sudan, particularly in the South, whom I know best, are vibrant, with lots of pride, fond of jokes and smiling, hauntingly beautiful in their singing. But in the 15 years of this phase of Sudan's war, they have known more suffering, terror, and death than any other population on earth" (Winter 1999). According to the U.S. Committee for Refugees' *Sudan Fact Sheet* (1999b), more than 1.9 million people in south and central Sudan died between 1955 and 1999 as a result of war. The massive loss of life surpasses the civilian death toll in any war since World War II. Over four million southerners have been compelled to flee their homes and have become displaced internally and internationally.

This conflict, which figures prominently as a determinant in the current migratory streams to the United States and Canada, reflects a quandary that the majority of postcolonial African states have had to grapple with since independence from European rule (Abusharaf 1998c). The current borders of the Sudan were drawn by the British in 1899 when the Condominium Agreement was signed. Yet for the duration of British colonialism in the Sudan, the north-south division was administratively enforced. Fearful of the spread of northern cultural practices (such as female circumcision), the Arabic language, and Islam, the British governed the two regions as separate political units. This was accomplished by way of the Closed Doors Ordinance, which diminished interaction between the two regions (Abdel Rahim 1969). In so doing, British colonial policies planted the seeds of disunion in a country with such remarkable ethnic diversity, pitting northerners versus southerners and "Arabs" versus "Africans." Indifferent to the long history dividing and connecting the two regions (as well as the internal diversity of each), and failing to allow contact to develop between their peoples, the British combined both portions into a unified Sudan at independence in 1956. So, like other modern African states, the Sudan may claim that the British colonial regime was responsible for blending disparate ethnic groups into one country.

The question of north-south relations became widely seen as an "ethnic" conflict between "Arabs" and "Africans" at the time of independence. However, just as there is no monolithic "Arab" north, the south also is a land of extraordinary ethnic variety. Ethnographers of southern populations depict marked differences in kinship structures, ethnolinguistic groups, social organization, and modes of subsistence (Wai 1973). According to Mohamed Omer Beshir (1968), southern Sudanese could be distinguished into three groups: the Niolitics, comprising the Dinka, Nuer, Shiluk, and Anuak; the Nilo-Hamitics, including the Murle, Didinga, Boya, Toposa, and Latuka; and the Sudanic peoples, including the Azande among other smaller social formations. In light of the heterogeneity of both south and north, it can be argued that the civil war has been prompted mainly by political objectives, and that ethnicity is but one component. More widely, as Talal Asad argues: "In any attempt to treat political domination as a central problem, it is necessary to inquire into such questions as the institutional sources of power deriving from the overall social and economic structure" (1970, 8). For southerners, "ethnic" or "racial" difference became exacerbated in the large scheme of power relations in Sudanese society. As Manning Marable explains: "Race only becomes real as a social force when individuals or groups behave towards each other in ways that either reflect or perpetuate the hegemonic ideology of subordination" (1995, 364).

Following independence, the new national leadership was not successful at mobilizing the Sudanese peoples, southerners and northerners alike, behind a political and economic program that could fulfill basic needs and ensure stability. Political authority was then seized by military governments after short-lived interludes of democratic rule. This reality has perpetuated a political arrangement that has encouraged the continuation of the war and subjected the Sudan in general and the southern region in particular to widespread instability, destruction of the economy, disruption of social cohesion, and death and displacement on a large scale (Abusharaf 1998c; Bechtold 1992; Deng 1995; Holt and Daly 1988; Khalid 1989). Bona Malwal is right to argue that the causes of the war "stem from a lack of basic democracy. This has led to a situation in which those who exercise power abuse the right of those who are excluded from state power; the exclusion of the vast majority of the people of the regions from state power has led to a perpetual state of tension, civil war and conflict" (1993, 3).

The Sudan is a perfect illustration of an African country unable to achieve nationhood despite a successful struggle for independence. In *Nations and Nationalism since 1780*, Eric Hobsbawm points to the impact of the colonial legacy on the question of postcolonial nationalism:

> Decolonization meant that, by and large, independent states were created out of existing areas of colonial administration, within their colonial frontiers. These had, obviously, been drawn without any reference to, or sometimes even without the knowledge of, their inhabitants and therefore had no national or even protonational significance for their populations; except for colonial-educated and westernized native minorities of varying, but generally exiguous size. Alternatively, where such territories were too small and scattered, as in many colonized archipelagos, they were combined or broken up according to convenience or local politics. Hence the constant, and eventually often vain, calls of the leaders of such new states to surmount "tribalism," "communalism," or whatever forces were made responsible for the failure of the new inhabitants of the Republic of X to feel themselves to be primarily patriotic citizens of X rather than members of some other collectivity. (1990, 170)

Extensive border crossings have been a consequence of the Sudan's civil war. For example, an estimated 71,500 refugees had fled the Sudan to neighboring Ethiopia by 1970. In addition, there were unknown, yet enormous, numbers of refugees in Chad and Kenya (Holborn 1975). Policies toward the south continued to swing between warfare and short-lived peaceful resolutions. One resolution toward peace was the Addis Ababa Agreement in 1972, which provided for the unification of the southern

[51]

provinces into a single region with full administrative and political autonomy. This agreement put a temporary end to years of internecine strife and
granted recognition to the pluralistic nature of Sudanese society (Warburg
1992, 92).

The peace agreement encouraged refugees to return home. The recognition of the south as an autonomous administrative and political unit was a
positive step toward ensuring the right of self-rule for southerners. According to Philister Baya, her own family, which had lived in exile in Uganda
since 1966, decided to repatriate along with thousands of refugees. "We
enjoyed a relative peace for eleven years. After a decade the peace col-
lapsed and the armed hostilities resumed" (1999, 61). The resumption of
the war can be attributed to President Gaafar Nemeiri's decision in 1983 to
revoke the Addis Ababa Agreement. By fragmenting the south again, Nemeiri prompted another war, made worse this time around by his espousal
of the hegemonic policy of Islamization. Since then, the adoption and firm
application of *sharia* law has developed further, irrespective of the complex
nature of the multiethnic, multireligious Sudan. In his 1998 book *Politics
and Islam in Contemporary Sudan*, Abdel Salam Sidahmed explains that
Islamization incorporates legal, political, and ideological aspects to legitimize central power. The legal component addresses offenses such as theft,
consumption of alcohol, apostasy, and rebellion against the state. The firm
application of sharia under the current regime since 1989 has been accompanied by the imposition of jihad (holy war) and the official imposition of
the Arabic language, creating a situation best described as "a tyranny of the
majority" (see Guinier 1994). Consequently, these impositions have in-
flamed the strife. As Deng puts it: "The conflict has increasingly been
viewed in religious terms. Although this has the effect of oversimplifying
the situation, it makes religion symbolic of all that is contested, a critical
factor in the definition of the national identity and in the shaping and sharing of unity of the country that is becoming increasingly accepted while religion, paradoxically is becoming a highly divisive factor" (1991, 25–26).

Since the recurrence of war under the current military regime, the mass
departure of refugees has begun all over again. Large movements have
taken place internally as well as across the national border. According to Sudanese geographer M. E. Abu Sin, human dislocation due to the war
reached its acme during 1989–90, when a million southerners took refuge
in northern Sudan. Statistics published in the *United States Committee for
Refugees News* (1999) show that, with four million southerners now living
in the north, the Sudan leads the world in internally displaced persons. Furthermore, many of them have been displaced more than once, and often repeatedly, since 1989.

As can be expected during a time of war, human distress multiplies and takes on different forms. The displacement of southerners is not the sole outcome of the war. Another adverse consequence that southerners talk about has manifested itself in the resuscitation of slavery. In 2000, slave raids were reported to have been taking place routinely in some parts of the south. Several news programs in the United States addressed the efforts of one group of American school children who donated their lunch money to redeem the freedom of slaves in the Sudan. About 25,000 slaves have been freed—redeemed for about fifty dollars each—with the help of Christian Solidarity International in Switzerland (Sudanet, September 7, 2000). Although this organization has been criticized, many southern Sudanese confirm its views.

Slavery is intimately linked to a war economy (Bales 1999, 2000). War slavery has been documented as a disturbing effect of the government's military operations. Bhatia Shyam describes a pattern in which Arab militias from the northern part of the country, including officers in the army, have engaged in kidnapping children and women from villages in the south and forcing them to work as field laborers, domestic servants, or sexual concubines (U.S. Committee for Refugees 1999a). As many as 100,000 Sudanese are enslaved, according to Charles Jacob, president of the Anti-Slavery Group in Boston (Sudanet, September 7, 2000). Some are also sold to countries in north Africa or the Persian Gulf. War-induced interethnic conflict among southerners was also reported as a cause of slave raids.

The most obvious example of interethnic conflict is that between the Nuer and Dinka. Hiram Ruiz (1998) provides a helpful analysis of the displacement of Sudanese and points out that in East Equatoria Province the overwhelming majority of the displaced are Dinka from the Bor region, all of whom have been displaced two or three times by Nuer raids. But as Kevin Bales points out, tribes that have been victims of slave raiding have sometimes themselves raided other tribes (Bales 2000, 18).

Rebecca, a Dinka woman, last saw her home seven years ago. She says combatants from neighboring ethnic Nuer attacked her town in the Jongli region and killed and raided Dinka (U.S. Committee for Refugees 1999a). However, in October of 1999 the leaders of both the Nuer and the Dinka met to discuss the return of women, children, and cattle captured in raids or abducted during the years of hostility. These talks were facilitated through the People to People Peace East Bank Niolitics Reconciliation Conference that was launched on May 8, 1999. The October conference was the second called to end hostilities, halt further displacement, and reconcile the Nuer and Dinka (Sudanet, May 2, 2000).

Displacement and Migration

Before 1955 southern communities perceived migration efforts as threatening to the well-being of both the individual and the collectivity, and out-migration from the southern region of the Sudan was extremely uncommon. "To a Dinka, his country with all its deprivations and troubles is the best in the world. Until very recently going to foreign lands was not only a rarity, but a shame. For a Dinka to threaten his relatives of leaving Dinkaland was seen as little short of a suicide. What a lot to give up, and for what?" (Deng 1972, 6). Ator Ayiik, a Dinka, confirmed this view when she said, "It is difficult for someone like me to depart my own land. Although we have difficulties here, it is my own land. If I die, I will die here. In another country you are not free. My land is better" (U.S. Committee for Refugees 1999a, 52).

This view has changed only with great unwillingness as millions of people were forced to flee their region. The southern Sudanese experience is different from other Sudanese migrations, then, in that these are refugees under direct coercion of war. As Kunz has noted, "It is this reluctance to uproot oneself and the absence of positive original motivations to settle elsewhere, which characterize all refugee decisions and distinguish refugees from voluntary migrants" (cited in Bariagaber 1995, 209). As a result, southern migration has become a solution of last resort.

This spatial dislodging has had profound social ramifications. Devastation of the social cohesiveness of entire communities occurred as a result of population dispersal (see Bascom 1995). The most severe impact of war on southerners manifested itself in the eroding of lineage and family structures, destruction of traditions such as initiation and other rites of passage, homelessness, and abject poverty within the receiving communities. Southerner Christina Dudu, herself displaced in Khartoum, argues that the majority of the refugees were originally agriculturists or agro-pastoralists whose rural skills do not provide them with opportunities to make a living in their new urban surroundings (1999, 51). In the words of Salah El Din El Shazali, the powerlessness of southerners is linked to lack of access to "objects and symbols that are central to the maintenance and propagation of sociocultural identity, value systems and practices" (1995, 42). Added to these problems are intensified intercommunity conflicts, personal bafflement, and social confusion.

Although displacement is typically hurtful for everyone involved, it is far worse for women (Baya 1999; Eastmond 1993; Hackett 1996; Indra 1999). Dudu's (1999) study on southern displaced women delineates gendered forms of exploitation that have accompanied the displacement. She has cast light on sexual abuse, prostitution, harassment, and other practices that were hitherto virtually absent among these societies.

Mary, a forty-five-year-old southern Sudanese war-displaced woman in Khartoum. 1998.

I discovered this abuse during my own fieldwork in the Sudan, where I was informed by a social worker at a Sudanese nongovernmental organization that one of the most distressing aspects of the experiences of the internally displaced is that they began to adopt cultural practices previously unknown to them, including female circumcision. With no money to pay a traditional wedding dowry, women are barred from marriage and become outcasts in the eyes of their fellow countrymen (Adam 2001). Mary, a nurse, explains: "These people lost everything back home. Practicing circumcision is a way to imitate their neighbors, to be like them; and to become more marriageable."

These newly transmitted customs of the "north" to southerners is a source of concern to southern Sudanese scholars. The cultural borrowing underway is seen, for instance, by Pressla Joseph, professor at Bahr El Ghazal University, in this way: "The cultures of Southern Sudanese suffer from the borrowing of Northern Sudanese practices. For example, marriage practices are changing. Now the bride asks for *shaila* (a dowry which consists of money, jewelry and other goods). Also in funeral services, Southerners started to mimic Northerners. Dinka language is also in jeopardy of extinction as Southerners now speak Arabic among themselves. I am fearful that this will entail loss of identity" (Adam 2001).

When southern Sudanese cross the border to neighboring African coun-

[55]

tries, their problems transcend those of cultural borrowing. Southerners who go to Cairo, for instance, embark on a journey that promises trouble as much as it offers hope and optimism. The journey by train lasts for several days in crammed conditions, and is fraught with hardship and suffering. Once in Ramsis Station in Cairo, they head for the Catholic church in Zamalik, Abbassia, and to various Anglican churches. The Catholic church on Ahmed Said Avenue in Cairo is the official residence of southerners. The church oversees their affairs in Egypt and helps in their resettlement applications to the United Nations High Commissioner for Refugees. The arrival rate is 500 per month, and by 1989 over forty thousand had come.

Needless to say, they meet a life that is proportionately filled with strain and anxiety. Unemployment, homelessness, and overcrowding while waiting to be resettled are some of the many challenges they face (Daughtry 2001). Twenty people share an apartment with little to do but work as servants or peddle herbs and small items in the market. A resident in the Abbassia neighborhood where large numbers of southerners live maintained that almost seventy men and women who were kicked out of their apartments in summer 2000 for not paying rent became homeless (*Rose El Youssif* 2000). A southern Sudanese refugee woman described the situation eloquently when she remarked that Sudanese here face another war. A recent article published in *Rose El Youssif* (2000), a prestigious Egyptian magazine, was titled "Migration to Egypt: Are Refugees Guests or Criminals?" The incident that precipitated the article involved a fight in Cairo between southern Sudanese refugees and Egyptians. Some accused the refugees of dealing in drugs. A Catholic priest from the church came to their defense. "I was in the church when people came in to tell me about the fight. When I arrived at the gas station [*benzina*], I saw Sudanese and Egyptians there. I tried to talk the Sudanese into going back to the church. In the meantime Egyptians picked up wood logs and tried to beat them up. People must know that the Sudanese who were arrested because of this did not instigate the fight. They were not drunk either, as people reported to the police. The injury done to these people was extensive. At the time of the fight, we already had 400 people in the church. Everything was just chaotic."

This incident depicts a bleak picture, one in which tension is building in areas where refugees are concentrated. The criminalization of these refugees also points to strong sentiments of exasperation and resentment on the part of the Egyptian hosts. The southerners' reaction to the incident also reflects strong refugee emotionality—produced and sustained by an unfriendly atmosphere. In spite of this, what gives southern Sudanese some hope and optimism is the knowledge that Cairo is only a transit station from which they move to the United States, Australia, New Zealand, or Canada. By summer 2000, 3,230 claims for resettlement had been processed (*Rose*

El Youssif 2000). The happy news that their application has been accepted invites celebration and delight for those waiting their turn to relocate.

Arrival in the United States and Canada

Probably one of the most highly acclaimed fashion models in the United States and Europe today is Alek Wek, a Dinka woman who lived with her family as a refugee in England. Alek Wek, who has graced the covers of magazines and made appearances on several talk shows in the United States, now resides in Manhattan—"a model life," as Constance White (2000), a magazine writer, describes her current existence of elegance and affluence. Alek Wek's trajectory does not mirror that of the majority of southerners, even though she herself is a refugee. One cannot belittle her experience, but the grief that thousands of southern Sudanese have endured remains unspeakable, and almost inarticulable.

The following account of Philister Baya communicates the more typical traumas that southern Sudanese, especially women, are forced to withstand. She writes:

> I came to live in Khartoum in 1987 and worked in the Council for the South until it was dissolved in January 1991. Soon, in March 1991, the Sudan People's Liberation Army (SPLA) occupied the town of Maridi. As Mundri, my home place, is just few miles from Maridi, the government army decided to evacuate Mundri, walking away on foot and accompanied by the civilian population, including my family. Upon their arrival at Rokon, fighting took place between the army and the Sudan People's Liberation Army. Many civilians were killed in crossfire. My dear father, sister and cousin were amongst those killed in that incident on Good Friday. (1999, 62)

Baya's story is by no means an anomaly: it echoes those of thousands of men and women. No wonder that the southern Sudanese see the current Islamic government as an extremely aggressive regime in relation to defenseless civilian populations. For southerners, the problem is aggravated by racial, political, and economic exclusion via the twin processes of Arabization and Islamization. All of this has converged in what they perceive as nothing less than a total annihilation of their indigenous cultures and beliefs.

To learn more about southern Sudanese migration to the United States and Canada, I interviewed southerners in New York City, Washington, D.C., Michigan, and Toronto. Others who resided in Texas, Arizona, California, and New Jersey responded to my survey (see also Holtzman 2000). Although these interviewees were of different ages, occupations, ethnicity,

[57]

gender, and class backgrounds, they all considered migration as a means to sidestep war, Islamization, and militarism.

The arduous processes of transformation for southerners are reflected in their stories of their experiences in exile. These southern Sudanese were mainly young or middle-aged individuals who began arriving in the United States and Canada in the 1980s and have continued to arrive (up to the time of this writing in early 2002) as a result of the civil war. Civil war refugees are mostly Christians, and those I encountered were generally highly educated, having either completed college or at least secondary education at the time of arrival (but compare to Holtzman 2000). The majority have high levels of proficiency in English. Most of the respondents indicated that they received substantial help from refugee resettlement organizations like the U.S. Catholic Conference, Christian Outreach, and the World Council of Churches. Although one interviewee maintained that the resettlement process is a highly selective procedure that automatically rejects illiterate displaced people, current reality refutes this view.

Civil war migrants who make it to North America can be grouped into three migratory streams according to individual histories. The first consists of a number of migrants who resided in Kenya, Ethiopia, Zaire, Uganda, Egypt, and Central African Republic before their move abroad, which was facilitated by refugee resettlement programs. (Most civil war migrants reported that their last place of residence prior to coming to North America was another African country). Leaving the Sudan to enter these countries was only the first step in their migration journey; most had to wait months, sometimes years, before placement and resettlement in a new country. A second stream consists of university scholars and government employees who had already been in North America for training programs and who, like their northern counterparts, preferred to remain. These, who arrived directly from the Sudan, were commonly government employees, some of whom resided and worked in the north prior to migration. Third was a small number of Sudanese who migrated to North America from Europe. The majority of these civil war migrants received refugee resettlement services.

Of paramount importance in all these cases was the role of political and religious factors, with the government's policies of Islamization adding to a preexisting sense of subordination and relegation to second-class citizenry. The polemics of identity—and its manipulation for political purposes—thus plays a significant role in both the civil war and the resulting migratory phenomena. (This is highlighted in the experiences of northern Sudanese Christians as well—see chapter 6.)

One of the first people I interviewed in 1993 was Peter. He was thirty-three years old and was born in Ngusuluku, in the western part of Bahr El

Ghazal Province. Peter arrived in Washington, D.C., in 1987, four years after the revival of the civil war. Peter voiced the motives behind migration of the majority of southerners I interviewed: "Education, political unrest, and persecution of Christians are the reasons why I came." He explained that the church helped him to settle by providing financial aid. He also related a personal revelation that became a recurring theme in my research. "The best thing about living here is discovering myself as an African. In the U.S. I continue to suffer, namely in the form of arbitrary police arrest and questioning. I see no possibility of assimilation, and I very much keep my relations with other Sudanese. This experience forces me to never loose sight of where I came from and of going back if the conditions that pushed me here in the first place end."

Peter went on to say that the subordination of the south is a concern for every southern Sudanese here in the United States and Canada, as well as in the Sudan. The exclusion of the region from socioeconomic development, the unequal distribution of resources, and the underrepresentation of southerners in the political sphere are seen by Peter as significant factors in the underdevelopment of the south and in the war.

The survey and interviews also identified the particular "pull factors" important in the experience of these southern Sudanese. Factors such as political and religious freedom in North America, assistance provided by churches and refugee resettlement organizations, and encouragement by family members and friends who were already here. As Joseph, a thirty-six-year-old refugee living in Connecticut, put it: "Almost everybody knows what is happening in the Sudan. The reasons for my leaving are religious persecution, disrespect for human lives, political oppression, and the war in the Sudan. I had no home in the Sudan. I was just living as a refugee in another African country, in Kenya. The reason why I am here is because of the freedom of worship and the respect of human rights." Joseph's viewpoint was reflected in the survey: although only 21 percent of Muslim northerners indicated they had migrated for political reasons, 82 percent of Christian southerners specified this as the main reason. Here are some representative stories.

John

Like many other Sudanese professionals, John describes his migrant experience like someone who is unexpectedly stranded away from home. As he spoke, I could see he was reliving the trauma of discovering the impossibility of returning there. Normally a quiet gentleman, he became animated and spoke passionately as he told his story, his voice often rising with anger, as if feeling it for the first time.

I am forty-one years old. I was born in Equatoria Province. I am a Latuka. I am Christian. I arrived in the U.S. in 1981. I completed my education up to my Ph.D. in the United States. Before joining the University of Khartoum, I used to live in Uganda and then Zaire. I left for Khartoum to go to college. I was a teaching assistant at the University of Khartoum. So I came as an exchange student with the sponsorship of a church organization. When I came here I worked like everybody else very hard to make ends meet. I worked odd jobs here and there till I finished. But still I don't have a full-time job. I am not really satisfied with the job situation, because I have to send remittances to family members back home.

The main reasons for staying on after my degree was finished are war and persecution. I would like to go back to the Sudan once peace [and] racial, religious, and cultural equality is established. Because life here is not problem-free. Loneliness, stress, and racism are the most common problems. But I try to overcome this feeling by socializing with Sudanese and by joining the Sudanese Pax Sudani Network with other southerners. I feel these things help me keep my Sudanese culture, which, consciously, I feel not too strongly about it, but unconsciously I do feel strongly about keeping.

William

Most of the southerners I interviewed understandably perceived Islamic law as a mechanism of northerner-forced Islamization and Arabization in the southern region.

Among these was William, a fifty-year-old Presbyterian minister born in Akobo. His wife, also a southern Sudanese, from Rumbek, and children moved with him to Chicago in October 1984, a year after the imposition of Islamic law in the Sudan.

In the Sudan, I was chairman and managing director of a pastoral organization. Now I work on an international development project and my interest in it emphasizes development at the grassroots level. I also worked for two years in Addis Ababa [Ethiopia] as host for Radio Voice of Gospel Liberation. I left that job to take up a ministerial appointment in the Sudan. I left the Sudan as protest against the Islamization and Arabization of southern Sudan, which continues to be a marginal region. Once we arrived, we received a lot of support. Church groups, friends, and nongovernmental organizations spared no effort in helping us. My friends here also helped us tremendously—not only did they provide us with a place to live when we first came but assisted in the process of settlement itself. They offered us accommodations and showed us where to find shops and the best deals for clothing.

Life here is a lot easier in terms of access to material goods. But overall there is something about the Sudan that makes your life easier there, it is home. Sure you struggle to obtain basic necessities like milk, sugar, and gas, but you know it is easier, because life in America has its problems such as the exaggerated individualism with all its implications and consequences, and the inability of citizens to try to understand people who are different. But my relations with Americans are good, although generally business is humanly superficial. My thoughts of my culture are very frequent and deeply ingrained inside of me. I am unequivocal about going back home when the [government's] pursuit of Islamic and Arabic policies changes. I hope that the Sudanese people will work and struggle to influence the return to a secular constitution. Believe me, life is much easier there.

Like the majority of interviewees, William maintained that permitting the continuation of the war is tantamount to the disintegration in civil society of the Sudan as he knew it. Southerners recognized that a depoliticization of religion and an acknowledgment of the multicultural character of the Sudan are critical to any peaceful resolution. Putting an end to the war is an important precondition for refugees to reclaim their lands and their lives. Nevertheless, they do not hold any conviction that this goal is within range under current political circumstances.

Morris

Morris, forty-six years old, was born in Yei. He is Catholic and married to a woman from Kajo-Keji. Morris was resettled in the United States in 1991 with the sponsorship of the U.S. Catholic Conference; until then, he was living in Kenya. Morris first worked in a government job in the United States. After a period on welfare, he now works as a supervisor in a different field and reports feeling underemployed. Morris is attending school in New Jersey.

> My problems in the Sudan are religious and political. I will only go back if the south becomes independent. The United States refugee and asylum seekers admission enabled me to be resettled here. The United Nations High Commissioner for Refugees and the World Council of Churches are the main organizations that provide resettlement services in refugee camps. I encountered many problems here: loneliness, racial discrimination, and cultural shock are only some. Subjection in the cultural sphere stems primarily from the current Sudan government's attempts to create a "unicultural" Islamic society.

For Morris, as for a considerable number of respondents, total secession of the south is the only condition under which they will be ready to return. According to Lado, another refugee, "The time to let our people go is long overdue. We cannot continue to be a nation of masters and slaves; pursuing peace in the context of a unified Sudan sustains Arab hegemony over

[61]

Africans in Sudan. Partitioning the country would deliver African Sudanese from centuries of bondage at the hands of the Arabs" (Lado 1994, 10).

David and Lisa

David and Lisa were both born in the town of Rumbek, he in 1953 and she in 1959. David held an administrative position at Juba University until 1987, when he left the Sudan with Lisa and their three children. They lived in Kenya for two years until the U.S. Catholic Conference was able to resettle them in Virginia. Eventually David brought his family to New Jersey, where he attended graduate school with outside financial assistance. David sees their migration as a temporary situation: "Home is home, and when the war is over I will go back. Right now at home people are barely surviving bullets. They should run for their lives."

Lisa told me that she was a housewife in the Sudan but, with the help of her friends, currently works at a daycare center in her neighborhood. "Before I was attending to my family; in the U.S.A. I have to leave my own children to a baby-sitter and leave early for work outside my house. I was well-off in the Sudan. Here our salary can't afford a thing. Bringing our children was also very expensive. I can't wait for the war to end and go home."

Michael

Michael, thirty-four, was born in Juba. He owned a business in the Sudan but currently has a part-time job and attends school, working toward a bachelor's degree in business. As a refugee, Michael was resettled in Connecticut with the assistance of Church World Service. When he arrived, says Michael, he met with a "Good Samaritan" who helped him.

I was given the basic necessities for life: food and accommodation and winter clothing. I found life here a lot easier because of religious freedom and my physical well-being. I was driven from the Sudan by war, resulting from our resistance to northerners' forced Islamization and the marginalization of the south in social, economic, and political spheres. Life became intolerable as a result of the northern Sudanese government policies. It torments me to see my other fellow southerners on TV, and I think about the harrowing conditions they live under. I wish there were something that could be done fast to save them. People have to realize that they are entitled to live as humans. It is obvious that I am here because of the war. The relentless attempts by the Islamic government to isolate the South and policies limiting our participation in areas of power and influence make me believe that secession is the answer to the southern predicament. It is the only legitimate solution, and southerners should fight until this goal is reached.

Frank

Frank now lives in Toronto, Canada. Originally from Equatoria Province, Frank is Bari and a Christian. He provided a detailed account that offers insight into the inner life of a southern migrant.

I moved to Toronto with my wife and children in 1992 after living as refugees in Kampala, Uganda. I graduated from college in Sudan and currently attend school part-time in Canada, hoping eventually to obtain a graduate degree in Divinity Studies. Before my departure to Uganda, I was working as a civil engineer and the principal of a vocational training center in Juba. Currently, I do not have a job and in fact I have not been able to get one since I landed in Canada. Depending on government assistance, I volunteer as a community worker. I really worked so hard to find a job, tried to network, mailed in my applications, and physically went from one place to the next, stopping by, asking for a job, but to no use.

Coming to Canada was a blessing because I prayed for safety, but it was hard because coming as a refugee makes you feel that as a human being you can't have choices, you are forced to leave and stay abroad indefinitely. Before I came I was corresponding with church groups and other people I knew from home. The Canadian government was responsible for my resettlement and really helped me a lot to get a visa, arrange travel plans, and provide airfare and a lot of things. They were very helpful to our families.

I came from a country where people's lives are worthless, people die everyday. But coming here with that knowledge makes one very emotional, it is very upsetting when people die like that. The good part of living in Toronto, however, is the presence of so many Sudanese northerners and southerners. We get along very well with everyone. We celebrate national events, play cards on weekends and keep in contact. That is what is lifting the pressure off our shoulders, the fact that we were forced into leaving. As far as thousands of southerners in Canada are concerned, let me say that the war and the Islamic religious oppression are the reasons why they are here.

No one seems to understand the pain of leaving your home, your relatives, friends, just everything. You can never recover from that. But you try your best to adjust the best you can. The moral support and other kinds of help that we provide each other here are essential. Maybe if I manage to get a job, that will also help alleviate the pressure.

Now, my family and I have Sudanese roommates, and we live in government-subsidized housing. We cannot afford anything else. This neighborhood is infested with drugs and problems. As a visible minority, a Black, I encounter racist attitudes here as well. This is a problem, when you find yourself confronted with so many differences, especially cultural differences. But again we go back and forth, we have lived through a lot and we just feel lucky to be alive. For that we feel very grateful. But we are still anxious and worried about family members and relatives who did not get out. This is a nagging worry that never goes away, no matter what you do to occupy your mind. I feel like I want to help, but I have no means.

I do hope that more Sudanese will be able to come to Canada until the situation gets better. For them, coming here will be an eye-opener. Different people have different experiences, but it will be educational for our Sudanese folk who have only heard about modern life but have not seen it. I want to stress that regardless of what I do here, I want to return if or when the southern question is resolved. If that happens today, I will go home.

A recurring theme in these statements is that being able to flee subjection, war, and marginalization is only one step toward freedom. This perspective underpins southern Sudanese patterns of adjustment and adaptation in North American society. It makes for a lingering discontent, whereas the greater number of northern migrants expressed complacency and satisfaction with their move.

However, like northerners, southerners do join activities and associations like the political Pax Sudani Organization that not only help them maintain ties with fellow southerners but also help raise awareness in the international community about conditions in the Sudan. Like the rest of Sudanese migrants, southerners yearn to go home should political conditions change, either through the return of democracy or, for some, after their region secedes.

Naya

It is mid-morning on July 18, 2000, when I receive a telephone call. A social worker from a hospital in New Britain, Connecticut, is trying desperately to locate a Nuer interpreter who can translate for twenty-two-year-old Naya. She had been brought to the hospital by her sixteen-year-old brother-in-law, who himself speaks very little English. Naya had fled with her family to a refugee camp in Ethiopia after the renewal of the war in 1983, as had her future husband with his two brothers. In spite of the hardship and uncertainty associated with life there, it was the only home that Naya had known since she was a child. Then, early in 2000, she and her husband— along with her husband's two younger brothers, both born in the camp— were finally resettled with the help of Catholic Charities and the Archdiocese of Hartford. It took me two days to locate a Nuer interpreter in Wisconsin, and he proved extremely helpful and cooperative with the hospital staff. Through a series of conference phone calls, Naya and her family were able to communicate their innermost thoughts and concerns about their loneliness and their homesickness in this new place. An invitation was extended to me to join a meeting with hospital staff, a representative of Catholic Charities, and the two social workers who were in charge of her case. Along with a fellow Sudanese in Connecticut, we attended the meeting, which turned out to be extremely informative about the predicaments of exile and uprootedness. The nurse practitioner began by identifying Naya's problem.

Her brothers-in-law, who are sixteen and twelve years old, brought Naya here. Her husband never came with her before. We were so concerned and frustrated because no one could communicate with them. I have the phone number of a northern Sudanese who kindly came to help, but since she did not speak their language she was not able to communicate either. The hospital staff then managed to contact a southern Sudanese family in Hartford, but they apologized because they are not Nuer-speaking. The person you helped us get in touch with is really helpful. Naya's brother-in-law was talking to him the whole time about how lonely and bored they are, and that they don't want to stay here. But what concerned me was that in the beginning of our conference call with him, Naya was reluctant and embarrassed to tell him about her symptoms. She is four months pregnant and her symptoms indicated the possibility of serious problems with her pregnancy. We ran a series of tests. Our resident obstetrician felt that the interpreter should explain to Naya that there are problems with her pregnancy and with the fetus. We wanted to make sure that she understands why she was undergoing these laborious procedures and why the doctor is very anxious to know how she feels about the next stage, which might entail termination of the pregnancy. That, too, proved to be difficult because we have to make absolutely certain that is what she and her husband want. I am not sure how they would feel about it. Is this something done or acceptable in their culture? This is the most emotionally draining case for us. We are so worried about Naya but we are not able to inform her with the details and the medical information. We are going to call the interpreter today to share with him the latest diagnosis.

Listening to the most intimate problems of Naya's encounters in the hospital was at the same time fatiguing and difficult. The discussion then moved from Naya's health to the subject of their life in New Britain. A social worker started to tell us about her experience with them.

I have been very busy with this family since they came because of the fact that they don't speak English, and they don't speak the language of other people from their country who live here in New Britain. I take them to the store for grocery shopping. I also take them to the bank, and I taught Shol, the sixteen-year-old, how to use the ATM machine. This was very hard. It took a while to explain to him that the money they get is enough for the rent, utilities, and phone bill. I also showed them how to use the stove and told them to make sure that the burners are turned off if they are not in use. Almost every little thing that seems obvious turns out to be very difficult because of their particular situation. Also, with the use of electricity, I try to explain to them that the bill can be very high. I told them to be careful with that too. Also about the monthly rent—that they have to pay it every month so that the landlord should not throw them out.

I think that Shol is very smart and he pays attention to everything, but still, he is a teen-ager who is in charge of the family now. His brother, Naya's husband, is very quiet and he did not take any English lessons at the camp. So for the most part, he is home day and night and doesn't leave except when he comes with us to the store. This is the other problem. I tell Shol that I am very busy and I can't come more than once a week to drive them to the store. I told them to buy enough groceries, but every time I take them, oh, they buy so little all the time. They buy milk, bread, and meat. I don't know how three people can survive for the whole week on so little.

At this point the other social worker added,

I worry about this family so much. They are very nice people and my heart goes out to them. But I don't want them to get in trouble. The other day the little boy was riding a brand new bike. When I asked him where he got it, he pointed at the sky. I did not know what he meant by that, whether it belongs to someone in the building who lives upstairs, or whether it fell from the sky [she added jokingly]. We have to mention to the interpreter to tell them that if they find things sitting around in front of the building they should not touch it, so that they will not be accused of theft. See, there is a lot of work to be done.

When I told the representative of the Archdiocese of Hartford that there is a Nuer community in Minnesota (see Holtzman 2000) and that there might be a possibility of relocating Naya's family in a community in which they can belong, she explained that the logistics are quite involved, and that their resettlement here was only possible because they had a sponsor in Connecticut. However, after our meeting, things did change dramatically for Naya and her family. The twelve-year-old started school and joined the school's track and field and soccer teams. I was told that he was "absorbing English like a sponge," while sixteen-year-old Shol now insisted he wanted a job. The three brothers all enrolled in English as a second language (ESL) classes. Naya, however, lost her baby two months later. The hospital social worker told me, "Naya sobbed and cried bitterly. She did not want to see the baby or hold him. She was in shock. We were so sad. She is a very sweet girl. She knew that we cared for her so deeply."

In January 2001, the two Nuer families in New Britain boarded a bus to New York City and then traveled to Minnesota. I learned they were soon in touch with other Nuer families, probably introduced to them by the Wisconsin interpreter. They left ready and anxious for their reunification with other Nuer in the Twin Cities. The social worker added:

> We were very worried about what they were going to do once they get to Port Authority—and all these bus connections. But obviously they got concrete directions and in fact the tickets were sent to them by the people there in Minnesota. I am convinced that these people are survivors. If they survived the camp, I am sure they will survive here. When we got a call from Shol to thank us for everything, one forgets that Shol is just a teenager. He is so mature, so responsible. I think they will make it.

Naya's experience is very similar to those described by Jon Holtzman (2000) who studied the Nuer community in Minnesota. He identified problems in dealing with the new environment, from landlords to housekeeping. Holtzman found similar patterns in the resettlement process, the development of community ties, and relations to American hosts. Yet the great ingenuity and resourcefulness of a community that has suffered life's worst blows to human dignity and imagination was also apparent as Nuer migrants carry on in yet another challenging habitat.

The southern Sudanese refugees' ties to their American and Canadian hosts are increasingly mobilized to increase public awareness about the continuing tribulation of their kith and kin in the Sudan. For example, the southern Sudanese community in Alexandria, Virginia, called upon Sudanese and non-Sudanese to join them on July 29, 1998, for a morning protest march on Pennsylvania Avenue in front of the White House. This event was an effort to bring the displacement, starvation, and death of millions of southerners to the attention of the American government. Professional athlete Manut Bol has initiated dozens of similar events; the seven-foot, seven-inch retired center in the National Basketball Association has used his physical stature and popular notoriety to raise the awareness of the international community to the political impasse in the southern Sudan. Although Bol later reconciled with the Sudanese government and was appointed by President Omer El-Bashir as a cabinet member in the Ministry of Youth and Sports, his earlier efforts registered widely.

Another large protest took place in September 2000 when the United Nations in New York City celebrated its Millennium Summit. The assembled diplomats faced waves of Sudanese migrants, exiles, and their supporters who were protesting the presence of President El-Bashir. Their protest centered on the claim that El-Bashir's military regime had perpetuated atrocities and was responsible for the conditions that propelled them to leave their homeland. This demonstration was not the first; Sudanese migrants and refugees had protested numerous times in front of the Sudanese Mission to the United Nations. Protesters have expressed their concern about a wide range of issues, including slavery and human rights abuses in their homeland.

One account in particular stands out: the story of Bak, who comes from a Catholic Dinka village in southern Sudan. Bak was one of the protesters demanding the arrest of President El-Bashir for directing his military forces to make slaves of civilian captives. In an article entitled "Outside the Summit, a Former Slave Speaks Out," Bak described her ordeal. When she was twelve years old, Muslim horsemen galloped into her Catholic village. According to her, they "burned our houses, and killed many people—including my grandfather, right there in front of my eyes. The attacking Muslim militiamen sold the women and children into slavery as domestics and shepherds. I was like an animal. I escaped one night after my nomadic master tried to rape me. I resisted, and he cut my leg with a knife. I slipped away, got on a truck and hid among the animals." Bak eventually ended up in Khartoum, where she met a fellow Dinka named Majak. In 1998 she married his brother, and six months later was resettled by the United Nations. Bak concluded by stating: "I am dismayed to learn that El-Bashir is walking the streets of New York City, a great city of freedom" (Sudanet, September 7, 2000).

The "Lost Boys and Girls of the Sudan"

On a sunny Khartoum morning in December 1998, I left for Takamul Camp along with two Sudanese social workers whose job often took them to various locations where the internally displaced are concentrated. We traveled for about an hour in congested traffic until we reached the outskirts of the city, a distance of about fifteen to twenty miles. Quite suddenly, the noise and traffic thinned, and for the next mile or two as we drove into Takamul Camp passed the densely packed buildings, we were acutely aware of the extent of poverty and hardship everywhere. Stopping at the clinic, we found ourselves in a relatively quiet sector where a group of dwellings made with *gana* (a bamboo-like plant) had been erected by the displaced themselves. The two social workers noted that even for housing these people are more often than not left to their own devices. And indeed, the absence of any substantial building materials or personal possessions in and around these huts was as glaring as the stark sun. In a nearby stall, some refugees were selling salt, peanut butter, and bread, which they had walked several miles to purchase at the market. Although it was very sunny, the weather was cold by Khartoum standards. Still, a group of thirty little boys who might have been in school had they been home were outside barefoot, playing *dafori*, a soccer game using a ball made of socks and old clothes, and wearing only thin handmade cotton pants and shirts tattered from years of wear. During that winter, I visited many similar settlements where displaced southerners live in Sudan: Jebel Awaliaa, Salama, Wad El-bashir, Soba, Mayo, and Magzoob. All reminded me of Takamul, with similar living conditions and surrounded by disease and suffering.

At Takamul I talked to Mary, a nurse who worked in a nearby clinic which provided limited assistance to the migrants with supplies from the government. She told me the residents of the camps were mostly mothers and children. There are few men, a situation typical of other refugee camps, since most of the men are either killed, join militias, or try to cross the border alone. Many camp girls are employed as maids nearby, and some employers even send the girls to school when they are not working. There is a reluctance to hire southern boys, however, who are less docile and often feared. They are stigmatized, called *shamasa* (thugs), and are largely left alone.

Beyond our conversation, the camp was quiet, except for the sound of younger boys playing. Mary and I decided to talk with them. As soon as they saw us approaching, they stopped their game and ran to us, speaking fluent Arabic. Several of them wanted to hold my camera; one lifted it to his face, pretending to take pictures. When I asked them if I could take their picture, their faces shone as they quickly lined up for their photo to be taken. In their adversity, I thought, these young boys had not lost their purity of heart or their charm. These, and tens of thousands of boys like them, are biding their time uselessly in refugee camps. They are unlikely to be resettled while they remain within the Sudan. Their lives are being wasted by a relentless war and by neglect. Thousands of Sudan's youth, driven from their homes, are hoping against hope that the United States will give them a chance at a new life (Corbett 2001; Simmons 2000).

Unlike the refugee boys within Sudan, the experience of those in neighboring Kenya and Ethiopia—now recognized as "the lost boys of the Sudan"—has received considerable media attention in the United States as they leave life in refugee camps to resettle in American cities. Many of these refugees have been living in Kenya for nearly ten years after being orphaned in southern Sudan and fleeing in the late 1980s. Their original number was estimated at 30,000, but it is believed that only 12,000 made it to Kakuma, Kenya, avoiding the wild animals, combat, hunger, and disease that killed others. They have forged their own self-created society in the chaotic world of a northern Kenya refugee camp. Of these, some 3,800 "lost boys" have been cleared for resettlement in the United States.

The lost boys and girls of the Sudan's civil war. Khartoum, 1998.

Numerous reports in the *Los Angeles Times*, the *Atlanta Constitution Journal*, *USA Today*, the *New York Times Magazine*, and the *Lincoln Journal Star* have addressed the subject of resettlement of the "lost boys" in the United States. The move was recommended by the United Nations High Commissioner for Refugees and is overseen by the U.S. Department of State. It is the first time the UNHCR has approved the overseas resettlement of such a large number of unaccompanied minors. The UNHCR has said the move was approved after fruitless efforts by the Red Cross to locate relatives of the boys still in the Sudan (Sudanet, November 13, 2000).

In November 2000, fifty of the boys arrived in the United States and settled in Omaha and Lincoln, Nebraska, with assistance from Lutheran Family Services, Catholic Charities, and other church groups. The plan is to place them together because, as one social worker put it, "We're very conscientious of the kin relationship they have established. We will put people who have grown up together as family in the same apartment or apartments in the same building." About 300 more teens are being resettled via charitable agencies in Lansing, Fargo, Phoenix, Boston, Grand Rapids, Philadelphia, Seattle, and Washington, D.C. They will live with foster families, some of whom are Sudanese. Other cities being considered in this resettlement effort include Richmond, Virginia, and Jackson, Mississippi, as well as sites where substantial Sudanese communities already exist in Minnesota, North and South Dakota, and Texas. The difficulties that resettlement services have identified are numerous. According to the executive director of Church World Service in Nebraska: "It is going to be a challenge. . . . The world to them is what is in this camp. They have no sense of money. No sense of cooking, shopping, driving, social interaction with adults. The only constant they have is each other" (see Lange-Kubick 2000).

Experienced charity organizations are key to the transition of these Sudanese boys into American life. Already the Roman Catholic Archdiocese of Atlanta has relocated refugees to safe houses in parishes where volunteers sponsor them (Teegardin 2000). Aowe, a refugee in Atlanta, for instance, has an entire parish dedicated to helping him make it in the United States; volunteers from All Saints Catholic Church help him pay his rent and provide childcare while he and his wife attended ESL classes. Like most refugees, the skills he brings from rural Africa are not easily transferable to the American job market, the same problem the "lost boys of the Sudan" will face.

Many southerners in the United States maintain that this longest civil war in history has not achieved any of the goals of either warring party. On the contrary, they maintain, allowing the war to continue only results in the wearing down of Sudanese society. Despite good intentions of charitable organizations helping to resettle refugees, as long as the war continues, the depletion of the southern Sudan's human capital will also persist—at escalating cost. The only certainty is that "lost boys" will be joined by more lost boys and girls who remain trapped within the Sudan.

[4]

Beyond the Storm: Sudanese Post–Gulf War Migration

We were forced to leave Kuwait because the Sudanese government supported Saddam Hussein. All Sudanese were seen as a big family. This was one way to take revenge.

>   Bab Allah, a former Sudanese worker in Kuwait. Khartoum,
>   December 1996

One of the noticeable aspects of Sudanese migration to North America from 1991–2000 is the arrival of persons who lived in the oil-rich Arab countries of the Persian Gulf region (e.g., Saudi Arabia, Kuwait, Qatar, Oman, and the United Arab Emirates) before coming to the United States or Canada. By 2000, they made up one of the principal migratory streams. A brief account of Sudanese migration to the Gulf region prior to the crisis of 1991 is pertinent to understanding not only the past trends but also this new post–Gulf War Sudanese migration to North America.

Prior to the Iraqi invasion of Kuwait in 1990, Sudanese were an important component of migration to these countries, which represented major attractions for migrant labor throughout the greater Middle Eastern swath of countries. Although other developing countries had witnessed declining economic performance in varying degrees, the explosion of oil prices in 1973 increased the wealth and prosperity of the oil-rich countries. As a result of the subsequent large-scale development projects undertaken by governments in the Gulf, substantial numbers of migrants were attracted to the region by employment opportunities. The total number of migrants in these countries in the 1970s was estimated to be 884,000, and by 1985 there were an estimated 7.2 million foreigners, constituting 70 percent of the entire Gulf labor force (Russell 1992).

Specific realities of the oil-rich Arab countries had shaped the increasing demand for migrant labor. Among these realities were the exceptionally small local population and the absence of economic participation by women, which dramatically diminished the number of available domestic workers. Massive investments in infrastructure also created an expanded need for imported labor.

Studies undertaken on Sudanese migration to oil-rich Arab countries have noted that since 1969, when the Nemeiri regime came to power, the movement of highly qualified Sudanese manpower reached such an extent that the Sudan, which in the 1960s trailed numerically all other labor-exporting countries in Africa and the Middle East, emerged as the largest exporter of migrant labor in Northeast Africa. This manpower loss was associated with locally rising costs of living, deteriorating economic conditions, and reduced civil service benefits. The wide income disparities over relatively short distances prompted people to seek higher incomes and better standards of living in the Gulf countries (Halliday 1984; Mahmoud 1983; Roy 1989).

One of the attractions of the Gulf countries to Sudanese was their geographical proximity. The trip from major Gulf cities to the Sudan takes two to three hours by airplane. Many found it possible to visit home frequently for social occasions and religious events.

Another significant factor underlying migration to the Gulf, especially by northerners, was that the Gulf countries, being Islamic and Arab, offered lifestyles roughly analogous to their own, and sociocultural adjustment in these receiving societies presented no formidable impediment (Birks and Sinclair 1980). As a result of these factors—lucrative employment opportunities, higher standards of living, proximity, and cultural similarities—the overall number of Sudanese migrants increased to approximately one million by 1990 (Amin and Mahmoud 1991). Moreover, Sudanese Gulf migrants generally represented the better-educated segment of the population, since it was professional and highly skilled work for which there was increasing demand in the Gulf (Galal el Din 1988; Roy 1989).

The phenomenon of *ightirab* (working abroad) that began to gain momentum in the late 1970s thus opened doors for Sudanese to material prosperity and financial security. The term *ightirab* was in fact coined in response to this mass exodus of Sudanese to the Gulf. There is no doubt that those who work in the Gulf (*mughtaribeen*) made tremendous contributions to their homeland through remittances invested in real estate, transportation, and other businesses. Entire shopping areas in the Sudan are

[73]

A returned Gulf migrant in his store. Saad Qishra Market, Khartoum North, 1996.

owned by mughtaribeen. A good example is Saad Qishra Market in Khartoum North, where a spice and perfume shop owner told me that his shop is
jointly owned (*sharaka*) by himself and his brother, who worked in the
United Arab Emirates. The ightirab became a dream for many in the face of
overwhelming economic hardship at home and made it possible for them to
lead comfortable lives.

The mughtaribeen came to be considered model prospective husbands.
To marry a Gulf migrant was not only a dream for young women but also
the most preferred avenue to security and well being. This remains true,
despite the later attendant difficulties. As the Sudanese folk singer Gisma
laments:

> *Ya Yumma ana zawli ma ja*
> *ya youma min el-khalij malu ja*
> *Yumma min el-khalij malu ma ja,*
> *ya Yumma ana halti rajia*
>
> Oh mother! my man did not come,
> Oh why did not he come back from the Gulf?
> Oh mother! From the Gulf he did not come,
> Oh mother! I have been waiting for him.

The Exodus during the Gulf War

I interviewed many migrants in the United States who reported that the Gulf War was the primary factor redirecting their "traditional" migration from that region to North America, because their once-welcomed arrival there was adversely affected by the Sudanese military regime's support of the Iraqi invasion in 1990. A thirty-six-year-old Sudanese whom I interviewed in Khartoum in 1998 was working in Kuwait at the time. He fled with a group of five to Saudi Arabia before the U.S.-led coalition forces arrived in Kuwait. Bab Allah, who had worked as a clerk in Kuwait City, recalls:

When we heard about the invasion of Kuwait, we watched the events very closely. My roommates and myself were very sure that if Saddam were kicked out, the Kuwaitis would make sure that they clean up the country. Even before the invasion, migrant workers were on their guard all the time, just trying to keep their mouths shut. After the Sudanese government was supportive of Iraq, we were certain that we are finished. We left in a big hurry. We did not care what we would leave behind; although I did not have that much anyway because I was there for two years. My family was not there with me, so I sent more than half of my income to my family. I still remember the day of our escape like yesterday. We packed our stuff, a few things, and we stopped by so many supermarkets to get some food for the road. We could not find anything; people emptied the shelves, and all we found was bug repellent [*Pif Paf*]. We made it to Saudi Arabia and then to the Sudan. The loss of our jobs was painful and unfair. But we knew that we had no alternative. The situation was boiling there. Now I am employed as a driver in a high school. What can I say? I have a family to take care of. If I find the opportunity to go somewhere again it will be a gift from Allah.

Like Bab Allah and his roommates, the instantaneous impact of the Gulf War on Sudanese was a forced departure, either before or after the liberation by the coalition. Tens of thousands of Sudanese who remained were unceremoniously expelled after liberation, as the Kuwaiti government targeted for reprisals the nationals of states that supported the Iraqi invasion (Addelton 1991).

Numerous Sudanese post–Gulf War migrants in the United States and Canada argue that they were all subjected to harassment and deportation in spite of their opposition to the Iraqi invasion. I was told that many of them had joined the Kuwaiti resistance movements. Still, overall public and official actions after liberation were sweeping. "Official and popular attitudes remain hostile towards the presence of Yemenis, Palestinians, Jordanians, and Sudanese in Kuwait. These groups have been targeted for arrest, interrogation, and harassment at random checkpoints and neighborhood sweeps. In addition to official actions, many Kuwaitis blame citizens of these countries, which supported the invasion, for acts of collaboration, and for policies of their governments" (World Refugee Report 1992, 150). The majority was then compelled to leave. According to results of the Migration and Labor Force Survey, return migration to the Sudan during the Gulf War period was estimated at 153,000 (Amin and Mahmoud 1991).

After Desert Storm, massive losses experienced by the Sudanese Persian Gulf migrants included material possessions and savings. As a result of the war, an estimated 1,800,000 persons fled Kuwait and Iraq (Refugee Board and Documentation Center 1991). They felt resentful of both their government's action and the Kuwaitis for whom they had worked. As Khidir, a forty-four-year-old Sudanese engineer who worked in one of the Gulf states before coming to Los Angeles, put it: "I was not sure why the Sudanese government had to support the Iraqi invasion. I also don't know why the Kuwaitis have to punish the Sudanese people working there for years. We were there because of conditions created by bad governments. Because of that we lost the opportunity to get jobs there but still be able to be close to our families. We were treated unfairly in the Sudan and also in the Gulf."

The invasion of Kuwait by Iraq immediately precipitated a massive exodus of migrant workers to neighboring Middle Eastern countries, with numerous Sudanese among the thousands who entered Jordan, which maintained an open-door policy to the refugees. Jordan provided housing while international refugee organizations arranged transportation to the refugees' home countries. I was told by Hisham, a Sudanese migrant in New York City, that "Sudanese migrants found temporary refuge in Jordan before being transported to the Sudan on special chartered planes or ships. Others found their way into Saudi Arabia, but I do not know what their situation was there. Also some went into Jordan or Saudi Arabia, but the majority returned to Sudan." A 1991 Canadian report on the condition of migrant workers during the war, however, stated that many Sudanese, along with other migrants, were stranded in Jordan because of troubles besetting their home country (Refugee Board and Documentation Center 1991). Nooreldin, forty-one years old and living in Brooklyn, was displaced by war.

I had been working in Kuwait for nearly three years. I was forced to leave because of the war and the uncertainty of my future after the war was over. A lot of Sudanese migrants fled Kuwait through the Jordanian desert because the highways were closed. The only route for people to leave Kuwait was across the Amman Desert. So what we needed was to find someone to guide us towards the Amman Desert. We talked about this with other Sudanese, and we decided that instead of moving in small groups, we would rather move as a convoy. The conditions were extremely difficult; we left without our possessions. I managed to bring a small handbag with change of clothes. We also took large amounts of canned food and bottled water. For many Sudanese who worked for a long time in Kuwait, their material losses were more profound.

Before we reached the desert, we had to wait in lines for fuel for hours. So, many people got discouraged and frightened, and many felt they should go to Baghdad. We continued until we reached Jordan. In Jordan the authorities housed refugees in camps in northeast Amman. Living conditions were especially difficult. We stayed there, and despite all these problems, the Jordanians treated us very well. We waited in Jordan to be transported to Sudan by Sudan Airways, other chartered planes, and by ships in Aqaba port. For Sudanese who managed to take their cars to Jordan, they were transported to Port Sudan. This was generally the condition during the war. But after the liberation, many more Sudanese were forced to leave because they were accused of collaborating with the Iraqis. In fact, only a small number did, but the majority, just like others, felt violated and devastated. That did not matter for the Kuwaitis anyway. However, there were some Sudanese who refused to leave Kuwait in the beginning, but eventually they were antagonized enough to leave. In Saudi Arabia, the condition of Sudanese was slightly better; they were on the verge of being expelled, just like the Yemenis. Sayed Mohammed Osman el Marghani [a Sudanese political and spiritual leader] was believed to have persuaded King Fahd that Sudanese who already left their country to work for decades in Saudi Arabia could not possibly be held responsible for the actions of the military regime. So, some Sudanese managed to keep their jobs. But recently a lot of people feel threatened by the Saudi strategies for cutting back on salaries. And employment in that country does not seem to be as satisfactory as it used to be.

After I returned to the Sudan I stayed six months before I managed to obtain the entry visa to come to the U.S. After the unfortunate experience we had in the Gulf, many had come directly from Saudi Arabia to the United States and Canada, because now these are the only viable alternatives for them.

After Liberation: The Closing of Migration Alternatives

Three new Sudanese migratory movements emerged as an outcome of Operation Desert Storm. First, mughtaribeen, who came either directly from the Persian Gulf region or first returned to the Sudan, managed to reach the United States or Canada after their expulsion. A second group now came to North America because opportunities in the Middle East were closed. Finally, some mughtaribeen families, mindful of political and social realities, decided to resettle wives and children in Canada while the husbands stay on to work in the Gulf states.

After the liberation of Kuwait, Sudanese and other migrant communities in the Gulf region were largely dismantled. Apart from the initial evacuations, a series of new measures propelled most remaining migrants to leave, including a Kuwaitization strategy aimed at replacing non-Kuwaiti workers with Kuwaiti nationals. In Saudi Arabia, the same policy has been enacted. In the words of a Sudanese post–Gulf War migrant now in the United States: "In Saudi Arabia we were asked to provide training for Saudis for the same occupations we were doing. For many, after the training is over, your job is over. We spent a long time training Saudis, knowing that these trainees were going to replace us. This created pressure and insecurity. Working under this pressure, I decided with other migrants to leave as soon as possible."

Kuwaitization, which reduced the presence of expatriate employees, was undertaken to ensure that Kuwaitis occupy major positions in key economic sectors (Addelton 1991). Added to these policies were more rigorous requirements for residence permits, yet another measure to eliminate the reliance on migrants. Finally, new regulations created obstacles to recruitment of laborers from outside Kuwait. In Saudi Arabia, reductions in monthly pay by nearly one-half led many Sudanese to leave: Only a few accepted the cuts and continued there. The overall situation of Sudanese migrants in Saudi Arabia remained better than for those in Kuwait, because the latter group was collectively held responsible for their government's support of Iraq.

These measures undertaken by other oil-rich Arab countries meant a significant restructuring of labor markets in the Persian Gulf region. This has entailed shifts in ethnic compositions, now well documented in the post-Gulf War era. South and Southeast Asian migrants are increasingly replacing Arabs, and these changes have resulted in skill shortages in the Gulf countries in the service, manufacturing, and public utilities sectors. Moreover, there has been a growing increase in the number of female migrants from Bangladesh, Sri Lanka, and Indonesia doing domestic work (Addelton 1991; Appleyard 1991; Russell 1992; Shah 2000; U.S. Department of State 1991).

Aside from the new circumstances in Kuwait and Saudi Arabia, the work situation in other parts of the Gulf region was less affected by the Sudan's support of Iraq. In the words of a Sudanese who migrated to the United States from Qatar:

On the eve of the Sudanese government's support of Iraq, the Sudanese migrants in Qatar expressed their support for free Kuwait, and their delegation made it clear that the Sudan government position did not necessarily represent them in any way. However, the political climate overall remained sensitive toward Sudanese. For instance, I was forced to leave my job, because I was accused of making negative statements about the repressive nature of the political systems of the Gulf countries. That is why I moved to the United States, because the overall climate is marked with hostile attitudes toward Sudanese.

Other Sudanese migrants in Washington, D.C., some of whom even hold positions with Gulf Arab Embassies, stress many new Sudanese migrants continue to come directly from Saudi Arabia and other Gulf countries. One explained: "I have a lot of relatives who work now in Saudi Arabia and who wish to migrate to America, since many of their friends have already come here. For them their migration to Saudi Arabia is just a temporary situation to try to secure money and travel expenses to come here." Another migrant in New York commented: "In my neighborhood alone I heard that in one week thirteen migrants, who are also relatives, arrived from Saudi Arabia, and are being assisted by Sudanese friends to find jobs and housing." Many statements like "My migration to the Gulf was temporary," or "After the Gulf War, we do not have any alternative to migration" were encountered from informants now in North America. For many post–Gulf War migrants, relocating to the Sudan after the Gulf crisis was "irrational." As one migrant put it: "For many Sudanese Gulf War returnees in the Sudan, those who were lucky enough to be able to bring their cars have used them as taxicabs or as emergency transportation [*el nagl el tari*]. Due to the problems in the Sudan, they are only allowed a small ration of gas per week. For the others like myself, we did not have anything, and if you want to start from the beginning, I thought I had better come to the U.S." United States and Canadian immigration policies with respect to this category of Sudanese migrant are the same as for nonimmigrant temporary arrivals. However, claims for asylum can be filed after arrival, as a considerable number of ex–Gulf War Sudanese migrants have done.

The responses to my survey indicate that 17 percent of Sudanese immigrants, predominantly northerners, worked in the oil-rich Arab countries prior to their migration to the United States and Canada. Many of these resided in Washington, D.C., but increasing numbers have settled in New York, Texas, and California. But wherever I talked to Sudanese about the make-up of their communities, the presence of "the Gulf people" (*nas elkhalij*) was pointed out.

Although the majority left the Gulf at the time of the war, others have come since. In 1992 Mubarak migrated from the United Arab Emirates. He is forty-eight years old and worked there as a journalist. Now living in Virginia with his wife and children, his main reason for migrating was to seek job security. Mutasim, who worked in the Emirates as an oil company clerk since 1982, concurs that job security is the reason: "My young brother here in Washington helped me to come. I came to secure a future. I never felt secure in the Gulf; all the time there was a fear of uncertainty. I am doing well here now. My biggest problem is that I miss the Sudan."

The political implications of the closed Gulf States migration opportunities point to the end of Pan-Arab nationalism, a bond that both oil-rich and oil-poor countries historically glorified and extolled. The closure of work opportunities and ethnic restructuring in the Gulf testify to new policies, now less defined by older ethnoreligious stereotypes. According to Shah (2000), by 1994 and 1995 labor migrants in Kuwait included four to five million workers from India, Sri Lanka, Bangladesh, and Pakistan.

The consequences for the Middle Eastern displaced laborers have been devastating. For Sudanese, securing another place to work has meant a redirection of migration from the Gulf to North America.

[5]

The Copts: A Perpetual Diaspora

And the orator said, speak to us of freedom. And he answered: verily all things move within your being, in constant half embrace, the desired and the dreaded, the repugnant and the cherished, the pursued and that which you would escape. These things move within you as lights and shadows in pairs that cling. And when the shadow fades and is no more, the light that lingers becomes a shadow to another light. And thus your freedom when it loses its fetters becomes itself the fetter of a greater freedom.

Khalil Gibran, *The Prophet*, 1923

No one can appreciate the gravity of the recent international migration of the Sudanese Copts without a solid grasp of who they are. Their legacy in the Sudan is ancient and their experience has been deeply conditioned by its religious contexts. With their expertise and industry, the Copts have contributed much to Sudanese society. As an ethnic and religious minority, the Copts have experienced an exodus from Sudan, one that started in 1969 during the military regime of Gaafar Nemeiri and climaxed after 1989 with the application of Islamic sharia law. Yet, as Edward Wakin writes of their coreligionists' earlier emigration from Egypt: "They leave with reluctance, talking not of greener pastures elsewhere but of closed doors at home. Feeling deprived of the traditional Coptic right to market their skills at a reasonably high price, they turn to the last resort of departure and dispersion" (1963, 160).

Who Are the Sudanese Copts?

Linguistically, the word *Copt* is derived from the Greek *Aigyptos*, a corruption of the ancient Egyptian word *hakkaptah,* or *Egyptian.* Thus, the term *Copt* originally referred to nationality rather than religion (Davis 1973, 678). However, after the Islamic conquest of Egypt, the term was used to distinguish the Christians from the Muslim newcomers (Zarroug 1991). As a new ethnic identity, *Copt* assumed both an experiential and a practical salience for those who bore it. It entailed the complementary assertion of the collective self and the negation of the collective other; it called into question shared humanity and its substance, reflecting the tensions embodied in relations of inequality (Comaroff 1997, 73). Under Arab rule, the Copts moved from being a majority to becoming a religious minority, and the label signified new boundaries between the conquerors and the conquered.

The Copts have been called "the modern sons of Pharaohs," "the passive survivors," "the endangered Christians," and "the lonely minority" (see Meinardus 1970; Vatini 1978; Wakin 1963; Yanney 1989). As Egyptian writer Mohamed Hasanain Haykal describes them in his *Autumn of Fury:* "In the face of systematic persecution, they remain a prodigy of survival." Coptic historian Aziz Attia describes them in this way:

> Like a great and solitary Egyptian temple standing sorrowfully on the edge of the desert and weathering sandstorms over the years until it became submerged by the accretions of time, the ancient Coptic church led its lonely life unnoticed on the fringe of Christian civilization and was buried in the sands of oblivion. Like the same massive temple, too, it has proved itself to be indestructible, though battered by the winds of change. As an organism, its potential vitality, though enfeebled by sustained fighting, has survived in a latent form under the weight of accumulated rubble. In the last few decades, with increasing security and liberty from within and support and sympathy from without, its sons have started removing the sands of time from around the edifice, which has shown signs of shining again. (1983, 30)

The Copts belong to the Egyptian Orthodox Church founded by St. Mark, who preached Christianity in Egypt during the reign of the Roman Empire and authored the earliest of the four canonical gospels. Throughout their history, the Copts have been subjected to various forms of persecution and repression, and some were propelled to seek safety by leaving Egypt. The Coptic presence in the Sudan dates to the Byzantine era, when monks "of the oases of the western desert and beyond the first cataract in Nubia in Egypt penetrated the Southern region as soldiers of Christ" (Attia 1979, 16).

More recent migrations occurred after the Turco-Egyptian invasion of the Sudan by Mohamed Ali in 1821. At that time, Egyptian Copts came to occupy leading positions as civil servants, financiers, clerks, and traders, and others arrived as craftsmen, weavers, leather-binders, painters, carpenters, and tailors. Copts came to live in urban areas throughout northern Sudan, in Khartoum, El Obeid, Atbara, Wad Medani, Port Sudan, Omdurman, Shendi, and Gadarif. Gadarif, in fact, was named after Gadroof Saad, a Coptic farmer who founded a farming community in the eighteenth century (Faraj 1998). For decades, Sudanese Muslim attitudes toward the Copts were accommodating and tolerant. However, with the advent of the Mahdist rule (1885–98) and the establishment of an Islamic state, non-Muslims were pressured to convert to Islam. "Even after conversion to Islam," however, Copts found "their property often was seized and confiscated and their mobility was severely curtailed" (Kramer 1993, 1). One sixty-six-year-old Coptic businessman whom I interviewed in Virginia told me: "When the Khalifa's soldiers came to my grandmother's place, they entered the house without knocking on the door. They started to tell her to say 'There is no God but Allah' (*la ilah ila allah*); my grandmother refused and she was saying loudly 'Jesus is the Son of God' (*yasou ibin allah*); the soldiers burned her alive." Massive conversions of non-Muslims eventually created a distinctive community known as *masalma*, although others converted only temporarily until Mahdist rule ended. Still others refused to convert and fled to Egypt.

A renewed Coptic migration from Egypt to the Sudan began with the establishment of British rule in 1898 (Waller 1988). Since then, the Copts have retained their identity as Christians, even tattooing a small green crucifix on the inside of their wrists to distinguish themselves. The Copts openly made pilgrimages to their monasteries around feast days and sought the intercession of saints in times of need. In the Sudan, they enjoyed freedom of worship, built new cathedrals, and established social clubs and community centers.

The Copts' contribution to Sudanese society during British rule and after independence included a significant presence in all branches of government. Coptic religious identity in the Sudan did not displace Sudanese identity, and whether Muslim or Copt, all Nile Valley people continued to engage in, and share, similar ways of life. In the Sudan, Copts were considered Sudanese, not foreigners. Muslims I interviewed in 1998 often expressed sadness at the departure of Coptic neighbors. In El Zuhoor, a neighborhood in Khartoum, Abdul Rahim, sixty-six years old, told me: "Sudanese people do not pay attention to what religion you believe in, but to the human relations among common folk. In the Sudan you find that Muslim and Christian relations are not shaken by the different beliefs. I like my Coptic neighbors very much. When our *eid* celebration comes, we share with them the meat and whatever we have: They do the same thing during their celebration. It is a neighborly thing." A Sudanese woman explained:

The Copts are part of the Sudanese society. In fact, celebration of religious holidays is not complete without visiting the Coptic-owned fabric stores and the Coptic dressmakers. Prior to the application of the *sharia*, these Sudanese Copts lived happily with neighbors and enjoyed rights like everyone else. In Omdurman we had so many Coptic friends. My father, who worked in the post office, had many [Coptic] friends. In fact, he spent most of his time with them. They used to get together in the evening and they sat for hours outside the house chatting and listening to the radio. I will never forget Banat Machaeil, who used to sew and embroider for the people here in our neighborhood. They were very talented and very warm and loving. When I remember how everything used to be, I regret what is happening to the Sudan now. Copts owned my favorite stores. And a Copt, Abu Nakhala, also owned the best neighborhood pharmacy. The most significant memory we have of the Copts is that they touched our life in a positive way. Everything was peaceful then.

In Khartoum, eighty-one-year-old Abdel Mutaal had many Coptic friends who were his colleagues at the Sudan Railway Company, where he worked as an accountant after graduating from Gordon Memorial College in Khartoum.

To give you an example of the tolerant nature of the Copts, a long time ago when people needed money for the Omdurman mosque, a Coptic poet, Butrous, published a persuasive poem urging people to donate money to complete the mosque. It is also important to remember that many Copts were active members of political parties and shared many responsibilities and duties at the times of the Graduate Congress which called for independence from the British. At the level of the civil service, they worked diligently in the postal service and the Sudan railways and made tremendous contributions to the economy. The Copts have a glittering past, and history is the witness.

During my fieldwork visit in the fall of 1998, I noticed several incidents reflecting the extent of the recent Coptic emigration from the Sudan.

The first occurred during my visit to Souq Eljumaa (Friday Market), located in Sahafa, a suburb of Khartoum. Since the day I arrived home, friends had promised they would take me to this engaging place, where I could buy anything I liked. Indeed, Souq Eljumaa was everything they promised me. Market goods ranged from spices to furniture, from antiques and household gadgets to car parts. After roving and strolling from one stand to the next, and hearing the loud voices of vendors telling us to take a look at their products and urging us, "Please buy this, pay whatever you want, it is yours now," we decided to go to the fabrics area. I was determined to buy a *farda,* an elaborately woven piece of cotton cloth that can be used as a *tobe* (a Sudanese dress resembling the Indian *sari*) or as a bedspread. I was happy to find a design I liked and ready to pay for it, despite an outrageously high price. After five minutes of bargaining, a satisfactory compromise was reached. While the owner of the stand started to measure the fabric, he explained why the price was so high. "Do you know that this is an original, Coptic-woven farda? You will never be able to find this kind again, because most of the Coptic weavers have left the Sudan. I am Coptic too. I can tell you honestly that this weaving industry does not exist anymore. The Copts did not train many people to do it; this was their way to make a living. Please take advantage now. Get another one or two. I tell you, if you come back you might not be able to find another one."

A second incident took place when I visited the Coptic Kanisat Elshahidein Church in Amarat. Anba Filsouth Faraj, pastor of the church, entered my appointment on his calendar and invited me to attend the following night's ceremony for the martyred Saints George and Mark. I returned and headed to the main sanctuary, where fumes of incense filled the air. Men and women of varying ages, including a few Ethiopians, were seated in gender-segregated fashion. The choir sang while a church volunteer moved from one aisle to the next with a red velvet bag and presented it to people, who thrust their hands in it for blessing. Pastor Filsouth Faraj finally appeared to conclude the service by offering a sermon commemorating the saints' legacy of martyrdom and persecution. At the close of a three-hour service, he led a prayer for the saints, for the Coptic congregants who were present, and for those in "the diaspora" who had emigrated because they could no longer endure conditions in the Sudan.

A third incident took place in downtown Khartoum. In the Sudan today, a popular mode of public transportation is the *ragsha*, a four-seat motor vehicle formerly used for delivering gas canisters door-to-door. With the pressure on public transportation in the capital growing due to increased rural-urban migration, the ragshas now provide a way of getting around at an affordable fare. When I inquired how long ragshas had been used for public transportation, I was told that Sudanese Copts were the first to import them for that purpose. I was informed that Coptic emigration had resulted in large revenue losses to their churches and that Copts began to invest in ragshas to earn a side income that enabled them to help maintain their congregation's activities. This story was corroborated by many people who agreed that it was the out-migration of Copts that produced the raghsa boom among those who remained.

A final incident took place at the Khartoum Airport when I was leaving the country. A moving scene was unfolding. A Coptic family of eight people was saying their good-byes to relatives who had come to see them off, embracing and weeping. The emigrants were heading to Bahrain, then Singapore, and finally to Sydney, Australia. On our flight to Bahrain, the mother,

Teresa, and her two-year-old sat next to me. We struck up a conversation as she asked where I was going, what part of Khartoum I had come from, and what did I do. I responded and asked her the same. Teresa said that had it not been for the bad situation in the Sudan, especially for Copts, they would never have left their home and their friends in Sennar, a town in central Sudan. "The Sudan is deteriorating very fast. We were waiting patiently for four years to emigrate to Australia. Once we settle we will send documents to sponsor our family back home." Teresa kept comforting her two-year-old, promising that grandma (*taita*) would join them—hopefully very soon. She added:

> This is very sad. My heart is aching for this separation. We are a close family and it is unfair for our kids not to enjoy the grandparents. But can you believe that a lot of people have already departed or are waiting to leave? At this time, they do not even think about missing their families. I am convinced that it will be very hard for us to come back. This is a sad farewell to everything we cared about. But we will see. There is a big Coptic community in Sydney and hopefully we will meet people from the Sudan there.

Why Are They Migrating?

The present migration of Sudanese Copts began in 1969 and 1970, due in part to the confiscation of Coptic-owned businesses by President Gaafar Nemeiri's government. Religious oppression is cited by Copts as the primary force behind their migration to the United States, Canada, Australia, and Western Europe, and statements such as, "I migrated because of the religious persecution of non-Muslims" recurred from my Coptic informants.

In 1983, the Nemeiri government proclaimed its intent to transform the country into an Islamic theocratic state, a goal maintained in Article 1 of the current government's Constitutional Decree. The subsequent adoption of the sharia and penal codes known as the *hudud* was pointed to by Copts such as Gabriel, age forty-seven, as "restrictive and constraining." Under these laws, all crimes, including consumption of alcohol, are judged according to the Quran. As Rizq Allah, a fifty-five-year-old former civil servant who migrated to Canada six years ago, maintained:

> Since Nemeiri decided to save his skin by adopting Islamic laws, a lot of damage was done to everyone, especially to the Copts. Nemeiri's security people literally had raided spirit shops that were owned by Copts and destroyed them. This was how many Copts made a living. The *hudud* deprived them of their livelihood. The political exploitation of religion had created a stressful

climate. At this age, I would not accept being flogged because my breath smells of alcohol. I came here to enjoy some freedom.

Another Copt immigrant told me about a Coptic grocer who was arrested and his daughter flogged because they raised their prices.

In the Islamic state, the well-assimilated Copts became more conscious of their identity as a non-Muslim ethnic minority. Coptic community activists expressed their opposition to the Islamization of the country, but ever-increasing numbers of Coptic people abandon their homes to seek refuge overseas. The volume of the new Coptic exodus reached a high point in the period between 1983–89, even though the 1985 April uprising that overthrew Nemeiri's regime returned a glimmer of hope to many Sudanese, including Copts. After Nemeiri's fall, the slogan *eldin lil allah wa el watan liljami* (Religion is for God, the nation is for all) was widely proclaimed. The Copts participated actively in the 1986 elections, which installed a democratic government after sixteen years of military rule, and they joined efforts to restore the secular constitution in effect before 1983. Political leaders were invited to Coptic social clubs, now open to the public to discuss Sudan's political future and the restoration of the 1973 constitution.

Coptic participation in the Sudanese elections of 1987 reflected their opposition to sharia, socioeconomic deterioration, and a repressive regime. They voted for candidates explicitly opposed to the Islamic state: 68 percent for candidates of the Sudanese Communist Party, 17 percent for the Umma Party, and 9 percent for the National Unionist Party (Abdel Nur 1989). Coptic opposition to sharia law did not reflect any antagonism to Islam but rather indicated a commitment by the Copts to a role within Sudanese society. A Coptic migrant, Tadrous, reiterated what his grandfather told him.

My grandparents had to flee the Sudan. They were originally from Atbara and then moved to Khartoum. There my grandfather held an excellent position in the Department of Electricity. He had a great command of English and was one of the minorities there. His being Christian was the reason behind his colleagues' attempt to frame him on fraud charges at work. Being a strong man, he knew immediately that he would not be able to tolerate working with such people. He thought of his children and their future and decided to go to either Canada or Australia. Just before he decided to leave, Islamic groups began to penetrate Sudanese political life. My grandfather has good and bad memories of the Sudan. From the best country in the world, it turned into living hell.

The fact that Islamic law remained intact after the overthrow of Nemeiri in 1985, coupled with discriminatory policies of the regime that seized power in 1989, forced still more Copts to leave. In the words of Antoinette, now living in Maryland: "The government policies of Islamization and intimidation of Copts through those policies had left us with bitterness and anger. Many of my relatives who were harassed and their businesses shut down by authorities have escaped already. For me, I came because of the harassment of Coptic children who had been teased in school by other, Muslim children." And in the words of another migrant: "Before I migrated to the U.S. three years ago, I came for a short training course. My boss told me that I could apply for a permanent job here, but I refused and went back to the Sudan after my training was over. One of the main reasons which forced me to migrate is the changing attitude of some Sudanese toward non-Muslims. All we faced for the past years is hostility and discrimination, just because we are Christians."

For another Sudanese Copt migrant, religious subjugation had deeper political roots. "It is true that Copts had been harassed and dismissed. But harassment and dismissal have been a feature of the current regime's policies, which continue to detain, execute, and dismiss hundreds of Sudanese Muslims on the grounds of their affiliation to other political parties. What is going on in the Sudan and forcing people to move is not religious, but it is a battle between Islamists and non-Islamists—including both Muslims and non-Muslims."

Although Copts used to live in equanimity and peace with other Sudanese, fully integrated in Sudanese society, this has changed radically. According to Edward, age forty-eight, now living in Virginia: "Many Copts equate the application of sharia with their ostracism and relegation to the status of second-class citizens." Subjected to laws restricting their ability to build places of worship and other rights enjoyed by full citizens, the Copts' consciousness of themselves as a minority was heightened. Sudanese legal scholar Abdullah An-Na'im concedes:

Non-Muslim minorities within an Islamic state do not enjoy rights equal to those of the Muslim majority. [*Sharia*] classifies the subjects of an Islamic state into three major religious categories: Muslims; People of the Book, being non-Muslims who believe in one of the heavenly revealed scriptures, mainly Christians and Jews; and unbelievers, being non-Muslims who do not believe in the heavenly revealed scriptures. Muslim males are the only full citizens of an Islamic state. People of the Book may be granted some rights as citizens if they submit to Muslim sovereignty under what is known as the pact of *dhimmh,* a charter of rights and duties with the Islamic state. Non-believers are not even entitled to this option of limited citizenship under temporary *Amman,* safe conduct. (1987, 1)

Dhimmis are not allowed to participate in the public affairs of an Islamic state and may not hold any position of authority over Muslims (compare to Sanasarian 1995). They may practice their religion in private, but they are not able to proselytize or preach in public (An-Na'im 1987, 11).

In the realm of education, Islamist rule has resulted in the abolition of teaching the Christian religion to Christians. During one of my fieldwork visits to a Christian church in Khartoum, a Coptic woman arrived in a rage at the way school children were becoming indifferent since the teaching of Christianity in schools had been abandoned. "For them, coming to church for religious instruction is not convenient, so they do not pay attention." Other Copts have complained that Islamic studies predominate in the teaching of history and other aspects of educational syllabi, for all students. Reportedly, the Christian heritage section has been removed from the National Museum in Khartoum. Other Islamist policies include the requirement that all Sudanese citizens wear the *hijab* (Islamic dress). Copts also are now grossly underrepresented in the top ranks of government, the judiciary, and the army (Africa Watch 1993).

On the whole, Coptic Sudanese migrants to the United States affirm that life has become unbearable in the Sudan and that their sense of belonging to Sudanese society has been undermined. Islamic impositions under the current regime are, in fact, perceived "as an effort to force the Copts to migrate." A legal assistant in an immigration law firm in Toronto stated that often dozens of refugee claims were made by Sudanese Copts weekly, and those filed as "religious" are always successful. Increased restrictions in the Sudan on international travel, however, impede the exodus.

One more reason influencing the Copts' decision to leave is universal conscription into the People's Defense Force, where young people are forced to take part in military training. Bolis and Wahiba came to Toronto in 1984 as part of Canada's family reunification policy after their son, Milad, migrated to that country to attend graduate school and decided to become a landed immigrant (and, therefore, was allowed permanent residence in Canada). Wahiba "misses the Sudan terribly" and confesses that "no matter how long I stay in Canada, I am not getting used to it and I never feel part of it even with my husband and son being there." Bolis is aware of "hundreds of Coptic families who came to the United States and Canada to escape extremism. Many Copts do not want their children to be drafted and forced to join the government's army in southern Sudan. They will be forced to kill innocent people and they do not want to be part of it. They do not want to participate in killing anyone, let alone fellow Christians."

Migration through the Eyes of a Coptic Pastor

In November 1998, I interviewed Anba Filsouth Faraj, the pastor introduced earlier, in his spacious office on the first floor of his church. Large
photographs of Coptic priests adorned the wall, along with a painting of
Jesus. Anba Filsouth was exhorting a church employee to take good care of
two chairs he was borrowing, as they were irreplaceable objects which the
church had acquired when times were more benevolent (*ayam elzaman
zein*). Turning to me, he said, "Oh, maybe I can give you some of the things
I wrote about the need for religious tolerance in the Sudan. I wrote a newspaper article reflecting on an occasion during the month of Ramadan when
the Coptic community hosted a Ramadan event for Muslims in the Coptic
Club, and several community leaders were invited to attend." Anba Filsouth then continued:

In order to understand the effect of the migration of the Copts [from Sudan],
I have to say that I have been in this church since 1968. I would not have fore-
seen a migration of congregation members like this. In the past, if people show
up a few minutes late for Sunday service, they would not find a place to sit.
This church was packed with people. Today, this is not the case. From this
church alone, one thousand families have migrated [since] a little bit before
1989. People sold their properties and left the country in a hurry. They lived in
fear of the military conscription.

   This migration is extremely disruptive to those left behind. A long time ago,
the Copts hardly moved. In fact if one moves from Khartoum to Medani
[about 80 miles away], the person is bid farewell as if he is going to the moon.
Again, the reason that forced them to go is the application of the *sharia*. The
Copts are not hostile to Islam; we have excellent Muslim/Christian relations.
That is not what the Copts are objecting to. Instead, the *sharia* court with its
imposition of flogging and harsh punishment became a source of fear and anxiety. Also, what is known as public order (*elnizam alam*) allows security people
to stop women on the street and harass them for not wearing Islamic dress and
covering their hair. In our religion, except for modesty, women's hair is considered part of their femininity and beauty. Why do they have to cover their
hair to conform to a religious order?

   Naturally, under these pressures people leave. I am inclined to believe that
migration complicates the situation. Because if everyone leaves, what is going
to happen to our country? People should sacrifice and persevere. In Coptic
culture we were taught to endure, persevere, and overcome. Now, I can describe the impact of several members of my congregation leaving as devastating. They supported all the church activities, because they were in a good financial situation. Now our air conditioners and furniture are broken, and
honestly, there is no money. So in terms of sustaining the church, it has been a
blow. The psychological impact on those of us [remaining] is terrible. After

Father Filsouth Faraj, pastor of Kanisat Elshahidain Coptic Church. Amarat, a suburb of Khartoum, 1998.

knowing these people for decades, seeing them leave is painful. Every Sunday morning you wonder who is going to be there. Those who stayed lost too. They lost family members and friends.

The Sudan has lost too, through the migration of very qualified Coptic doctors, bankers, and engineers. Many members moved to Europe and Australia and the United States. We don't know if they will ever come back. If they do, they have to start from square one.

Father Filsouth continued to reflect on the impact of Coptic emigration on his congregation.

For us as pastors, we mourn the departure and the shrinking of our church. There are of course some Copts who believe that it is home, and they don't want to move. Others do have the means to venture into migration. Whatever their reasons, they felt that they had no place in the Sudan. It is regretful, because they are Sudanese and not foreigners. What is going on alienates them. But we have to remind ourselves of the good things the Copts have done. They are bearers of civilization; they are good citizens, who served this country earnestly. They cared about this land. In spite of this, those of us who remained will continue to plant love and to restore a good relationship among all the people in the Sudan. We are Sudanese regardless of whether we wear black turbans or white turbans.

[91]

Despite the fact that some have already moved to Australia, England, and other European countries, many Copts contend that North America is the most viable migratory destination for them and for other potential migrants. A report by *Africa Watch* describes the constrained alternatives:

> The Copts cannot escape to Egypt this time, as most of them have been born in the Sudan and no longer have connections in Egypt. The greater obstacle to flight, however, is the growth of Islamic absolutism in Egypt, with its encouragement of sectarian hatred and violence. Facing such dangers, and the fact that Egypt and Sudan do not officially recognize refugees from each other's countries, Copts now face a dilemma over asylum. Some Sudanese Copts' applications for asylum have been rejected in Germany and Canada, and they are left with no option. The days are gone when Coptic monks used to hide in the desert monasteries: even the desert is no longer a safe hiding place. (1993, 2)

Driven to preserve their forms of worship in foreign lands, Coptic newcomers have not become part of existing North American congregations but have founded their own churches in cities throughout the United States and Canada. New cathedrals in Coptic style are located in Detroit, Chicago, East Brunswick, Toronto, New Orleans, Cleveland, and Los Angeles. A monastery named after St. Anthony was also founded in California (USA Copts Home Page 2001).

[6]

Migration with a Feminine Face:
Breaking the Cultural Mold

> Travel, migration and movement invariably bring us up against the limits of
> our Inheritance. We may choose to withdraw from this impact and only select
> a confirmation of our initial views. In this case whatever lies on the other side
> remains in the shadows, in obscurity. We could, however, opt to slacken con-
> trol, to let ourselves go, and respond to the challenge of a world that is more
> extensive than the one we have been accustomed to inhabiting.
>
> Iain Chambers, *Migrancy, Culture, Identity*, 1994

The migration of women has received scant attention in most studies of
population movements (Agger 1992; Hackett 1996; Indra 1999). At best,
women are treated as dependent variables who move only as part of family
units. For some, the notion of women traveling by themselves is unimaginable, a threat to the well-being of the family and community. In her book,
Bint Arab: Arab and Arab American Women in the United States, Evelyn
Shakir says of such female migration: "In a society where male protection
and patronage were essential guarantors of a woman's respectability, to go
alone among strangers—especially for young, unmarried women—was a
daring if not a brazen act" (1997, 27). Sudanese attitudes toward the migration of single women should be understood in this light. An elderly woman
whom I met in Khartoum expressed nostalgia for the good old days, when
women were not allowed such mobility. She remarked: "Sudanese women
are becoming increasingly free; they cut all these distances to go to distant
countries all by themselves. I swear to Allah all of them are *matalig*"—a Sudanese Arabic term meaning "free or unrestrained," with the pejorative
connotations of uncontrolled or reckless behavior.

Yet, paradoxically, underlying this perceived "freedom" is the increased relegation of Sudanese women at home to a subordinate position (Khaleefa et al. 1996). "Under the current regime women will not occupy formal political positions, such as minister. With the declaration of sharia, which enhanced the *guama* [guardianship] of men, women must always have a lower status" (El Amin and El Sanusi 1994, 682). Restrictions on women's participation in public life, local decrees and curfews, and the imposition of hijab, the Islamic code covering women's dress and behavior, have all converged to narrow the lives of Sudanese women. According to Eltigani and Khaled of the Omdurman Center for Women's Studies, in recent years Sudanese women have been subjected to discriminatory practices and "too many have also been subjected to detention, ill treatment and torture. Whipping has been introduced by the state as a punishment, and women are specifically targeted for this harsh treatment. The current regime has enacted many laws to undermine women's rights in the name of Islam" (1998, 223).

In the 1940s, when the Bahhara arrived as single men in North America, no one could have envisioned a later stream of women without the company of their menfolk. Until recently, the only migration of Sudanese women by themselves was the migration of female schoolteachers to the Gulf countries, especially to the United Arab Emirates, Yemen, and Oman. These "women of exceptional merit" secured contracts ranging from three to five years, arranged by the Sudanese Ministry of Education. During the 1990s, however, I encountered a clear trend of Sudanese women migrating to North America by themselves. Circumstances at home and abroad have now intersected to transform gender traditions, resulting in a new feminization of international migration.

A clarification needs to be made at the outset: I make no assumption of the existence of an undifferentiated homogenous category "Sudanese women." The personal histories and individual experiences that prompt them to come to North America are many, and their premigratory backgrounds and biographies need to be explored.

So who are these women whose migration is so widely talked about both back home and in their new societies? I observed five categories. First are women who are unmarried, relatively young, and educated. In their demographic as well as socioeconomic characteristics, they approximate Sudanese male migrants, especially in their occupational status. The majority of women in this category hold white-collar jobs before coming to the United States or Canada. Entering as visitors, they subsequently decide to apply for asylum because of their fears of returning home.

Second are southern Sudanese refugee women who live in other countries before their resettlement in the United States. Unlike the larger number of Sudanese women who arrive first and then seek asylum, these southern women's claims of persecution are recognized officially prior to their migration.

A third group consists of single women who enter the United States as winners of green cards in the U.S. Diversity Visa Lottery Program established in 1990. The Sudan was allocated nearly 5,000 such visas annually, and offices that process applications are scattered among the Sudan's provinces. The majority of these women I encountered either applied from the Sudan or had contacts in the United States who applied on their behalf. As Ahmed, age thirty-five and living in Colorado, explained: "I really want to get married to a woman from the Sudan. But these days everyone knows that Sudanese at home are starting to call America 'Armica,' meaning in Arabic 'to throw out,' because people go home, get married, but cannot bring their wives. I decided to apply for six women from my home neighborhood for the [visa] lottery. Any of them who wins, I am willing to marry."

Fourth are married women who are expecting children and come with the sole intention of giving birth to "American children." Rarely accompanied by husbands, these women plan with Sudanese already here to facilitate their stay until babies are born and return home afterward.

A fifth category of migrants includes women whose husbands are still working in Persian Gulf countries and who move with their children to a more secure place to live. This group largely is concentrated in metropolitan Toronto (see Noivo 1997 on a similar migration of Portuguese women).

The stories that these Sudanese female migrants told me demonstrate the self-reliance, resourcefulness, and agency of many who opted to migrate. The magnitude of female migration, moreover, testifies to the fact that gender is no greater a stumbling block to mobility than ethnicity or class. Whether they are refugees, visa lottery winners, or wives traveling without their husbands, the arrival of women in North America has forced Sudanese to revisit some of the most basic organizing principles of their lives. By the end of 2001, several hundred Sudanese women unaccompanied by men were spread throughout the United States, and several thousand resided in Canada. Family and friends in Toronto helped me to navigate the city's subways and streetcars and quickly begin interviews, which resulted in the narratives that follow.

Eight Refugees

Hanan

Hanan, a thirty-two-year-old Sudanese Muslim woman, was born in El Damer, a town in the northern province of Shimalia. Prior to her migration, she attended college in the Sudan and earned a bachelor's degree in commerce. Subsequently, she held a position in the Ministry of Finance for three years and "was very satisfied with it." But fearing interrogation about her activities in an opposition political party, Hanan arrived in Minneapolis in 1993, four years after the Islamic government seized power. In her view, she was compelled to leave.

> In the Sudan I was very outspoken politically. During the Intifada [the April 1985 popular uprising against the Nemeiri regime] and the return of democracy, we were very relieved to be able to express ourselves. Heated debates in our office about Islam, the *sharia*, and Islamic leaders were something we all talked about freely. I was and am still clear on my position against the application of the Islamic *sharia* because not everyone in the country is a Muslim. After Omer Elbashir came to power and the Islamicists took control, everybody was insecure. The conversations that we had about *sharia* were a source of worry to me. I decided to leave.
>
> I went to Egypt first to process my visa from there. With the assistance of one of my old neighborhood friends residing in Minnesota, I was able to find initial residence [in Egypt] from which my quest for asylum in North America was launched. I have other Sudanese women whom I am friendly with in Cairo who were also in search of an avenue to the United States. Their situation in Egypt is very difficult because of unemployment and financial need. I feel lucky to be here, especially when I remember the stress and worry I went through in the Sudan. But, as I promised the family back home, I intend to return when the rule of this regime ends.

Contrary to any belief that migration for political reasons is an activity limited to men, Hanan's story demonstrates the strong political agenda behind her migration. Hanan's participation in the Intifada also illustrates that women were a part of the challenge to authoritarian rule. The impact of Sudan's policies has been to form a North America refugee community whose female members advance an oppositional vision of the Sudan and their place within it. Hanan's vocal opposition to sharia law during the short-lived democratic rule created feelings of uneasiness and anxiety about her future in the Sudan. Although after her arrival she could obtain only a low-skilled job in a nearby shopping center, the realization that she was "free from military oppression" outweighed disappointment on the job market, and she expects opportunities to improve in time.

Mahasin

Mahasin, thirty-seven, was born in Elfashir in Western Sudan. She is a Muslim and a single woman. Before her arrival in Canada she worked in

Yemen as an officer with a European organization running an agricultural experiment.

> I worked in Sanaa, Yemen, for two years during which I was a community development specialist, working especially with rural Yemeni women. When my job ended in Yemen, I decided that I would not go to the Sudan under the present situation, which is bad for almost everyone, but especially for women. My reason behind coming [to Canada] is the bad government, which discriminates against women. My other equally important reason was getting a degree to enable me to obtain a career in a good field of specialization. I wanted to be independent. I came to Canada in 1992 with the assistance of a friend who sent me an invitation. This helped me very much when I presented it to the officials in the American embassy. So I got an entry visa to the United States. This was the most exciting thing that had ever happened to me. I was staying at this friend's place, but I had my own savings in American dollars from my job in Yemen. I am satisfied with my decision to immigrate.
>
> After I came to Canada, I found that health care and education are my rights as immigrant. Having the freedom of expressing opinions is also something that I hoped for. Life is very short, and going back to the Sudan to live under a military dictatorship would have been like poking out my own eye. My life in Canada is good; I have a lot of Sudanese friends. I also think that being independent of social restrictions is something that was worth migrating for. I really think that Sudanese women should learn from this experience to be assertive and forget about the feminine ideals of being shy and docile. This is something I always believed in, and now I am validated by my own experience.

Mahasin's statement stresses the importance of gender discrimination as a factor determining her migration decision. Is Mahasin a permanent migrant? Her answer is that she is not. "Had there been a democratic government in Sudan, what are my reasons for not staying at home?"

Amna

Born in Omdurman, Amna, like Hanan and Mahasin, is a political migrant. Now thirty-eight, she is a Muslim, a college graduate, and unmarried. Amna migrated to Toronto in 1990 after living in Virginia with friends who facilitated her tourist entry visa by sending affidavits of support.

> In the Sudan, I was a government employee in the Ministry of Development and Economic Planning. I graduated from Cairo University, Khartoum branch. I was determined to get out of the Sudan. The decision itself was very

hard because I have to leave my sisters and my parents. My departure was a bittersweet thing. I was very happy when I was finally able to leave, and at the same time the day of my departure was the most painful event in my whole life. Before I came here in 1995, the situation was tough in the Sudan. Every move you make is calculated, and you feel watched the whole time. I like to lead a normal life, and being a woman should not be used by officials to rob me of my most basic rights. I think what is happening to women in the Sudan is not right. The Sudanese woman by nature is one who cannot take any degradation. This generation especially is suffering, because they are the first to be laid off from their jobs. These women are becoming very desperate. I was a secretary in the Sudan; all the money I got was put into savings to be able to get out. When I arrived in Canada, I realized I was not alone. I met a lot of Sudanese refugee women. Many of them are unmarried, generally young, in their thirties maybe. Like other refugee women, I can summarize my reasons for coming here: military oppression, imposition of laws that threaten me as a woman, and shrinking opportunities to get ahead, have a decent life. Definitely, my migration was the answer.

Amna highlights the double-edged nature of exile; she cheered at the idea of coming, but at the same time she felt an extreme sense of sadness and loss. The overall conditions at home forced her decision to migrate, a decision linked to her yearning for self-fulfillment and to the inability to achieve such satisfaction in the Sudan because of her gender.

Safia

Safia was born in 1967 in El Obeid, a commercial center in Kordofan Province in Western Sudan, but her family migrated to Khartoum, where she grew up. As a health worker in a foreign nonprofit organization, she was able to move to New York in 1992, and unlike many Sudanese, she was able to get a job shortly after her arrival. Safia maintained that the security officers in the Sudan harassed her for wearing pants. She was called *dakaria* (lesbian), reprimanded, and nearly lashed for her "indecent appearance."

I was very mad about what happened to me in the Sudan. The people from El-nizam Alam [Public Order] were very disrespectful to me just because I was not *muhajaba* [covered]. Some were repeatedly talking among themselves that I was a *habashia* [Ethiopian] maybe. The whole ordeal was painful, and every time I remember it I feel sick to my stomach. I did not immediately move after that, but that incident stayed with me for some time. A year later I came to New York and got a job as international staff. I got married to a European man I met here, and I am happy. I assisted my sister to obtain a tourist visa, and she too is looking for a life of freedom and welfare here. Things went very well and I feel that going back is not in my outlook.

The military regime's claim to be reinventing Sudanese "authenticity" supports Shahnaz Khan's argument that "the body of the Muslim woman often becomes contested terrain between competing visions of authenticity" (1995, 146). Safia's mode of dress brought interrogation and harassment. Yet as Sondra Hale states, the government's "attempts to remold Sudanese women to fit a Muslim ideal were not totally accepted by either left or right" (1996, 116, 210). Since Safia's departure, as Sudanese Women's Union president Fatima Ahmed Ibrahim explains: "In 1994 the government issued a law, which considers the Sudanese women's [dress] not Islamic, and legislated that women should put on the Iranian costume, *chador,* instead. Our Union organized a campaign against the law, and issued a declaration in which it challenged the government to publish the verse of the Quran that considers the Iranian costume the official Islamic uniform. It also revealed the fact that Iran had given them tens of thousands of these costumes for free. They made *chador* compulsory in order to make a profit from its sale"(1996, 10).

Arafa

When I visited forty-two-year-old Arafa, her studio apartment in Toronto was impeccably clean and her magazines placed neatly in a woven basket underneath a coffee table. Arafa was born in Omdurman, one of the three cities comprising the capital.

Before I came to Toronto, I was a government employee. I lived with my parents, and although my salary was small, I managed my financial situation very well. I was saving for this moment for a long time. I joined a savings plan [*sandug*], and I did not have to pay rent, though I always brought back a bag of bread or fruit to contribute something to my parents. My experience is very similar to that of other Sudanese women here. It started in 1993 after it became clear to me that the Islamicists [*kaizan*] were not leaving power in my lifetime. I felt that the political situation was going from bad to worse, and I felt suffocated [*makhnooga*].

I am not married and you know in the Sudan a woman my age is considered an unwanted commodity [*baira*]. People always asked me whether there was a guy [*wad el halal*] who wanted to marry me. I was, in short, sick and tired of everybody. Of course I did not come here because I am not married, but for the political repression in the country; after all, marriage is fate and luck [*qisma wa nasib*]. Anyway, as a Sudanese woman, the social pressure reflects lack of freedom, and the political situation meant more restrictions and poor economic conditions, with no opportunity for self-improvement. Besides, I was very outspoken about my political views during the democratic government. I made my position clear that I am against the Islamic leaders when they were trying to force themselves into different government positions against the wishes of the people. A lot of people I know from our office were laid off "for the common good" [a government policy of dismissal called *lil Salih Alam*]. I was afraid and angry.

So what can I tell you? I started moving fast, before things got worse. My friend in New York helped me to get a visitor's visa. I also have a lot of friends in Washington, D.C., and Ontario. My friends from Canada knew the process very well because almost none of them arrived directly from the Sudan. They had to make a stop somewhere. So I was told to take the bus, or ask my friend to arrange for me to go to Buffalo, and then go straight to immigration in Canada.

The day of my departure from New York was a lot easier than that from the Sudan. I knew if anything happened I could go back to my friend and his wife, who were very helpful to me. The bus ride from New York City was the longest. My brain was working. I had a lot of questions, and I was worried about what lay ahead. I did exactly as I was told, and told the immigration officer about my situation and my request for asylum. They started the paperwork but he told me to go back to the U.S. and return to the border a month later.

Some Sudanese who face similar decisions usually go to churches and shelters if they don't have friends in the area. I had mixed feelings—should I go back or should I go to the shelter? I said to myself, "a devil you know is better than a devil you don't know" [*jinan tarafu akhair min jinan taghaba*]. I returned to the city for one more month during which I was able to work under the table to save money for Canada. Finally, when the time arrived, I returned to the border and was admitted. I had my friend's address in St. Catharines. I contacted him and thus started another cycle. He helped me a great deal. I stayed again with him for a few days till I found a place of my own.

Arafa continued her narrative by highlighting the paramount role that her friend played—a role which reflects the primacy of kin and social networks in the lives of the new arrivals (Pohjola 1991).

Through him I contacted a lawyer who helped thousands of refugees. The day for my claim in court arrived and I was scared to death. I knew that as someone who fled for political reasons I had a case, but still you never know. Fear and anticipation gave me the worst stomachache. I reminded myself of the stories of other Sudanese women who got asylum in Toronto. I calmed a little before fear swept over me again. A few friends accompanied me and when my claim was granted asylum, we were very happy. People were congratulating me, and I really felt that my life had begun with that moment.

Now I am living legally in Canada as a landed immigrant, thank God. I finished a community college degree focusing on computer programming and am working for a reasonable income. I have a good life here as part of the Sudanese community in Canada. At the same time I am glad that I am able to send money and medications to my family in the Sudan whenever I have the opportunity, and I am very glad that I was able to beat the odds. I've come a long way.

The five narratives above exemplify the insurrection of Sudanese women against the state's "symbolic politics" and patriarchal ideology. They show women's attempts to ward off gender oppression under a totalitarian ideology and highlight the tension between women and nation (Chow 1995; Kaplan et al. 1999). In their migrations to the United States and Canada, these women challenged stereotypes of female passivity and dependency. These are clearly politically conscious women whose migration to the United States and Canada is perceived by them as a necessary step. The political crisis of their country has entailed a corresponding personal crisis they set out to resolve via international migration. Like other women I interviewed in Toronto and the United States, they viewed their migration as a forced movement carried out under the pressure of the state.

Before their migration, these particular women enjoyed greater social mobility than thousands of Sudanese women who could not entertain migratory decisions. Despite their educational attainments and previous occupational status, however, the exigencies of being refugees have propelled Sudanese women to take jobs that they would have shunned at home, including grocery store cashier, nanny, and janitor, among others. Some have done well economically, but others are on welfare assistance: A majority, like their Sudanese male counterparts, have experienced forced proletarianization. Nevertheless, it is fair to say that Sudanese women have shown strength and self-reliance in remaking their lives and struggling to overcome the psychological and physical pressures of being a refugee in another country. As Safia pointed out, feelings of fear, anxiety, and confusion while awaiting court decisions can "drive you crazy."

Next we turn to three narratives of women from southern Sudan. Despite the specific context of the civil war, significant similarities exist between them and their northern countrywomen. Southern Sudanese were forced to accept migration, and they see it as a disruptive development. "The migration of our youth in general and our women in particular is a new phenomenon. In spite of its forced nature, it still created a negative impact on the Southern Sudanese community. The notion of women traveling overseas is equally disconcerting and worrisome. This demonstrates the extent to which individualism has replaced our cherished ideals of collectivism" (*Alayam,* October 30, 2000, 5).

Veronica

Forty-two-year-old Veronica, a scientist, is a Latuka who was born in Juba, the capital of Equatoria Province, 745 miles south of Khartoum and a site of military operations and refugee dispersals. Like most southerners arriving here, Veronica is Christian. When she was in elementary school, her family was forced to leave the Sudan to seek a safe haven in Uganda. Although she has been in the United States since 1977, Veronica views her migration as a temporary situation and has every intention of going back to the Sudan.

> We left the Sudan because of the war. In Uganda, where I received my education up to high school, Sudanese were very successful in the Cambridge College Admission Certificate, but the Uganda government issued a decree prohibiting Sudanese from signing up for these exams. So I was looking for a place to sponsor me to go to college, and indeed I was awarded a scholarship as an undergraduate in a college in Pennsylvania. My experience was good; once I entered college I was able to work on campus and put myself through school.
>
> As I remember from my early youth, living conditions were far better in the Sudan. No worries, no stress, safe, carefree, no fear of danger in the street. My memories are happy ones. I did not face any problems here. I was lucky to have lived in Uganda; perhaps that is what made me ready for any situation that I come in contact with. I did not face any discrimination. I find Americans to be kind and warm. They greatly admired my uniqueness as a Sudanese.
>
> As many years as I spent here, I must say that I am very much the Sudanese who arrived here twenty years ago. Nothing has changed a bit. I join Sudanese activities, dinners, social gatherings, and demonstrations. My friends are all Sudanese, whom I contact on regular basis. Emotionally I am a Sudanese in every way. I am here as a refugee. I just wait for the war to end because I cannot spend the rest of my life outside. I should say that many Sudanese, especially those coming here recently, tend to change faster than people in the Sudan, especially in the south, who are just trying to stay alive, due to bombing and starvation. What they need right now is just to make it out to safety anywhere and not necessarily to the U.S. or Canada. But if anyone makes it to America, I don't have any negative reason for why they should not be here.

Susan

Like Victoria, Susan was born in Juba and was propelled to move with her family to Uganda. At age thirty-nine, Susan, also a scientist, lives in Washington, D.C. She too completed her undergraduate degree and graduate education in the United States. Like millions of southern Sudanese, Susan's migration was prompted by war. She told me that she is determined to return to the Sudan "when there is freedom of religion and when the south becomes independent." Similar to most southern Sudanese I interviewed, she is not favorably disposed to the notion of a united Sudan and holds deep disagreement with those who think a unified Sudanese nation is a good idea. "We have suffered enough with the problems with the north. We have to decide for ourselves and govern the region as an autonomous country. I think the people who think that the south has problems within the same community and cannot govern itself—I think that is very paternalistic. Southerners are deserving of a chance to prove themselves." Susan went on to argue: "When we hear now that most of the southern Sudanese displaced women in Khartoum are in prison because they make alcohol, I say to myself that there is no justification for us to stay in an Islamic state. Southerners are Christians, some of them have their own religion, and a small number are Muslims. I think that we deserve our independence. That is the only way out."

Josephine

Josephine, a twenty-eight-year-old southerner, left the Sudan as a nanny with a northern Sudanese family. Josephine has only finished third grade and enrolled in a church school at a local church in Virginia. Her story is a compelling example of what can happen to migrant women who are un-equipped socially and economically to deal with their new role.

> Before I moved with a northern family to Maryland in 1989, I was working for them also in Kuwait. Once we came to the U.S. this family refused to pay me my salary. They claimed that they were already paying for my food and shelter. They did not allow me to leave the house or learn English. My life was terrible; I wanted to go back to the Sudan so bad. Some Sudanese friends told me that in this country I have rights. If I am not happy, there are things I can do. That is true, because there is nothing I liked about living here; if I could help it, I would have left immediately, but I was not able to do that. That is why the Sudanese people to whom I told my story were very angry, and they advised me to leave this family. So I did. I am lonely here; most of the people I am friendly with are busy. My life was better in the Sudan in spite of all the problems. But the war is going on in the Sudan. I can't go now. I think of home and a lot of times I cry, but there is nothing I can do now. If things change, I will go back.

In 1996 I attended a gathering at the Harbourfront Center in Toronto to listen to a discussion on the role of Sudanese women in peacemaking in the Sudan. The Inter-Church Coalition on Africa, a Canadian organization, sponsored the event. About four hundred people congregated in the auditorium, including Sudanese, other Canadians, and other African immigrants. The first speaker, Fatima Ahmed Ibrahim of the Sudanese Women's

Union, a northerner, started by stating her purpose: "to explain to the Canadian people how this regime has misused Islam to wage a civil war and suppress Muslims in the north." Both Fatima and Anisia Achieng Olworo, a southerner and the coordinator for Sudan's Women's Voice for Peace, had been delegates at the September 1995 conference "Harvest for Sudan: Women's Peace Initiative" in Nairobi. There, more than thirty women from all parts of the country—south, north, east, the Nuba Mountains, the Ingessena Hills—discussed the religious, ethnic, and political oppression of the military regime and adopted a stand against atrocities committed in every part of the country. A declaration signed by all these Sudanese women appealed to regional and international bodies, in particular the United Nations Security Council, to review the situation in the Sudan, ensure that the rights of every Sudanese are respected, and support all options to bring lasting peace and justice. The two women read from this declaration: "We, Sudanese women participants—recognizing our diversity, differences, and commonalties—agree to call on the warring parties and the people of the Sudan to engage in serious negotiations to end the long lasting war and to achieve sustainable peace." The *Toronto Star* covered the event, assisting the conferees' desire to broaden public consciousness about conditions in the Sudan. This kind of political action by Sudanese women is now imaginable because of the independence they have gained during this most recent migration to the United States and Canada.

"I Don't Need a Guardian": Aftermath of Operation Desert Storm

As Sudanese migratory choices and alternatives shifted following the Gulf War, those few male Sudanese migrants working in the Persian Gulf region who managed to keep their jobs became increasingly aware of their vulnerability. Since 1994, the wives of these workers have constituted a significant flow of female migration to North America. Once started, it gained a life of its own, with friends from the Gulf region following others who came before them and settling in the same area. Today, there are hundreds of such Sudanese women in Canada and others in the United States. As one, Rashida, explained: "We cannot and will not ever go back except maybe for visits. My husband finished his degree and now he has to worry about the children. When we came here we wanted to go back to the Sudan. In fact, my first year here was a very emotional time for me. I felt isolated and really missed my family back home. But as I started to get used to New York and the cold weather, I was fine. In the course of the years, our plans have changed. I felt that my children deserve a good life here. There is no stability in the Sudan, and no future. I used all different kinds of plans to convince my husband, but finally he yielded because, deep down, he is also convinced that he should not go back."

In 1998, I conducted interviews with Sudanese wives in Toronto who had migrated from countries in the Persian Gulf with their children. All but one had come without their husbands. Most of these women have settled in an affluent neighborhood unaffordable to other Sudanese in Canada.

Manal, thirty-six years old, was among the first of these women I interviewed. She is married to Ali, who still works in Oman, where he has been a highly paid computer specialist for the last fourteen years. Since arriving with her two children, ages ten and thirteen, she has rented an apartment next to two other ex-Gulf Sudanese women who came earlier. In her elegant and spacious apartment, tastefully decorated with expensive furniture, paintings, oriental rugs, and elegant window treatments, Manal prepared mint tea served on a gold-plated set.

I decided to migrate to Canada for several reasons. First, the insecurities that were created after the Gulf War, especially the fear of instability of the Gulf region in general. We were forced to think about a place to go if another war erupted. We cannot go back to the Sudan, because we will not be able to maintain the life that our families are accustomed to. Actually, I did try for a year to go back to the Sudan, but it was very hard on the children. Our second reason is the education of our children. Because we put them in private schools in Oman, we found that it is much better if they come here, where they can still get good education without spending so much money. We found that the immigration procedures to Canada were a lot easier compared to other countries like Australia and New Zealand. We do have friends who applied for Australia and New Zealand; some managed to go, the others are still waiting. We did explore the opportunities, and decided to go to Canada. Also in the Gulf now, there are many lawyers and agents who provide legal assistance in processing your application for landed immigration in Canada. We paid $5,000 [Canadian] for the whole thing, and it took about a year from beginning to end till we got the papers.

We knew that it was going to be tough from the standpoint of family separation. Ali is very well paid, and we did not feel that he should leave his job and start from zero. The decision was made for the welfare of the family; the kids will get the best education. Now my husband sends enough money for us here, and I also want to go back to school for additional training. I also want to say that not everybody in the Gulf can make this decision. Only people with very good incomes are financially able to bring their families. But, of course, there many people talk to us to find out exactly how we went about this.

The Gulf employment can no longer provide the security and the expectations they had decades ago when Sudanese communities were established there. This sense of insecurity led people to resettle elsewhere. The family decision was hard in the beginning, but I always felt that I did not need a guardian to accompany me. Coming without my husband, of course, put a lot of pressure on me for assuming the responsibilities of two parents, but it was worth it. My husband comes once a year during his vacation. Although he was reluctant in the beginning, I was very firm, and I made my intentions known that he will be supportive of the decision, and we can still be a family, but I am going by myself [anyway]. Keeping in touch with the family proved to be very expensive, since we have to save every penny. This decision of course had an impact on the family, but I think it is a positive one.

Wijdan also came from Oman to Toronto in 1995. Whereas Manal arrived alone, Wijdan's husband accompanied her and subsequently returned after getting the family situated in a beautiful three-story home. At the time of our interview, her husband Omer, a physician, was visiting on his vacation. Four of us, including Manal, were seated in a tasteful wall-to-wall carpeted living room with impressionist paintings on the walls and sandalwood incense releasing a sweet scent. Wijdan's pearl jewelry and sky-blue silk outfit left no doubt she led a very different life from the refugee women in Toronto. Manal and Wijdan exchanged a joke about how wonderful it is to be "free of husbands" and how smoothly their lives were running. Husband Omer began.

Since the Gulf War we decided that we must find a secure place to live. Going back to the Sudan was not a feasible thing to do, because our children are in high school now and soon will be going on to college. Schooling is not stable in the Sudan: Education is always interrupted by government decisions to close down the schools for fear of demonstrations. Staying in the Gulf was also questionable. I have to say that my position as a physician in the Sultanate is secure, and I have no financial problems supporting my family in Canada. I was sure that my wife would be very capable of being here and quite good at managing her own affairs.

When they came here it was difficult; just the idea of being so far from them was troubling to me. But we are increasingly becoming e-mail parents. I e-mail my children everyday, and they ask me sometimes to help them with homework via the internet. I know that other migrants in the Gulf have tried to bring their wives [to Canada], but [their wives] couldn't take it. The wives were always on the phone with them, so it did not work. I think my wife's background, as someone who worked before, is important. Here she is doing well, and after sending the children to Catholic schools, she feels that they have a good education.

The husbands back in the Gulf often get together on the weekends, play cards, and exchange news. The family separation is easier for some than for others, but this type of migration is really increasing. As far as marital relations are concerned, I think that I have a good relationship with my wife and it does not matter to me whether she is there or here. Others, however, find it difficult and we hear some rumors of husbands who start to fool around. I think that the decision to come to Canada was in the family's best interest.

Wijdan continued to comment on her migratory experience:

Coming to Canada was a good decision. After all this time I am very used to it, and I have an independent life. My children are at a stage now where they are reliable and responsible. They realize that I am responsible here, and rarely do they make any decision without consulting me. I also found it necessary to bring them every summer to the Sudan. I feel that raising them as Sudanese, not Canadian, children will make them more accepting of my advice.

The responsibilities here are big. I have to budget our income, although we get more than enough, but I feel I have to be careful and secure savings for the family. I decided to enroll in a community college in Toronto to get ready for a job so that we can also have an extra security. I think that I have changed. In the Gulf I had maids, and I had people do things for me all the time. My adjustment experience in Canada in the beginning was hard in assuming the role of a maid, driver, teacher, mother, and father, but I got used to it and I organized myself. What I also find encouraging is that whatever difficult issue you become confronted with, you don't run to the husband for answers. I am figuring everything out on my own. Our life here is nice; especially my social life is rich because of the presence of other friends who are in the same position as me. Rare is the day when we don't talk to each other or visit one another. Every way you look at it, coming to Canada was a wise decision. When I go to the Sudan in the summer, I get the emotional support I need for the whole year until I go back again. There are no problems.

Migration brought about significant transformations in the life of these privileged migrant women, including increased freedom and mobility, especially the opportunity to socialize with each other. They spend weekends together, attend social events, pay visits to others in the community in times of happy and sad occasions, or just call to chat (*wanasa*) or to exchange information. For many Sudanese women like these who came unaccompanied by their spouses, the decision to come to North America represented a threshold they have crossed successfully. Many point out that in the beginning their husbands and in-laws nagged them that it was not a good idea, but later accepted the situation.

The majority of these women in Canada had not previously worked in the Persian Gulf countries, although most had a college education in the Sudan. Once in Canada, and in spite of the funds sent by husbands to cover expenses, these women worked to secure their own financial independence. For example, Manal and Wijdan both started training in computer programming to ensure job access in the Canadian labor market. Others have started in similar occupations. The choices of Sudanese women in Toronto have enhanced their sense of control over resources, finances, and their own bodies. It is worth mentioning that the majority of these women have only two or three children, an extremely small number by Sudanese standards. Manal contrasts this with "living in the Gulf, where women have nothing to do except get golden jewelry and get pregnant annually." Family size has been transformed through migration.

The Sudanese community in Canada, however, is marked by class differentiation. Most Sudanese nationals in Canada are refugees who depend on government welfare programs, usually for two to three years, before they complete training and obtain jobs. This leads to a residential pattern in which families and groups of single men share housing to make ends meet. For the post–Gulf War women, this is never the case. As Leila, thirty-seven and originally from Khartoum North, pointed out: "The people who came from the Gulf maintain the same level of material prosperity as they used to have in the Gulf. Everybody knows that in the Gulf people do not have to pay for rent, taxes, or anything, so they have decent incomes, and the currency is strong compared to the Canadian money. There is no comparison between them and the poor [*masakin*] Sudanese who are on welfare."

"Too Many People Are Winning the Lottery Now": Ibtisam's Story

Originally from Shendi, a town between Khartoum and Atbara, Ibtisam moved to Khartoum to attend college and then obtained a government job as an accountant. In 1997 she migrated to New York under the Diversity Visa Lottery Program. Like thousands of her compatriots who have won the *lotteria*, as Sudanese call it, Ibtisam was an immigrant on her arrival rather than a refugee. I met Ibtisam one evening during an *eid* celebration in the Bronx. Wearing a traditional Sudanese *tobe*, Ibtisam was among nearly three hundred Sudanese attending a concert by Sudanese singer Sammy Elmagarabi with a banquet catered by a Sudanese chef, herself a lottery winner. I asked Ibtisam about her decision to come to New York.

> I have a lot of people here, in Brooklyn, both relatives and friends. I was working in the Sudan, but the working conditions there are hard in every way. The salary [*mahia*] is not enough. I get it at the beginning of each month, and by the end of the first week we start to scratch our heads wondering how to get by for the coming three weeks. We borrow money, try to cut down, ride a bus instead of a taxi, but everything you try to do is of no use.
>
> My economic situation was very strained. But all the time I was in the Sudan I wanted to get out of the hard life [*shagawa*], the oppressive heat, and

Advertisement for U.S. immigration lottery in a Sudanese newspaper announces "America in your hands."

the running around I did just to get by. I was keeping in touch through letters with my relatives here in New York and they were very helpful to me. I asked about the lottery, because if you do it yourself in the Sudan you have to pay someone to prepare it for you. I sent my information and when the lottery was announced it was big news. I felt like I wanted to fly on wings of joy.

The family, to tell the truth, did not object, because I am a single woman. Just the opposite: they were helpful and understanding. Even the oldest people in the family wished me success. In the Sudan, the American consul used to come from Egypt about once a month to process the visas for lottery winners. Now you have to go to Egypt to get a visa because the American consulate is shut down in the Sudan. Everything went well. I arrived in New York, where two of my very close friends met me, and brought me to their house. I have a job now in New York, but not as an accountant. I need to give myself time to learn English before I try for another job. I am sharing an apartment with other people here. I like New York except for the cold winter, but what can I do?

I am glad that I was lucky, and once I settle enough I can help my brothers and sisters. Already one of them works outside the Sudan in Jeddah, Saudi Arabia. As for women coming here, this has been a normal thing. People do not resent it like they did in the past, and your own family expects you to lift the financial burden from their shoulders when you send dollars. Even if you send twenty dollars, it amounts to a lot.

Ibtisam's case resonates with those of several women who obtained permanent residence through the lottery. It highlights the expectations of changing Sudanese socioeconomic life, with families becoming increasingly more tolerant and accepting of female migration.

"She Is Not Going Back until She Gets Her Child an American Passport"

"She is not going back until she gets her child an American passport" was what forty-one-year-old Salwa, a Sudanese migrant in Alexandria, Virginia, said about her neighbor's sister. Among the ever-growing numbers of Sudanese migrants in the Washington, D.C., area, this topic of women coming to the United States to give birth provoked much comment: "What would they do in case of an emergency?" "What are they thinking, coming on this trip while in the last stages of pregnancy?" "What if they give birth in the airplane?" These were all provoked by the new pattern of giving birth to "American children." Surprised by this shift in attitudes of Sudanese toward their homeland, Imad, thirty-eight years old, reflected on his own mother's circumstances. "Forty years ago, my father was a graduate student here in the United States. When my mother was expecting my older sister, she insisted on going back to the Sudan to deliver the child there. She wanted to be with her family and friends during this time, and she returned to the U.S. after my sister was born. The irony of fate is that my sister is here now as a graduate student, and she is trying her best to obtain permanent residence. Now it is the opposite; women come all the way here by themselves to make sure that their children will be American citizens by birth."

Several Sudanese migrants told me that in concentrations where large numbers of Sudanese migrants reside, women arrive frequently to give birth. Aziza, thirty-nine years old, had given birth in Brooklyn.

First of all, I have to say that if I did not have a relative here in the United States it could have been difficult to come here. When I made this decision, a lot of people in the Sudan thought that coming here for the reason of giving birth is a fad introduced by rich Sudanese women. In my case, I am a working person and I had to save money to do this. In the Sudan, people there will make comments that show you that they do not support the decision of traveling somewhere to give birth, but I did not mind. If the Sudan were stable, I think it would be a lot easier to stay there and be among family members. The important thing is that when I got everything organized, my husband was supportive and excited. I decided to come for the sake of the child's future. We don't know what is going to happen in the Sudan twenty years from now; certainly there is no sign that things will improve. I thought that at least my son could come back to the United States as a citizen. I am not worried about myself, but about my son's future. I am thankful that I had this opportunity. My son can come here to go to school and lead a good life, get good education and health care, just everything here. And it is true that in the Sudan women are coming here for that, in spite of the criticism of other people. When I go back, I will feel satisfied that I did everything in my power to make sure that the next generation has an easier life.

Patricia Nabti (1992) has pointed to the same strategy among Lebanese women, and it is no doubt occurring more widely. Whether this pattern was pioneered by "rich Sudanese women" is now a secondary issue, since it leads to the formation of a cohort of American-born children in the Sudan who will probably return one day. And it is women who are the prime movers in producing this cohort.

The stories told to me by Sudanese women in the United States and Canada illustrate trends and transformations that Sudanese people are experiencing at home as well as in the ghorba. Their stories reflect the changing nature of gender roles and expectations in Sudanese society, where social relations and societal values have unquestionably been more confining for women than men. The Sudanese saying, *"elmara kan fas ma bitkisr elras"* (even if the woman was an axe, she would not be able to break the head), denoting helplessness and passivity, receives no corroboration from these women living in North America. Unimaginable a generation ago, women are even migrating by themselves, without guardians (*awlia amr*). The stories also demonstrate how Sudanese women are carving a space for themselves in the social landscape of the receiving societies.

PART III

❋

THE GHORBA: LIFE IN EXILE

[7]

Economic Bearings

Migration is too often a dream followed by disillusion. For when he leaves home, the emigrant has idealized his new life so much that the reality is hard to accept, but the rapid and lasting social advance that he has longed for is often painfully slow in coming, and the awakening is as rude as the dream was delightful.

Abdel Wahab Bouhdiba, 1974

In Alexandria, Los Angeles, New York, and Washington, in addition to professionals and students, you can find Sudanese working in the service sector as taxi drivers, pizza deliverymen, gas station attendants, store cashiers, and restaurant workers. This phenomenon is part of a global era of transnational exchange—in labor, technology, and capital—that is marking "the end of geography" as we know it. Massive distance is no longer a hindrance to population mobility, and people's perpetual search for "the better" is less and less impeded by it. The world is shrinking in this transnational age, bringing the disparities in economic wealth and political power that exist within national boundaries more immediately to global attention (Bottomley 1992; Harvey 1989; Heyden 1991; Mahler 1995; Ueda 1994). Migrants see their movements as "An attempt to circumvent institutionalized inequalities, but in making this attempt migrants face many obstacles, including the historical legacies of colonialism and Empire, regional and class structures in their countries of origin and a further set of racial and class divisions in their countries of settlement" (Ballard 1987, 38–39).

Individual perception is greatly influenced by globalization, which shapes awareness of conditions elsewhere. Why else would a middle-age Sudanese, a vendor in Saad Qishra Market in Sudan, ask me about the drug Rogaine for balding; or a Sudanese woman ask her migrant nephew, "Just how effective is the American antidepressant medication Prozac?" adding, "Can I get a big sack of it?"

The international movement of peoples is principally a by-product of inequalities at both the national and transnational levels. Sudanese migration to North America thus can be seen as a viable alternative to economic hardship. Awareness of economic opportunities in the United States and Canada travels with migrants across borders. Before Abdel Jalil from Umm Doawan Ban village in eastern Khartoum came as a Diversity Visa Lottery Program winner, he drew his knowledge about life in the United States from acquaintances there. Formerly a merchant in the Arabic Market in downtown Khartoum, he has driven a taxi in New York since his arrival in 1989. Abdel Jalil maintains that his motive to migrate was purely economic. Once he accumulates enough capital, he intends to return to his homeland, and he tries to save money by sacrificing his own personal needs to reach that goal. Content with his situation, he concludes: "If I am asked about life here I will say that it is fine. If anyone wants to come—welcome, you can work hard and save. This is my advice to my friends: come. Just remember to stay away from drugs, alcohol, and sex." Another migrant, Khalifa, who comes from Kadougli in the Nuba Mountains, reports that his income and quality of life here are much better than in the Sudan, where he was unemployed before his departure.

For other people, aspired economic prosperity and sudden riches are not achievable. To the dismay of many, dreams are smashed by economic reality. Needless to say, Sudanese middle-class migrants do not cheer about downward mobility after their arrival.

Sudanese migrants and exiles are distributed by government and sponsor organizations to different locations in the labor markets of the United States and Canada. Among Sudanese, 48 percent I interviewed had held professional, white-collar occupations at home (as university professors, lawyers, pharmacists, engineers); 27 percent were students; 15 percent worked in the service sector; and 10 percent were unemployed. After arrival, only 22 percent had professional occupations; 38 percent were employed as service workers; 25 percent were students; and 13 percent were unemployed. This confirms informants' perceptions that those who held white-collar employment in the Sudan were most likely to experience downward mobility after their migration. Thus, it was not unusual to meet lawyers, pharmacists, and engineers now working as taxi drivers, pizza deliverymen, or parking lot attendants.

In my interviews with Sudanese migrants in the United States, they often related stories of "a rude awakening" after they arrived and realized that the long years of education and training in the Sudan were insignificant. Proletarianization and deskilling of the migrant were linked to other common problems faced by Sudanese in North America. For some Sudanese, downward occupational mobility was also accompanied by employer exploitation due to the migrant workers' undocumented status. As Walid, a migrant in New Jersey, put it: "Because the kind of jobs we get don't require documents or social security cards, and little experience, working under the table is the only way to survive—hoping that with the passage of time things would improve, like getting a green card. In the meantime we are all underemployed." In the four excerpts that follow, each of the migrants was seeking to legalize his stay at the time of the interview.

The "Rude Awakening" on the Job Market

Habib Allah

Habib Allah, age thirty-seven, worked as a high school teacher in the Sudan; now he drives a taxi in Brooklyn.

I came to New York with my cousin Hussein in July 1989, one month after Omer Elbashir's military government came to power. My reasons for leaving were economic and political. When we came, we stayed with a Sudanese couple from our neighborhood in Sudan until we both got jobs and then moved out. I thought that the economic opportunity here is much greater, but in no way does my present job match my expectations. On the one hand, I was happy that I am in a place where you can be free. But my biggest problems are working in unsafe conditions for little pay and for long hours. Sometimes we get phone calls to get somebody, and you hesitate—shall I go get this guy from this neighborhood? I can't tell you the extent of the psychological pressures I face everyday. I have no time for myself, and I really feel very strongly about going back to the Sudan after the restoration of democracy and a stable economy. I found life to be very, very hard here.

Awad

Awad, age thirty-six, born in Elnuhood in Kordofan Province in Western Sudan, was a lawyer before his migration to New York, and was working at a grocery store in Brooklyn when I interviewed him in 1994. Awad was a political activist in the Sudan and decided to leave. With financial help from two brothers working in Abu Dhabi in the Persian Gulf, and with encouragement from friends already in New York, Awad made his move. He indicated that his major problem has been his inability to secure a job as a lawyer, or even as a paralegal.

> When I came from the Sudan, I started work immediately in an immigrant-owned business in New York. I worked for little pay since I did not have legal documents. I had no benefits, no insurance, no nothing. My work was very intense; I had to unload boxes and boxes of merchandise from commercial trucks. Physically, I was not able to handle these kinds of jobs. In fact, I never dreamed in my life that after five years of law school this would be my destiny. I was only 120 pounds. I collapsed. I went to the storeowner and asked him for some days off because of my condition. My legs were swollen. I could barely move and it was winter. He told me that he would let me know by the end of the day. The following day my friend who found me the job came to me to tell me about the storeowner's answer to my request. My friend told me that the owner thinks that if I want to complain, tens of people can take my job today. I decided to stay in the job in spite of my pain, since I was thinking to myself if I get another job it is not going to be Mayor of New York. At that time I cannot tell you how disappointed I was. I was disappointed for coming here; I was disappointed in my country, and in my life. That is when I decided to leave the United States to seek asylum in Canada. At least in Canada you receive some assistance, most importantly health coverage, which I sorely needed.

El Riayah

El Riayah arrived in 1992. An engineer in the Sudan, he was a gas station attendant and a janitor at the time of my interview with him in 1993.

> I used to be an engineer in the Sudan. When I arrived, some Sudanese friends helped me find a job in a grocery store. The storeowner was merciless. He made me work for very long hours with very low pay. Later on, I became self-employed as a cab driver. However, I decided to quit because it is extremely dangerous to be a cab driver in New York. Now I work in a department store. What is really painful is that, at least in the foreseeable future, I will never be able to go back to my job in my field since I need further training, and I do not have the time to work and study. I have friends who face the same predicament. But we are all forced to take whatever jobs are available since there is a large stream of migrants waiting in line and ready to perform these kinds of low-wage jobs.

Jalal

Jalal was born in El Turabi village in Gezira Province in the Sudan. After earning a bachelor's degree in art in the Sudan, he worked as a high school teacher in Oman from 1988 to 1992. Jalal left his job in Oman to join his wife in Washington, D.C., where he works as a taxi driver. He explains:

> One of my biggest disappointments here is that I failed to secure a job in my field. I work hard as you can expect, in the taxi service. If I knew that was going to happen, I would not have left my teaching career to drive a cab in the U.S. But the grass is always greener on the other side, as people would have it. If I am to advise any of my friends or relatives who want to come here, I will be honest. I will tell them that life is tough in a different way. Yes, you will have electricity, water, and food. If they are married, I would advise them to stay, and not to take a risk of sacrificing your life for the unknown.

This underutilization of migrants' skills and qualifications tends to create a strata of Sudanese proletarianized intellectuals. These Sudanese perceive themselves as victims of dual oppression: in the Sudan, by current political and economic conditions, and in the United States, by a labor market that has little room for their social and professional advancement. In 1995, Sudanese political leader Fatima Ahmed Ibrahim met with over 150 Sudanese in Canada to decry the deskilling of the nation at home. The most productive segments of Sudanese society are those leaving or already abroad. This trend constitutes a drain of talent in a country that, ironically, fostered both the development and the displacement of these productive citizens. Ibrahim's message: "Do your best to go back to the Sudan to benefit your people. After years of delivering pizza and driving cabs and working as janitors, I don't think you will be able to remember the conspicuous high-quality education you received back home. When the political regime is overthrown, go back to your jobs as lawyers, engineers, and teachers. Your country is in serious need of your talents."

But as the migrant Mahgoub told me: "If one ventures to convey the truth about obstacles encountered in the U.S., people will accuse you of being envious [*hasid*], that you got there so now you do not want anyone to be as successful as you are. So the cycle of downward mobility remains unbreakable if people do not want the truth." Yet in the words of Abdel Rahman, thirty-three years old and living in El Sahafa, a suburb of Khartoum: "I just want to go to the U.S. I don't care if I have to sell melon seeds in the streets." A potential migrant, Abdel Rahman worked in a travel agency in Khartoum and was waiting to hear news about the visa lottery. Abdel Rahman expressed deep frustration with life under "a repressive environment and grim conditions in the Sudan." Seeking a way out, Abdel Rahman had little time to worry about downward mobility. He cannot leave as a refugee because as a resident in the north he is not considered to be affected by the civil war. Therefore, the lottery seems the only alternative for Abdel Rahman and many like him. He plans to apply every year until "an act of God changes his situation." His story echoes that of thousands of other Sudanese women and men hoping to depart.

Legal vs. Illegal Migration

Dramatic shifts in class identification are often related to migrants' legal status. Middle-class Sudanese or those who are trained professionals at home and who are "illegal" in North America must accept new class identities as workers in low-paying, low-skill occupations. For those who escape deportation, their irregular immigration status represents a formidable obstacle in adapting to their new life. Many stated that unless they manage to legalize their status, they would not be able to acquire high-paying jobs. Some Sudanese, like other migrant populations, have resorted to "green card" marriage to a U.S. citizen as a route to lawful permanent residence. However, these marriages are not without problems. Apart from the demands that migrants may experience from U.S. citizen spouses, they are still considered conditional migrants by the Immigration and Naturalization Service (U.S. Immigration and Naturalization Service 1991). As one Sudanese migrant explained:

> Chances to have a good life in this country are very slim because many have no legal status. But in order to legalize your status you have to wait for a very long time without guarantees. So some people are forced to get married to Americans. It happened to me and I got married to a Caribbean who had the green card, but after awhile the person who arranged this marriage told me that since it was a holiday season, I had to buy extra gifts. I was not happy at all since I have already paid a lot of money. I went to my so-called wife's house [since we never lived together] to give her the gifts. She opened the door and from her appearance it became clear to me that she was expecting more than the gifts. I dropped the gifts so fast and ran literally. On the way home, I was cursing the military dictatorship that forced me out of the Sudan. In short, trying to legalize your status is not without problems, even through marriage to Americans, and many people are getting smart enough not even to try it.

Sudanese migrants with irregular status are concentrated in low-wage jobs, at least at the first stage of their migration. Those that I interviewed were overwhelmingly dissatisfied with their lives in the United States and Canada. As one migrant put it: "When I arrived at the airport, I was not sure what I would be doing here. I had a very good job in the Sudan but I moved for political reasons. My friends here told me that I have to take whatever job I find. My present job pays very little. I am very exhausted, since I work seven days a week for long hours, with no health insurance, no rest. But I have no alternative."

By contrast, the adjustment experience of migrants with regular status is perceived as more satisfactory. For those in the asylum category who are found eligible for protection under the Canadian refugee determination process or the United States courts, adjustment is facilitated by their status, which entitles them to receive assistance from the respective governments. For those who acquire permanent residence ("the green card"), freedom of occupational mobility is open. In recent years, the majority of arrivals with regular status have chosen to reside in Canada.

How Are Sudanese Managing?

In 1994 I met a group of five Sudanese men in Silver Springs, Maryland, who had held white-collar jobs in the Sudan. They cut living costs by sharing apartments—sometimes six or seven people shared housing to reduce the cost of rent—and avoiding eating out. Their rule was "Never eat out and never go shopping for anything other than basic necessities." I was told that each had one day of the week assigned to buy and cook dinner for his roommates. That same person used leftovers from dinner to prepare lunches for the following day.

Another strategy adopted by Sudanese all over the United States and Canada is the use of a rotating credit association, or sandug. This method of saving is popular in the Sudan. A group of people each pay a part of their income to one sandug participant per month. Participants take turns receiving the pooled contributions from the rest until everyone has taken a turn, then the group begins the rotation again. Anthropologist Susan Kenyon writes of the sandug in the Sudan that it "provides a means for achieving significant material development which is readily available within everyone's grasp, for if one cannot find an existing sandug to accommodate one's saving needs, one can always start a box oneself" (1997, 3). The sandug also is used by Sudanese migrants to accumulate remittances to send to family members back home or to cover an emergency. In Michigan, Siham organizes a sandug that sometimes is as large as $3,000 in one month. The sandug is an effective coping mechanism for meeting financial needs, but it relies on Sudanese people's trust and confidence in one another. It becomes a feasible strategy only when a culture of trust among fellow migrants exists (see also Laguerre 1992; Park 1997).

A similar gesture of support among Sudanese migrants is a donor list, or *kashif,* that circulates at the time of a wedding, a death in the family, or another unexpected event. At these times, Sudanese pass along a kashif, on which one signs one's name with a pledged monetary contribution to the needy migrant. In 1996, for example, a group of migrants in Boston circulated a kashif to collect funds to cover funeral arrangements for a migrant who was killed in a car accident.

The Role of Women in Economic Adaptation

Migrant women often play a critical role in their family economies. Although few Sudanese women worked outside the home in the Sudan, in North America jobs outside the household are common. Well contented with this situation, a group of five women I interviewed in New York City asserted that paid jobs are empowering for women.

Balqis, age thirty-three, a woman who did not have much opportunity to find a job outside the home, decided to make good in spite of this. Originally from the western region of the Sudan near the commercial capital of El Obeid, and a daughter of a landowning peasant, Balqis started a babysitting business by taking care of two young children between 9 A.M. and 5 P.M. on weekdays. By babysitting over a period of two years, she was able to accumulate a sum of capital, which she did not disclose to her husband. Before she returned to the Sudan, Balqis was able to purchase two hundred twin-bed sheets, women's dresses, shoes, and handbags that she planned to sell there. She added: "When I subtract the money that I set aside for airport customs and other petty cash to help me until I leave, I still ended up with a respectable amount of money." Balqis's success in moneymaking was discussed by Sudanese friends after she left. Her close friend Manahil said, "If someone wants to go back to the Sudan, she has to be like Balqis. Do you know that Balqis is a very successful businesswoman now? First, she has a regular job as an administrative assistant, so she has a steady income from that. She sells Sudanese women's national dress, or *tiab* [described in Eltayeb 1987], which she purchases from Switzerland. I am sure that the money she used to earn here in the United States gave her a very good push."

Ibtihaj was born in Buri El Mahas, a suburb of Khartoum. Her husband is from Gezira Province. A secretary in the Sudan, she is now a factory worker in Toronto. She lives in a small two-bedroom apartment in downtown Toronto with her husband and two children:

> We arrived in the United States in December 1991, and I have been living in New York with my husband for a year. This was the hardest time emotionally.

We were not sure whether to go back or stay, but we followed tens of Sudanese who crossed the border and sought asylum in Canada. Once we arrived here and got refugee status, we received welfare assistance. It was very helpful, and although they pay exactly what they expect your family will require to get by, I tried to cut out a lot from the budget and get things that are very necessary. I looked for a job for a long time, but my attempts then were not successful. I decided to take a course in English as a second language, and over a period of a year my English was getting better. I was able to get a factory job, and it is really very hard but I make more than what I used to get on welfare. Besides, I looked at the whole welfare situation as temporary assistance, and unlike some people I know, I could not settle for it for the rest of my life. My husband now delivers pizza at night, and we alternate so that one of us will be around for the children. See, childcare here is very expensive. For that reason I thought if we were to start building a reasonable life for the family, I should not have any more children. In the Sudan women of my generation have five and six kids on average, we just can't afford this kind of behavior.

Now, more or less, we are settled comfortably. I want to work hard to save money to have the security for my family. I do a lot compared to what I did in the Sudan—driving, cleaning, cooking, and taking care of the children when I am not working—but I think that we are only paying the price for leaving.

The increased participation of Sudanese women in employment outside the household has expanded the scope of domestic duties and household work performed by men. Prior to migration, Sudanese men rarely did laundry, cooked, or cared for babies. As Sudanese migrant families lost the labor for these activities previously provided by extended family members, neighbors, and hired help (*khadadim*), the picture has shifted. The division of household labor is becoming more equitable since men and women no longer divide work along gender lines. This change, however, cannot be understood apart from the work opportunities and schedules that have shaped Sudanese migrants' lives. In the Sudan a regular workday lasts from 7:00 A.M. until 2:00 P.M., but the situation is very different here. Many of the migrant Sudanese men have evening jobs as gas station attendants, pizza deliverymen, or security guards, which leaves available time for household duties during the day. Ali, age forty-four, remarked: "I do a lot of things in the house. I even learned how to bake *kisra* bread. Doing dishes, changing diapers everything; you name it, I do it. When my mother came to Washington for a visit, I thought that a civil war between herself and my wife would erupt. She was really astounded at the work I do. But my wife was very reluctant to accommodate extra work while my mother was there. I told my mother that the days are gone when I did not have to do anything in the house—just go to work, eat, and sleep. She kept shaking her head."

Port Sudan, a popular restaurant for Sudanese and non-Sudanese visitors to downtown Toronto's Yonge Street. 1999.

These transformations account for a restructuring of gender boundaries in the migratory context. As a consequence, family politics tend to change, with women exerting greater influence in the household. In summary, in the ghorba, one of the chief organizing principles of Sudanese society has undergone a massive shift to accommodate economic adjustment strategies. Greater gender interdependence is the result.

Sudanese Small Businesses

To say that downward mobility has plagued a large number of Sudanese in North America is not to deny that other Sudanese have achieved comfortable lives. Some have managed to do so by establishing small businesses. In 1994 I interviewed Taha, who owned a hotdog stand on Pennsylvania Avenue in Washington, D.C. A graduate in philosophy from an Egyptian university, he acknowledged satisfaction with his business, and during a three-hour visit with Taha, dozens of customers stopped by. One only has to read the pages of Sudanese newspapers in North America to see the growth of other businesses. These include Sudan Corners and Port Sudan Restaurant in Toronto; Metro Towing Services, Nihad Travel, and Tire Mart in Texas; Blue Nile Travel in Silver Spring, Maryland; Nilien Insurance in Philadelphia; Khartoum Restaurant in Washington, D.C.; Rainbow Motors in Scarborough, Ontario; MH Bookkeeping and Nile Information Services in Brooklyn; Philio Photo Video Services in Ontario; Goba Carpentry and Abdul's Auto Repair in Pennsylvania.

In.May 1998, I visited Asia in her store, Sudan Corners, in Spadina, downtown Toronto. As I approached, the high-pitched voice of Sudanese folksinger Hanan Bolobolo boomed through the enormous loudspeakers placed in front of Asia's store. The singing, the incense inside, and the imported merchandise combined to give the shop a nostalgic atmosphere. Asia explained:

My husband, who is a maintenance mechanic, was among the first to settle in Canada. He came in 1971. Sudanese migration to Canada was not common. A few people came to school, but up to 1980 we were seven families in Toronto. I am the first woman to come here as a landed immigrant and also the first to obtain Canadian citizenship. I started my business in 1990. When my husband came here, life was easy, jobs were plenty. By the time of my arrival, little by little, the community started to grow. Forty Sudanese families decided to begin the *jalia* association. After 1990, immigration to Canada increased due to the coming of refugees. Almost weekly we hear that some Sudanese has arrived. They started to form the Sudanese society in *ghorba;* especially because of their life style and way of life, they are very much Sudanese. Right now at least 5,000 [Sudanese] people live in Toronto. For that reason, organizing ourselves in the *jalia* became'very important for the maintenance of our social and cultural life. We wanted to have an identity [*kainoona*] in Canadian society. We wanted to keep our traditions and know how to obtain our rights. We began to celebrate the *eid* [religious festivals], weddings, sporting events [soccer], and our focus is on the social aspect of life. When I arrived here, I brought with me the Sudanese customs that are very important here, because Canadians are very different and their concepts are very different from mine. We started a women's group [*jamia El Marraa*] especially because of male chauvinism. We decided to have meetings. Women migrate today by themselves, and they live alone. I finished high school here. I started my business in Spadina and the benefits are not only financial but also cultural.

When I asked Asia about what she meant by the benefits being "cultural," she provided a more nuanced explanation.

I feel that I am introducing Sudanese culture in Canadian society. My clientele is made of Sudanese, but the majority is Canadian men and women, Somalis, and Ethiopians. Canadians like to come for henna tattooing. It is a major source of income for me. I also import things from Saudi Arabia and the Emi-

Asia Elneil in front of her store, Sudan Corners. Toronto, 1999.

rates. My experience as a business owner is good, but I must say it requires very hard work. I have a husband who helps very much with my two sons, so I have time to work everyday. I think that Sudanese in Canada should think about small-businesses. Look here in Spadina and Chinatown; we must learn from them and learn how to take risks. Otherwise you have to fight in a country where the strong eats the weak.

Like Asia, other Sudanese women are also employing their knowledge of the folk art of henna tattooing to make a living and contribute to the family income. These Sudanese women establish a solid clientele of people, both within the migrant community and, increasingly, outside of it. American celebrities like Madonna and the artist formerly known as Prince have made henna familiar to young Americans. Kawther, a forty-six-year-old Sudanese woman living in Manhattan, was convinced by other friends to establish a henna salon to earn money from the elaborate styles that she had previously created for free. Their advice did not fall on deaf ears; the stylist founded her salon and is already making good income.

Another Sudanese folk art appropriated by migrant women for monetary reward is hair braiding, known as *mushat*. I was told by a Sudanese woman about another woman who started braiding hair for a living. A newly arrived refugee in Saskatoon, Saskatchewan, in Canada, supplemented the income she received through welfare. Even in predominantly white Saskatoon, Fawzia found a number of Africans who used her services. The commodification of folk art that has become a strategy for surviving under advanced capitalism is but one more irony of life in the ghorba.

[8]

Finding Refuge in the Shrine of Culture

Gharib wa el ghorba aqsa nidal.
(I am a stranger, and estrangement is the hardest struggle.)
                                        Sudanese song by Abdel Karim El Kabli

How do Sudanese migrants react when they realize that they are leaving their homeland behind to enter a foreign land; to be among foreign people who speak a foreign language? What kinds of obstacles do they encounter in the new environment? What strategies and coping mechanisms have they employed in everyday life to help them adapt in the new society? To unravel the intricacies of Sudanese life in exile, I begin with a concept that informs much of what a Sudanese in exile does to cope socially, culturally, spiritually, and economically.

Sudanese refer to life away from home as in the *ghorba,* an Arabic expression denoting more than physical separation, or even exile, for it has powerful psychological dimensions. In linguistic terms, *ghorba* is the antonym of *gurba* or *garaba,* which mean nearness, proximity, and kinship. For the Sudanese, the ghorba evokes loneliness, loss, uprootedness, nostalgia, and yearning for the familiar. It refers to a psychological state as well, a sense of alienation one finds away from family and friends back home. Fatima Ahmed Ibrahim eloquently captured this tormented state when she wrote: "Like a plant pulled from its soil, its roots withering in the cold air, I am out of my element in the West" (1994, 208). To give a flavor of the depth of the term in the Sudanese psyche and consciousness, a Sudanese will say *"Allah yarood ghorbatu"* (May God reverse the alienation) on two occasions: to wish someone a safe return home or to wish someone a speedy recovery from any form

A U.S. migrant, with his relatives, during a winter holiday in Amarat, a suburb of Khartoum, 1998.

of psychological stress. The physical state of being distant from one's home and the psychological state of mental pressure are equated.

The ghorba is therefore a cultural concept that enables Sudanese to focus upon their social norms, expectations, and collective representation (see Bouhdiba 1974, 204). With it, they conjure up their own sense of the world. As the late Omer Salih Eissa, a former diplomat and a migrant whom I interviewed in 1993 in Washington, D.C., put it: "In the ghorba many Sudanese see themselves as sojourners who will remain abroad until they save enough money to go back to the Sudan, or until whatever reason for being abroad is no longer there. They read Sudanese magazines, eat Sudanese food, associate with Sudanese friends only, almost every facet of their life is connected to their reality of being Sudanese. I am inclined to suggest to you that Sudanese in the United States have managed to create their own little Sudan. I tend to view Sudanese here in this country as long-term tourists."

Examining Sudanese life in the ghorba entails examining their social, cultural, and economic adjustment in the new North American societies. Factors affecting these processes in the United States and Canada include the immigrants' socioeconomic history, differential demographic characteristics, length of residence in the receiving society, motivations underlying their decision to migrate, presence of kin networks, past history of mobility, and level of exposure to diverse sociocultural environments. Anthony Rich-

[129]

mond, a Canadian migration scholar, has argued that the process of migrant adaptation is influenced by the migrant's level of interaction and identification with members of the new society (1988, 111). Richmond's definition of adaptation refers to "mutual interaction of individuals and collectivities and their response to particular social and physical environments" (1974, 194). The usefulness of the concept stems from the importance it places on the interrelatedness of the social, political, economic, and cultural elements of migrants' lives in the host societies.

This approach runs counter to functionalist "melting pot" assimilation models that stress the conformity by the individual migrant to dominant standards and values of the European majority, a presupposition, which is now widely questioned, of "linear progression of immigrant cultures towards a dominant American national character" (Miller 1990, 6). Richmond's more open adaptation model allows us to understand how Sudanese migrants cope under conditions of irregular immigration status, changing class positions, internal migrant community tensions, racialization experiences, the presence or absence of established kin and friendship networks, or other specific social contexts in North America in which these new international arrivals find themselves.

A critical place to examine the life of migrants in the ghorba is an exploration of Sudanese culture and how it affects processes of identity construction, continuity, and adaptation. As Abdou Maliqlim Simone writes of Sudanese culture: "While embodying so much ambiguity within it, the culture demonstrates little tolerance for ambiguity, yet is always willing to hold up the ambiguity of its Afro-Arab heritage as a calling card to the rest of the world" (1994, 28). Although Sudanese at home easily identify others as either "Arab" or "African," migrants in the ghorba find it harder to make such distinctions.

Like a magnificent symphony, the Sudanese cultural landscape has its own distinctive melodies, rhythms, harmonies, tones, and forms. Because of the variation within Sudanese peoples' outlooks, no assumption is made here that overseas Sudanese draw their cultural capital from a singular root or stock that shapes their survival abroad. But there are elements of Sudanese culture that, by and large, are shared by all Sudanese, whether Dinka or Nubian, Muslim or Christian, male or female, and their reality is sharpened and clarified by the ghorba experience. These elements are easily intelligible as revealing a common Sudanese origin. To a great extent, these symbols, idioms, and meanings embody a common cosmos that in the ghorba imbue them with a realization of what it means to be Sudanese.

When the noted northern Sudanese musician Abdel Karim El Kabli held a concert in Virginia, he was introduced by a young southerner who stated: "Kabli's music is appealing to everyone in Sudan. People in other neighboring African countries like Ethiopia and Somalia also find the music to be fantastic. We as Sudanese came to appreciate Kabli's music not just because of its brilliance, but because it really touches upon what all Sudanese have in common, our love for Sudan."

When I asked a southern Sudanese migrant in Boston about his views on commonality and differences among Sudanese, he reflected: "I know it might sound strange to some people, but I have been educated at the University of Khartoum. When I left Juba for college I did not know what to expect, really. Upon my arrival, I felt at home. Southerners and northerners have differences, but they also have shared traits. Just as a husband and wife who live together for a long time begin to look alike, so it is with northerners and southerners. Yes, interaction might not be as intimate, but the similarities are there in demeanor, ethics, and traits." Another southerner added: "To say that southerners and northerners are alike in many ways is a fair statement. You realize these commonalties when you are away from the Sudan. I know that the problem is deep. But most Sudanese people are generous and kind people. They share a lot in their warmth, their kindness. I think we have to distinguish between ordinary people and politicians. Because I worked in Saudi Arabia before I came here, I encountered an interesting experience. That all my friends there were northerners, and still some of my best friends really are northerners. I was also relieved to find some Arabic-speaking people in my workplace here in Boston. We vent a lot together. It is great."

Northern Sudanese who identify themselves as Arabs in the Sudanese context—more a linguistic than an ethnic signifier (see Mohamed 1980)—find they have more in common culturally with their southerner Dinka or Nuer counterparts than with Saudi Arabians, Iraqis, or Lebanese. One anecdote, which illustrates this assertion, is apropos. A group of Sudanese and Sudanist anthropologists attending a conference met together in a hotel room to socialize and talk about experiences in the Sudan. A waiter from room service arrived. My friend opened the door and asked him where he was from. "Sudan," he replied. When I heard that, I introduced myself and exchanged greetings and phone numbers. A southerner, he invited me, a northerner, to come to his house to meet his sister and his cousin, who just joined him from Egypt. He also offered to take me to the airport, adding that he had a car and I should not worry about transportation. On another occasion in Boston, a southern Sudanese friend and I met with three other Sudanese women and decided to go to an Ethiopian restaurant (the closest cuisine to Sudanese) for dinner. As the taxi stopped, we all reached for our purses. My friend, the only male in the group, insisted on paying. After dinner he paid for everyone, adding: "Just because Elbashir kicked us out of the country, that does not mean we stopped being Sudanese." These examples demonstrate the malleable nature of identity. Once in exile, a common Sudaneseness deeply affects people's comportment and outlook. Indeed, as Simone argues, ethnic or regional differences "make no sense removed from a tradition in which cultural identities of subgroups were established on the basis of how various ethnicities related to and interacted with people they considered themselves not to be" (1994, 29). In the ghorba, all Sudanese are Sudanese. Sudanese folklorist Sayyid Hurreiz has unraveled the subject of Sudanese commonality in the following terms.

> Close investigation of the study of Sudanese groups living along the Nile Valley, especially the northern and central parts, reveals a higher degree of such cultural similarity and continuity apparent in dress, food, customs and social institutions, religious beliefs, practices and institutions. For instance, religious practices prevalent throughout different parts of the Nile Valley show strong influences of sympathetic magic associated with traditional religion beside influences from Judaism, Christianity and Islam. Whether we are discussing facial marks, divine kingship or certain kinds of food, we point to continuity and similarity that runs across time from the meroitic period up to the present era; and that runs across space from Sennar to Shilluk and Dinka Land. (1989, 97)

Their mixed Afro-Arab heritage endows the Sudanese populace with a historical consciousness, which, when realized and refined in the crucible of the ghorba, may inspire unity and even harmony in the free Sudan of tomorrow. This vision is illustrated in a radio statement (April 27, 2000) by the Dinka leader of the Sudanese People's Liberation Army, John Garang: "Greetings in the name of the New Sudan. I salute the heroic struggle of the Sudanese people. I salute the youth, students, workers, farmers, professionals, trade unionists, and National Democratic Alliance activists. These are the forces of the intifada that overthrew the Abboud dictatorship in 1964 and brought down Nemeiri in 1985. I greet all the marginalized Sudanese everywhere: in the countryside, in the south, in the east, in the west, in the far north, in the center, in Khartoum, and in the camps for displaced people." What this carefully phrased salutation reveals is Garang's mindfulness of a common Sudanese denominator in spite of difference.

This commonality is sometimes also understood by non-Sudanese observers. On November 23, 1953, the British Broadcasting Corporation interviewed Sir K. D. Henderson for a "Mid-Week Talk." In response to a question about what kind of country the Sudan is, he stated: "The people are a mixture of Arab, Hamites, and black with one common characteristic: they are very easy to like. Some people are not, even for a British troop, who gets on with everybody. But you can't help liking the Sudanese and sympathizing with my nine year old daughter's tears on leaving them, at the prospect of spending the rest of her life surrounded by nothing but gloomy white faces. The Sudanese are really all the same, quick to anger and quick to laughter, brave in battle and vociferous in dispute, governed by the heart rather than the head, slow to forgive an injury or forget a kindness" (Henderson 1953). Despite the obvious racial categorization and condescension of Henderson's remarks, and the irony that British colonial administration worked for the better part of a century to divide the country's various ethnic groups, there is a recognizable element of truth concerning a common Sudanese predisposition toward generosity and emotional expressiveness.

More than any other factor, Sudaneseness and Sudanese identity define the country's migrants and exiles in North America and allow them, in spite of differences, to come together in the ghorba. Without romanticizing the Sudanese community as one in which unity and harmony prevail—for intercommunity tensions do exist—their common culture becomes an asset for dealing with new realities away from the homeland and leads people to develop closely knit networks in their attempt to overcome alienation and loneliness. Despite its heterogeneity, the expression of Sudanese Afro-Arab culture works to ensure a continuity of past and present—and of habits of the old place and the new.

When asked about problems encountered in the United States and Canada, both northern and southern respondents in my ethnographic sample gave similar responses about the importance of cultural factors in coping with the new society. Finding refuge in the shrine of Sudanese culture, they pursue their place in multicultural North America.

Coping in the Ghorba: Social Networks

Many scholars have long acknowledged the primacy of kin and social networks within migrant communities in shaping individual migratory actions (Bottomly 1992; Freeman 1995; Kasinitz 1992; Lessinger 1995). As Mullan puts it: "The act of migration is rarely undertaken as a completely independent event, rather it is often a decision made easier by being accompanied by, or received by, friends and relatives among whom a first or second-hand knowledge of the area of destination is almost a certainty. In fact, there exists an unwritten code of sorts among migrants stipulating that knowledge and information essential to facilitating the migration process is shared" (1989, 69). Moreover, among the most catastrophic losses sustained in the migratory process is the abrupt withdrawal of one's self from the closely knit community which for years provided moral support and emotional succor.

[133]

The experiences of the majority of Sudanese in North America are no exception to these general conclusions. As Tariq, twenty-five years old and living in Los Angeles, told me: "In this country I only deal with Sudanese. It is true that we live in America, but our life is very different and we do not have any relationship with anybody beside Sudanese. Here we live in our own zones." And Isam, a Sudanese cab driver in Queens, New York, stated: "If it wasn't for the help I received from my friends when I first arrived in New York, I don't know what I would have done. I just can't imagine." The pivotal role that kin, friends, and former neighbors play in migrants' social adaptation reflects the continuities in Sudanese culture which strongly enforce adherence to social and familial obligations toward fellow migrants as well as toward those who remain at home. These networks play a pronounced role in migrants' identity construction and preservation, and also reflect their noticeably limited interaction with Americans and Canadians, with most migrants describing such relationships as "superficial" or "nonexistent."

Sudanese hardly ever arrive without knowing in advance where they are going to stay, with whom, and how they will manage financially in their initial days. In my interviews, I was told repeatedly: "If it wasn't for the presence of friends we would not have come here." When crises arise, migrant networks again come into play. As Muntasir acknowledged: "When I came from the Sudan, I tried to contact an old friend from work, but I couldn't, since his telephone was disconnected. Fortunately I had a letter that I was supposed to give to another Sudanese whom I barely knew. I decided to go to him, feeling sure that he would do his best to help, and indeed my life in America started with the help of this Sudanese, whom I barely knew." A Nuer refugee in the United States was on the verge of deportation in 2000. A call for help and for a Nuer interpreter was posted by a young Sudanese woman. Northerners and southerners alike registered concern. One northerner advised: "Please tell your friend, if things go bad for him, to leave immediately for Canada. Life in Canada is generally better, especially for starters and families. I will be more than happy to help in any way" (Sudanet, May 3, 2000).

Kinship not only creates ties that transcend geography but also establishes "chain migration" and clusters of relatives from the same sending communities. When asked to identify sources of help in making the decision to migrate, more than 40 percent of respondents told me relatives and friends initiated the idea and provided information about how to execute it. When asked whether anyone had followed the migrants to North America, 56 percent responded that relatives, friends, or neighbors had joined them, and 44 percent were expecting such arrivals. Several added that ever since Sudanese immigrants found out about the Diversity Visa Lottery Program, many now apply on behalf of relatives in the Sudan. Several "lottery win-

Two friends in their traditional Sudanese *jallalib*, Boston, 1999.

ners" corroborated these claims. Amal, thirty-eight years old and a recent arrival in Phoenix, Arizona, told me that she applied for her sisters, one of whom "won" and was to join her in a few weeks. El Sadiq, a lottery appli-cant in Khartoum, the Sudan, explained: "I am asking Allah to make it easy for me to get this green card lottery. The stories I hear from my friends in

Washington—Oh Man! [*ya zoal*]—they are great; very good and encouraging. According to them, America is a paradise. My friends told me a joke—that judgment day has already arrived—those in America already died and went to heaven, those still living in the Sudan already died and went to hell."

The Sudanese case illustrates how established kin networks at the destination shape migration decisions and mold subsequent settlement. As Siraj in New York stated, "Before I moved to America, I always wanted to go to the Gulf but I couldn't. Some friends however moved here before me. They are very close friends from my neighborhood. They persuaded me that moving here is the best thing to do. They provided me with the necessary information and helped me to follow them. They are in fact the reason for me to move to the U.S." Abdel Raoof, fifty-eight years old and living in Washington, D.C., offered the established migrant's perspective: "I came to the U.S. in 1969 as an embassy employee. I worked for seven years and was supposed to return to the Sudan. However, I preferred to stay. I quit my job with the government and managed to secure another job here. The main reason for my decision at that time was to help my brothers and nephews to come here to get their education. After their arrival, I continued to pay for their education. I still continue to provide help for others who came recently."

Once in North America, Sudanese migrants' subsequent adaptation experience is also shaped by their social networks, which serve as indispensable sources of information about work and accommodations. In the words of Ibrahim, a migrant from Wad Medani: "Since my arrival from the Sudan, I stayed for one month with some friends. The same friends showed me where and how to find work. I managed to find a job on the third day here. When it was time for me to move, I wanted to pay my share of the rent, but my friends refused to accept it. They told me that it is customary among migrants to provide free food and lodging for the newly arrived in the first month. They told me that if you want to repay us, do exactly the same when a new person arrives from the Sudan—let him stay with you free for the first month."

Sudanese migration demonstrates that through these networks one's culture of origin is sustained, even as the location of the bearers of culture undergoes a radical shift. The networks also expand notions of "kinship," as fellow countrymen and women not genealogically related speak and think of themselves as kin for practical purposes. Ismael, an established businessman in New York City, illuminated how Sudanese develop these obligations: "I went to the airport to pick up my brother. I saw a young Sudanese man who also was there at the same time, and he looked quite distraught because he could not find his friend waiting for him. I took him home with me since it had been a very long and tiring flight, and he stayed with me for more than four days until he managed to locate another friend in another city. So then I helped him to go to this friend."

Social networks also affect in a remarkable fashion the residential distribution of migrants (Basch 1987; Chan 1992; Dinnerstein 1996; Handlin 1959; Miller 1990). Sudanese, like the majority of international migrants, seldom move to unfamiliar locations without knowing beforehand that kin network ties will be there. A neighborhood in Brooklyn came to be known to Sudanese as El Abbassia—the name of a neighborhood in Omdurman— because of the predominance of migrants from that home neighborhood. In Los Angeles, an apartment complex is referred to as Wad Nubawi, because the majority of its residents are from that area in the Sudan. Whether in El Abbassia or Wad Nubawi, kin and friendship networks provide advice and offer moral support as new arrivals experience feelings of loneliness and loss. For Sudanese, as anthropologist Maxine Margolis observed of Brazilian migrants in New York: "There is no question . . . that the presence of kin networks reduces the material and the psychological cost of migration" (1994, 102).

This social network–based pattern, however, is different for many southern Sudanese, whose residential choices are less influenced by kin than by church organizations, which resettle them as refugees. The largest concentrations of Sudanese refugees, mainly southerners, are in New York City, Washington, D.C., Iowa, Maine, Minnesota, North Dakota, South Dakota, Tennessee, Texas (cf. Holtzman 2000). In Canada, the largest refugee numbers are found in Alberta, British Columbia, Manitoba, and Ontario. Although most Sudanese migrants depend on kinship networks, those that come as refugees tend to settle where their church and organization sponsors are located.

Whether from north or south, the majority of Sudanese in North America do not become homeowners. What is most common is for groups of migrants to rent apartments or houses. Amin, fifty-eight years old, is a professor living in Silver Springs, Maryland. As he saw it, "The fact that they do not own their homes cannot be explained, in certain cases, neither in terms of incomes nor in light of their length of residence. I have known a lot of Sudanese who resided here over fifteen years, yet they resent the idea of buying a home while paying a monthly rent for the same amount of what they could have paid for a home mortgage. The only explanation from my point of view is that Sudanese exhibit profound commitment to going back to the Sudan one of these days. Buying a home is a step in the wrong direction since it entails acceptance of the idea that you migrated for good or you started a new life in another country."

At the symbolic level, home ownership comes to mean "abandoning their own country," as one migrant put it. Still, many Sudanese who share rented homes with other migrants do not have incomes sufficient to afford mortgages. In other cases, their status in the United States or Canada may discourage the thought of home ownership.

"Migrants Need Other Migrants": The Sudanese *Jalia*

Wherever they settle, Sudanese establish community associations known as *jalias* (pronounced jah-lyas), which sponsor events that preserve the cultural world of Sudanese and counter their experience of racialization, downward mobility, and peripherialization as newcomers from the developing world.

On May 10, 1998, I headed to 100 St. George Street, on the University of Toronto campus, to attend a general assembly meeting of the Sudanese jalia of Ontario. I was forty-five minutes late, but as I approached, I could see men in their Sudanese attire of jallalib and imam and women in their tiab heading to the same place. As I approached the auditorium, I collected flyers, the Sudanese Community Association of Ontario's Arabic newspaper, *El Niliain*, and miscellaneous advertisements. The jalia's hand-written Arabic newsletter conveyed congratulations from the Sudanese in Ontario "to everyone who won an asylum case in court, to everyone who became a landed-immigrant, to everyone who accomplished success, and to the St. Catharine, Ontario, Sudanese community, in celebration of Sudan Day."

After signing an attendance sheet presented to me by a Sudanese teenager, I entered the auditorium. The room was a portrait in diversity: two hundred Sudanese from all backgrounds: southerners, northerners, Nubians, Copts, women, men, young, and old. As I was reading the agenda, one woman, seeing that I was a newcomer, told me that the meeting was supposed to have started at 1:00 P.M., "but everyone seems to be taking their Sudanese time." The meeting finally started with greetings from the jalia's president, who then conveyed news of the sudden death of a Sudanese in St. Catharines. Everyone was asked to recite collectively the *fatiha*, the opening chapter of the Quran, in memory of the deceased. People were then urged to carpool or make other arrangements to go to St. Catharines for the *maattam*, the condolence ritual. A chilling silence and sense of grief permeated the room; not only was the deceased well liked in the jalia, but he was also a young man.

Next, the president read the meeting agenda and described goals of the jalia.

We have both a long-term and a short-term plan. We would like your support for purchasing a house as a community center. Our goal is to establish a school for our children to teach them our language, religion, and our cultural values. Establishing our own community center will help people to come together and to be with each other. We want to hold meetings like this in our own center. Our short-term plan for the Sudanese community is recreational, which will include sporting events [mostly soccer matches]. Also, we would like to provide migration and social services. For example, the Sudanese community in Kingston already started contacts with Canadian Parliament members to address the difficulties encountered by Sudanese to secure legal status as asylum seekers. Social services will be geared to helping Sudanese in finding jobs, legal consultation, and workshops, and to provide orientation to the newly arrived people.

Sudanese migrants turn to their established networks not only to overcome their sense of isolation in the new country, but also because of the linguistic difficulties most experience in North America. With low levels of English proficiency, Sudanese frequently indicate language difficulties as a problem in adapting to life in the United States and Canada. Although the majority has taken English courses during school years, they maintain that they nevertheless face difficulty in understanding North American spoken English. For many, especially women, language problems constitute a significant problem in their initial days of settlement. Ahmed, a restaurant worker in Toronto, told me: "To begin with, my wife does not speak Arabic, only Dongolawi dialect. She will join me in Canada, and she does not speak English. She will have problems talking to other Sudanese and to Canadians. With my long working hours, I do not know if she will be able to manage." As Mamoun explained: "I know a lot of Sudanese in Toronto who have been here from 1986, yet their level of English proficiency is very low. They spend a long time with other Sudanese. They often hesitate to talk with Canadians because the accent is hard for them to understand." Nur, a thirty-three-year-old migrant woman living in Virginia, maintained: "I was very interested in improving my English when I came from the Sudan, but after I moved to Washington, D.C., I only got the chance to practice English at a very limited level. Because mostly I talk to Sudanese all the time."

In addition to language problems, many Sudanese attributed their inability to interact and establish social relationships with North Americans to the discriminatory attitudes and overall hostility existing in this new society. Earle Waugh argues generally that "Muslim migrant populations in the United States are continually confronted with the portrayal of their religion as alien against an idealized, historical Judeo-Christian mirror" (1991, xi). More specifically, as one Sudanese migrant put it, "As blacks, Muslims, Arabs, and migrants, Americans do not hesitate to discriminate against us on the grounds of such attributes." So apart from maintaining responsibilities toward kin and friends through regular visits and frequent contacts, the networks linking migrants with other Sudanese allow them to preserve a sense of worth of their culture and identity in the diaspora.

The Northern Sudanese Wedding Ceremony

One significant way to understand migratory phenomena is to explore the forms in which cultural practices are preserved, changed, or modified in the migrants' new societies. As the Sudanese case demonstrates, although some aspects of culture persist with extraordinary tenacity, new conditions demand the selective adaptations which migrants consciously pursue. In addition to networks as cultural assets shaping adaptation in the ghorba, a plethora of cultural practices and events are no less important in the preservation of identity.

The northern Sudanese wedding ceremony in North America is an amalgamation of Indigenous and not-so-indigenous traditions. The ceremony is usually a two- to three-day event, beginning with *lailat el dukhla* or "night of entry," conducted in a similar fashion to Western-style celebrations: the bride and groom are dressed in a white dress with a veil and tuxedo. Large numbers of guests assemble for the festivities, which include singing and dancing. In March 1999 I attended a wedding ceremony at a Holiday Inn in Brookline, Massachusetts. Half an hour after our arrival, the *zagharid*, piercing ululations performed by the women, began a ritual expressing joy at the arrival of the bride and groom. The bride's appearance in a white dress, and sporting intricately designed henna decorations on her hands, exemplified a meeting of "modernity" and "tradition." After an extended period of greetings, everyone was invited to the buffet dinner. In the Sudan, a typical wedding feast consists of chicken, roast beef, fried meats, falafel, pickles, potato chips, sesame rolls, and *sanbooksa* (similar to Indian *samosa*). This Massachusetts meal was an ad hoc arrangement: in addition to the traditional fried meats, people loaded their plates with Basmati rice, turkey sandwiches, and Lebanese parsley salad, all prepared by a group of the bride's kinswomen. For dessert, there were cookie-like *khabeez* and a huge, professionally prepared, American-style wedding cake. The festivities began with a concert by the popular Sudanese singer Sammy Elmagherbi. The hundred or so male and female guests danced with such energy and joined the collective singing until it reached such a deafening roar that all seemed to enter an ecstatic trance. Despite the already painfully loud music, people constantly ran over to turn the volume on the loud speakers higher, as if trying to listen for something beyond the songs, perhaps a reminder that they were still connected to their homeland. This party lasted

A Sudanese Western-style wedding.

from 7:00 P.M. until 1:00 A.M. Just before it came to a close, the groom presented the bride with lavish gifts of gold jewelry, bracelets, rings, and a necklace purchased in one of the Persian Gulf states.

Despite the existence of Sudanese elements in this Western-style *dukhla*, the second part of the ceremony, the *jirtig*, retains its cultural roots and has persisted in the United States and Canada with far less change. In 1995 I was invited to a jirtig ceremony in Michigan. On the night before the festivities, I arrived at the home of Nafisa, who had assumed the responsibilities of the maid of honor (*wazirat elarous*) and had invited a number of guests to spend the night there. About twenty women and their adolescent daughters had arrived from the Detroit area and from as far away as Wisconsin and Washington, D.C. The proceedings were strikingly similar to wedding preparations in the Sudan. Nafisa and other friends gathered in the kitchen, where the drum music of Sudanese *dalooka* was playing. They started to prepare food for the jirtig and for the breakfast to be served to the guests the following day—fried meat, falafel, baklava, and *leigeimat* (fried dough)—and cooking lasted into the early hours of the morning. While the older women preoccupied themselves with the arduous frying, chopping, grinding, and baking, the adolescent girls kept busy with beautification, as some straightened their hair using hot combs and blow dryers while sharing happy laughter and "bad hairdo" stories. Afterward, everyone retired to sleeping mats and sofa beds. Nafisa's home was furnished like houses in the

Sudan, where even small spaces are equipped to receive many guests: Most of the bedrooms contained two or three beds, and both living room couches were sleeper sofas. Somehow everyone arose cheerful and happy and seemed well rested the following morning.

We all left for the wedding reception, which took place around 2:00 P.M. on a muggy summer afternoon. Meanwhile, Sudanese single men volunteered to give rides to guests. Given the high cost of weddings in the United States, the bride and groom celebrated the two parts of the wedding on the same day. The dukhla and reception lasted for three hours, after which the bride changed into her jirtig outfit. The jirtig fertility ritual prevents evil spirits from undermining the newlyweds' reproductive capabilities (see Boddy 1989; Kenyon 1991). A bride who does not take part in the jirtig, Sudanese say, will become infertile (*agir*), for her reproductive organs are filled (*itkabasat*) with evil spirits.

The jirtig is redolent with symbolism and cultural meaning, and the values it celebrates are deemed essential to the life of the married couple, whether at home or abroad. During this ceremony, the jirtig bed (*angaraib el jirtig*) was placed in the middle of a large hall, where two hundred Sudanese were seated. The bed was covered with a red velvet bedspread, which symbolizes fertility. The bride was also now dressed in red, while the groom wore the Sudanese jallabia, a long white robe-like outfit, with a red band tied around his forehead. Attached to the middle of the band was a golden crescent. Both bride and groom wore a jirtig bracelet of red silk adorned with beads and gold. Next to the bed, several objects were placed on a table in a tray, including a glass of milk and a large plate filled with henna paste into which white candles were placed. Both the bride and groom seated themselves on the bed, surrounded by spectators. The ceremony was quite typical. Those who officiated during the ceremony were older women who had given birth to at least four children. The jirtig began with chanting and the singing of popular songs. During the singing of *Alail lail el adil wal zein*, a mixture of perfumes and herbs called *darira* were placed on the bride's and groom's hair. Several other ornaments and necklaces were placed around their necks. The couple was given a glass of milk to sip and told to spray each other with the milk. (If the bride sprays the groom first, it means they will have a lot of children; if the groom sprays her first, they will have a lot of money.) After this, the groom stood on the bed and was handed a bottle of perfume, which he sprinkled on the spectators. The jirtig concluded with a bridal dance. Ideally in the Sudan, a procession to the Nile concludes the festivity, where ritual washing is recommended in an attempt to rid oneself of hurtful and maleficent spirits. Also in the Sudan, a lamb is slaughtered during the ritual proceedings and a feast combining sweet and sour foods—with fried lamb meat, sweet fried dough, or-

A Sudanese traditional wedding ceremony of fertility (*jirtig*). A ritual that persists in North America.

anges, and dates—is served afterward. In Michigan, the slaughtering of the lamb did not take place, but the rest of the feast followed. The crowd then dispersed after good-byes and good wishes to the bride and groom.

The majority of northern Sudanese weddings in the United States and Canada include the jirtig. The ritual, as I have observed it, remains exceptionally authentic, save for the procession to the Nile, which is the symbolic source of abundance, plenty, and blessing and for which no substitute is possible.

The *Simaya*: Naming Ceremony

The *simaya*, the northern Sudanese naming ceremony, is a ritual that has attracted the attention of anthropologists for its zestfully symbolic content. "A function of such ritual is to emphasize and impress beyond the shadow of a doubt that one phase of the life-cycle has been left behind and to announce and stress that henceforth he or she is in another phase. Another aspect is to make sure that the individual has received communion with the deepest cultural ideals" (Elguindi 1996, 3; see also Fakhouri 1987). Carefully replicated and cherished in the ghorba, the simaya solemnizes the

[143]

naming of the child as an important rite of passage and a source of blessings (*baraka*) and good omens. Generally, anywhere from one to two weeks after the birth of a child, a sacrificial lamb is slaughtered for the ritual naming of the newborn. It is celebrated with feasts, drumming, remembrance ceremonies, and concerts and marks the rite of passage from birth to initiation into the wider community. The spiritual and religious nature of birth is venerated by Sudanese Muslims and non-Muslims, but for Muslims it reflects their understanding of the Quranic verse, "children and money are the benison and benediction in life" (*elmal wal banoon zinat elhyat eldonia*). One adjustment that Sudanese adopt here is that a baby boy is circumcised immediately after birth, whereas in the Sudan, circumcision occurs between the ages of three and five, and among some ethnic groups as late as nine. The simaya for a Muslim male, thus, serves a dual function in North America, announcing his birth and, through his circumcision, initiating him into Muslim society. For girls, circumcision is not a part of their simaya ceremony in the Sudan.

A feast is held for the dozens of guests who come to the simaya ceremony with gifts of money and goods for the parents of the newborn. Among Sudanese immigrants, the simaya always involves singing. At one simaya ceremony I attended in New Hampshire, a popular Sudanese singer was flown in from Washington, D.C. Women and men dressed in their best clothes, danced for hours, ate, and presented gifts and kind words before leaving.

The *Eids*

The *eids* (*Eid Elfitr* and *Eid El Adha*) are cultural and religious events that are celebrated even more assiduously by the Sudanese Muslim migrant community in North America than at home. *Eid Elfitr* commemorates the end of the holy month of Ramadan; *Eid El Adha* marks the end of the pilgrimage season to Mecca. In the Sudan, *Eid Elfitr* lasts three days and *Eid El Adha* four. In North America migrants adapt to the secular calendar, condensing the celebrations to one day unless, happily, they happen to fall on a weekend.

Both are occasions for rituals that involve the sacrifice of animals, concerts, and the exchange of visits. After Muslim Sudanese first gather for prayers attended by men, women, and children at immigrant mosques throughout the United States and Canada, often they are joined by non-Muslims friends in parks, homes, or community centers where feasts are held with abundant amounts of food, and gifts are distributed to small children. Evening celebrations of the *eid* include concerts by popular Sudanese musicians that are open to the general public.

[144]

Eid Elftir party celebrating the end of Ramadan. New York City, 1999.

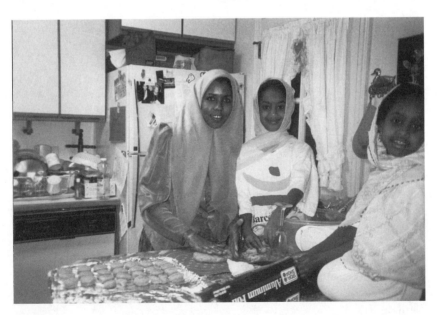

Baking day for *eid* celebration. Mansfield, Connecticut, 1997.

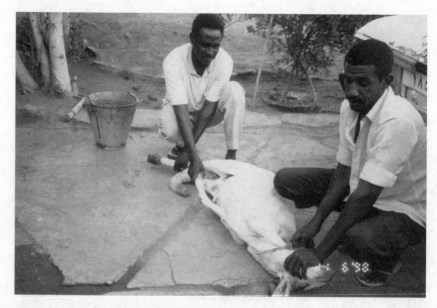

Eid El Adaha sacrificial slaughter. Khartoum, the Sudan 1998. This practice is disappearing among North American immigrants.

At one *Eid El Adha* I attended in the Bronx, at El Hadi Hall, which is owned by a Sudanese migrant, over three hundred people, including a small but enthusiastic group of southerners, danced and feasted on traditional foods supplied by a Sudanese caterer from Brooklyn. The music lasted until well after midnight and featured the singing of the ubiquitous Sammy Elmagharibi. The *eid* concert also featured a raffle, with prizes including telephone cards offering up to two hundred minutes of calls to the Sudan.

A flyer by from the Sudanese Community Association of Ontario for an *Eid El Adha* celebration in Toronto advertised that the festivities at its picnic would include lute (oud) music, volleyball (for "men and women"), jump rope for children, card playing, chess, and the African game *mangalah*, in addition to door prizes and a raffle. The flier included a note that videotapes would be made of the event and offered for sale, with proceeds to go toward the jalia's building project. "Our slogan," the flier announced, "is Love, Work, and Cooperation for Building the Sudan in the ghorba.'"

Some elements of these ritual events have changed in the ghorba. During *Eid El Adha,* Sudanese families obtain a sheep and either hire a butcher or slaughter it themselves. Here, those people who have purchased at sheep farms or *halal* (ritually clean) markets pay someone to conduct the slaughter. Others send money to their families in the Sudan to sacrifice on their behalf but still enjoy halal or kosher meat purchased from Muslim or Jewish butchers.

The *Mawlid El-Nabawi*

A third major Muslim festival, the *Mawlid Elnabawi,* begins on the eve of the eleventh day of *Rabi al-Awal,* the third month in the Islamic lunar calendar, and commemorates the birth of the Prophet Mohamed. This event involving remembrance feasts (*zikir*) and drumming ceremonies is an essential part of religious life in the Sudan, as it is throughout the Muslim world, where in largely Muslim countries it is a legal holiday.

In North America the Mawlid has only recently joined the constellation of community celebrations among Sudanese migrants. Principally in the Sudan, as elsewhere, the Mawlid is conducted separately by each of the numerous Islamic sects. There, each religious brotherhood (*el-turuq el-sufiya*) sponsors public festivities including drumming, recitations from the Quran, and praise (*madih*) to the Prophet based on the teachings of the sect's particular imam or religious authority. In the Sudan, each sect constitutes an "imagined community," with full sovereignty and autonomy, and even symbolizes this sense of communal nationhood with its own flag. In the Sudan, I have witnessed Mawlid processions (*zaffa*) consisting of whole villages, with thousands marching.

Until recently, local communities of Sudanese migrants in North America were too small or too religiously heterogeneous to celebrate the Mawlid in a way that recreated such sect-as-nation rituals. The first Sudanese Mawlid in North America of which I became aware was held in 1998 in Irvine, Texas, by a community of Mikashifiya Sufi Muslims, followers of the Imam El Mikashifi. Since that time, they celebrate their annual Mawlid in Texas with a festival that includes a sumptuous cultural performance that is unusual in being open to the public. The invitation extended by the Mikashifiya sect both to Sudanese and non-Sudanese reflects in a dramatic way the attempts of a migrant community to legitimize its religious heritage in the United States.

By attending the communal, festive portions of these Islamic religious events, Copts and southern Sudanese Christians enjoy a strong connection to the rest of the Sudanese migrant community in the United States and Canada. On the other hand, they celebrate their own Christian holidays in the same fashion as their North American hosts (save for Christmas, which Copts, like many Christians worldwide, celebrate on January 7). Bernard, a sixty-nine-year-old southerner, reflected on their ritual variations:

Like the rest of Sudanese, southerners, who are a very diversified group, go to dance parties, socialize, and visit. Most of the time they participate in northern Sudanese events. For example, we went to hear Kabli [a Sudanese singer] when he held a concert, and enjoyed it very much. However, for religious celebrations, southerners are more fluid, and the fact that they are not Muslims, at least the majority, means they tend to find their niche and blend in the new country as far as religious observance is concerned. But if you tell me that northerners preserve "traditional ways," for southerners I think the refugee situation they find themselves in makes it slightly different. For example, we cannot say that Dinka or Nuer weddings here resemble their weddings at home. This is so different; everyone in the situation of exile feels as if they are walking in their sleep. But like northerners in other spheres, I think creating networks with your own people is a very common way of survival.

The Congregation in Migrant Life

Of special importance to many Sudanese is the increased significance of religious practices in the ghorba. Elsewhere (Abusharaf 1998b) I have argued that participation in mosques has given migrants an opportunity to rearticulate their faith through distinctive adaptations to the host environment's dominant culture while still struggling to maintain the essential attributes of their faith and their culture.

Aisha, thirty-four years old and living in Colorado, stated: "One of the important things to us is the mosque. In the town where I live, there are only five Sudanese families. We go together to the Friday congregational *jumaa* prayer, and we take the children to Sunday school to learn Arabic and religion. The mosque is beautiful. We do a lot of things also like potluck dinners and getting together with other people. It plays an important part that way in the social life of a lot of friends I know." The adoption of Sunday for religious activities is one of the noticeable calendrical adjustments that immigrants to America are making (Warner 1994, 81). This is true for Sudanese as well. In the United States, Sunday becomes the day for family-oriented activities, even though Friday is the Muslim sacred day. Despite this temporal shift, in the process of teaching Sudanese children the principles of Islam and the Arabic language, congregational activities sustain identities in a dramatic way. As Stephen Warner argues: "As religion becomes less taken for granted under the conditions prevailing in the U.S., adherents become more conscious of their traditions, and many become more determined about its transmission. Religious identities that had been ascriptive from birth may become objects of active conversion, in order to counter actual or potential losses by defection" (1993, 13).

Religious and language education highlight the importance of the congregation for some immigrant northern Sudanese families, and the mosque
assumes the role of mediator between host and migrant cultures. Hence,
religious education aims at transmitting both revealed and cultural knowledge to a new generation of Sudanese children, whose educators spare no
effort in promoting moral, spiritual, and cultural accountability in the face
of daunting outside influences. Several Sudanese with whom I had conversations on religion stressed the role of congregational membership in pre-
serving the knowledge of "who you are." This, of course, is far more important in the ghorba than it was at home, where there is little need to ask this
question.

Changing Cultural Practices: Female Circumcision

In the preceding sections I have discussed persisting traditions in order to
demonstrate how culture can be a conscious factor for Sudanese dealing
with the experience of foreignness and alienation. From this vantage point, it
can be argued that culture is not merely a way of life but a strategic component in the migratory process. But other cultural practices are changing
under the influence and sway of powerful socioeconomic and political circumstances encountered in the receiving society. Cultural traditions which
were once revered and venerated by Sudanese for their symbolic and non-
symbolic power are forced to undergo substantial transformations in the
North American context. To illuminate how traditions change, I now focus
on a set of practices that have attracted wide notoriety and created an explo-
sive contemporary issue: female circumcision. In recent years female circumcision (referred to often as female genital mutilation) "has only paradoxes to offer" (Scott 1996). In the United States, the practice became
widely known through the story of Fawzia Kassindja, who fled her African
home country Togo to escape undergoing the ritual before her marriage
(Kassindja 1998).

To understand how the immigrant views surrounding this practice have
become transformed in the United States and Canada, I will first relate its
ideological configuration among Sudanese people at home.

The practice of female circumcision has existed in the Sudan for thousands of years and continues to this day. The practice comprises a variety of
surgeries that include clitoridectomy, excision, and infibulation (El Dareer
1982). These operations are performed on girls at different ages, ranging
from a few days old to puberty. Practitioners are usually trained midwives
or traditional birth attendants, but occasionally medical doctors do the pro-

Village women in Sudan provided powerful views on why they follow female circumcision.

cedures as well. In some areas, the ritual is a source of joyous celebration and elaborate festivities, whereas in others it is shrouded in secrecy. The ritual is embedded in complex sociocultural and religious beliefs and rests on a foundation of cultural notions regarding femininity, beauty, tradition, gender, sexuality, and religiosity (Abusharaf 1998a). Like all such rituals, female circumcision has no meaning apart from these dominant beliefs, and in turn these beliefs combine to shape community norms according to which the ritual is practiced (Abusharaf 2001).

No one can pinpoint the origin of the practice in the Sudan, but folk wisdom locates it in ancient Egypt. Ancient Egyptian myth stressed the bisexuality of the gods, and circumcision may have been introduced to clarify the femininity of girls (Meinardus 1967). At the very least, the ritual dates back more than a millennium, when the eighth-century poet El Farazdaq denounced the tribe of Azd on the Arabian Peninsula, writing that their women had never experienced the pain of circumcision and were therefore "of inferior stock" (Eltayeb 1955). Other writers speculate that the practice may have originated with the Red Sea tribes who introduced it to neighboring peoples, an assertion refutable on the grounds that several ethnic groups in the Red Sea region do not perform genital surgeries on women. The point, however, is that although circumcision is not a universal practice in the Sudan, those who adhere to it see it as an integral aspect of their identity. Where it is practiced, female circumcision is passionately embraced and closely safeguarded; it is regarded as an essential coming-of-age ritual that ensures chastity, promotes fertility and cleanliness, and enhances the beauty of a woman's body. In Arabic, the colloquial word for circumcision, *tahara*, means "to purify." When I interviewed women in the Sudan about the significance of the practice, it was clear that in their terms the ritual had many benefits and was indispensable to women's welfare. This view stands in stark contrast with the changing notions of Sudanese migrants in the United States and Canada.

Sudanese, along with other African refugees and immigrants arriving in Europe, Canada, and the United States, have recently brought female circumcision more immediately to Western public attention. On the basis of the 1990 Census, the U.S. Centers for Disease Control and Prevention in Atlanta estimated that at least 168,000 girls and women in the United States have either been circumcised or are at risk for undergoing the procedure. Since 1996 the U.S. Congress and nine state governments have criminalized the practice, and similar laws have been passed in several European countries. In the United States and Canada, the practice is now considered "a form of persecution sufficient for a refugee status" (Annas 1996, 335). A report on female genital mutilation (FGM) issued by the Center for Reproductive Law and Policy summarizes current efforts of the U.S. government to curtail the practice, both domestically and abroad:

> In 1996 Congress passed several legislative measures related to FGM. First, the practice of FGM on a minor is now a federal offense, unless the procedure is necessary to protect a young person's health. Second, the Department of Health and Human Services is required to compile data on FGM and to engage in education and outreach to the relevant communities. Third, the Immigration and Naturalization Service must provide information on all aliens issued U.S. visas as well as the consequences of FGM under criminal or child protection statutes. Finally, Congress enacted legislation requiring U.S. executive directors of international financial institutions such as the World Bank to oppose non-humanitarian loans to countries that have not undertaken educational measures designed to prevent FGM. (Center for Reproductive Law and Policy 1997; see also Toubia and Rahman 2000)

Within this context, Sudanese migrants coming from regions which adhere to female circumcision are being forced to reconsider this practice, which, as we have seen, is intricately interwoven with fundamental values and notions of virginity, feminine beauty, honor, and sexuality (Abusharaf 1998). Although Sudanese have striven to preserve many cultural practices, in this area where they detect dissonance and incompatibility, migrants are quick to modify if not abandon customary behavior. Attitudes of migrants are shifting, and circumcision is increasingly seen as an obsolete practice that must end. Many factors in addition to legal ones are facilitating the decision not to circumcise. Chief among these is the independence of the couple from the influence of the extended family and the authority of the elderly.

That the perspective of these elders has not changed was clear in several interviews. For example, a Sudanese grandmother who arrived for a visit in the United States indicated disappointment over her son's refusal to have his daughters circumcised; she voiced concern over the virtue and marriageability of her granddaughters should they remain uncircumcised (*ghuloof*). Fathia, a thirty-nine-year-old migrant living in Michigan, shed light on the significance of changing family arrangements with respect to female circumcision. "Before I came to the United States, I was convinced that I would not circumcise my daughter. We as Sudanese women have endured a lot of complications. Our families took the liberty to take away something very important. The decision was agreed upon between myself and my husband, who is very opposed to the circumcision of girls. But I really think that coming to this country made it easy for us. Right now there is no one who can interfere in my business. There are no mouths that will dip in your decisions. In a lot of ways, though we miss the relatives (*ahal*), we think this is a blessing in disguise. No one can force you to change your mind about doing this to your child."

Other women shared Fathia's sentiment, but Nadia, forty-two years old and living in Canada, had a somewhat different motive for not circumcising her daughters. "I was circumcised when I was very young. I experienced pharaonic circumcision [the most drastic type of genital operations]. When I got married I suffered, and when I had my baby in the Sudan I was in excruciating pain. The midwife, working under the instructions of other women, was told to reinfibulate me. I remember I could not sleep at night. I did not know what to do. When I came to Canada and delivered another baby in the hospital, I found that the doctor was very knowledgeable about the practice. My children are Canadians now; they are going to spend the rest of their lives here, so I don't want them to suffer like I did."

I also talked to Sudanese women who, due to infibulation, reported having trouble finding trained gynecologists to treat them. When asked, with respect to their daughters, whether they worry about the legal issues surrounding the practice, these women simply reply: "The thought of circumcising never crossed my mind." For example, thirty-nine-year-old Amani in Rhode Island explained: "Even before I got married, I was convinced that any daughters of mine will not be subjected to circumcision. I feel that it was a big mistake that our families committed. Female circumcision is cruel and harmful. I will not forget the pain I went through because of it. But of course, with coming here, there is no chance of something like this happening."

Changing attitudes toward this centuries-old practice serve as a reminder of the ability of migrant communities to modify and renegotiate once-revered traditions. This, however, was not the case for the Sudanese Bahara in the 1940s and 1950s. As Nubians, they gave the practice unquestioned importance in their cultural worldview. And at that time there were few African immigrants and refugees in the United States and Canada and no criminal legislation banning the practice, so it remained virtually invisible. As pioneering migrants from an African society which glorified the ritual and meanings of female genital surgeries, the Bahara were able to keep it alive.

Sudanese Culture in North American Society

The negative attention that female circumcision has drawn to African immigrants, including Sudanese, should not overshadow other gifts a migrant community can offer to its hosts. As Thomas Sowell argues: "Not all cultural interactions resulting from migrations are one way. Just as the larger society surrounding the immigrants may influence their culture, so can the immigrant culture affect the larger society" (1996, 48).

A website announcement for a public concert of Sudanese music sponsored by the Nubian club of Washington, D.C., illustrates this point.

> Finally! Mohamed El-Amin, the king of oud [lute] music is in America! The Sudanese community and their friends, especially the Ethiopians, Eritreans and Somalis will have the biggest Sudanese cultural event in North America. It is the first time for Mohamed El-Amin to visit North America. I bet it is going to be a new era for the Sudanese music in this part of the world. Wad El-Amin will tour the U.S.A. and Canada to introduce the Sudanese music and play the lute instrument which he masters as one of the best lute musicians in the world of today. Many Americans are eager to see and listen to his Sudanese lute "symphonies." Let us make our day. The Arlington Hilton Hotel, Virginia on June 6, 1998 from 8:00 p.m. till 1:00 p.m.

Mohamed El-Amin was not the first Sudanese musician to visit North America and attract a U.S. following (see Feather and Gitter 1999). Previously, in 1993, the master Hamza Alaa Eldin gave a sensational musical performance at the Boston Museum of Fine Art. Humbled by this opportunity, Alaa Eldin opened his performance with a few profound words: "I can't de-

Preparation for a *karama*, for Sudanese and American invitees. Hosted by the Sudanese mission to the United Nations. New York City, 1999.

Sudanese oud (lute) musician entertaining fellow migrants and refugees at a social gathering. Bear Brook, New Hampshire, 1997.

scribe my joy that Boston Museum of Fine Arts finds my art to be fine." The audience, the majority of whom were White Americans, stood up and applauded for nearly five minutes before silence returned to the auditorium. In the dim lights of the stage, Alaa Eldin, wearing white traditional dress, started a mesmerizing oud performance of an hour and a half. The reaction of many Sudanese in the audience afterward was a mixture of pride and fondness for Alaa Eldin's efforts at presenting Sudan's culture to North American society with such talent and grace. The sounds of ouds in the hands of Alaa Eldin, Mohamed El-Amin, and others not only serve to reduce the distance between migrants and hosts, but offer more favorable aspects of a country whose reputation in the last few years has been far from auspicious, especially after civil war, repression, and U.S. accusations of terrorism to justify its bombing of the Shiffa Pharmaceutical Factory in Khartoum in 1998.

[9]

Political Life

While exile is a political phenomenon that unlocks key aspects of the dictator-ship, it is, much more importantly, a moving human drama—it is the story of shattered dreams, broken families, and truncated dreams; a psychological and physical trauma; of the struggle to adapt to strange cultures and climates.
Thomas Wright and Rody Onate, *Flight from Chile: Voices of Exile*, 1998

The human drama of emigration referred to by historian Thomas Wright and Chilean journalist Rody Onate is powerfully illustrated in the post–1989 Sudanese exile, which now surpasses all other migratory movements in Sudanese history. As a political phenomenon, it has altered the Sudanese migratory landscape, producing the distressing and overwhelming experience of open-ended stays, uncertain futures, and unanswered questions. This chapter chronicles the political life of Sudanese in exile in North America.

Many Sudanese I encountered consistently acknowledged political forces as determinants of migration or future decisions about returning home. Burhan, a thirty-six-year-old living in Boston, stated: "I came to Washington in 1990 after I lost my job in the Sudan. My dismissal was purely political. I joined Sudanese opposition groups here. As long as this regime is in power, I will never go back." Mudathir, a forty-year-old from Sharaffa village in the Gezira Province now living in New York City stressed the same background forces. "The problem that led me to leaving is political. Lack of freedom and harassment by the agents of the Islamic Front was my biggest fear. My problem is a problem of the nation, of a country, and of a people who are exploited by a political party." When asked about his future goals, Mudathir was unequivocal: "to return to the Sudan when this regime is overthrown."

Others shared these aspirations to return home after "the restoration of democracy," and were quick to point to the October Revolution of 1964 and the 1985 April Uprising in which military dictatorships were overthrown by civilians "who were only carrying tree branches."

Sudanese political organizations in the United States and Canada now include the Sudan Human Rights Organization (Washington, D.C., and California chapters); the El Sudan Center for Democracy, Peace and Civil Rights; the Darb El-Intifada; the Voice of the Democratic Alliance; Sudanese Victims of Torture Group; the National Democratic Alliance (Washington, D.C., and California chapters); the Sudan Opposition Group (Colorado and Texas chapters); the Pax Sudani Organization; the Sudanese National Rally (Philadelphia and New England chapters); the Sudanese National Alliance in Canada; and the New Democratic Forces and the Zinjirab Party (both in Brooklyn).

Sudanese migrants driven to exile by recent political developments at home—and committed to return once the current military regime is out of power and democracy restored—are less inclined than other Sudanese to perceive their migration as permanent. On the contrary, they affirm their move to be temporary in nature, which prompts them to limit interaction and interpersonal relationships with North Americans. They also maintain transnational ties with Sudanese exiles who have fled Islamic ascendancy and militarist oppression and have sought refuge and asylum all over the globe. Yousif, a migrant in Texas, remarked: "Sudanese people are scattered everywhere. Wherever you go you either run into a Sudanese, or run into someone who tells you they met a Sudanese in some strange place. Now even if you pick up a stone from the ground, you will find a Sudanese underneath it."

How does this background affect political life in the North American ghorba? In examining this question, I encountered Sudanese celebrations of their country's independence—the October Revolution, and the April Uprising—and political rallies and demonstrations like the annual Day of Protest organized by the Sudanese Human Rights Organization on the anniversary of the June 30, 1989, coup d'etat. Political conferences also served as significant forums for Sudanese: the National Democratic Forces, for example, held a conference in Alexandria, Virginia, in 1998 to discuss the role of the opposition abroad in influencing political transformation in the Sudan. And Sudanese political leaders such as former Prime Minister Sadiq El Mahdi and Sudanese Women's Union leader Fatima Ahmed Ibrahim are often called upon by exiled groups to discuss such issues as the ending of the civil war, recognition of the Sudan as a culturally diverse nation, citizenship rights, and separation of religion and the state.

On April 25, 1998, 130 men and women gathered in front of the Canadian Parliament to voice their protest of the massacre of two hundred high-school boys who drowned in the Sudan while trying to escape the Sudanese army draft. The protesting Sudanese, living in the Ontario cities of Niagara Falls, London, Hamilton, Kitchner, and Toronto, had assembled after delivering a petition urging mobilization of the international community to address the Sudanese situation. The Sudanese community in the United States and Canada also expressed an outpouring of support during famine, which hit the southern Bahr El Ghazal region. Their "A Dollar to Save a Life Program" reached out to the international community and drew worldwide attention to their home communities during a time of dire need.

Sudanese exiles engaged in an international awareness campaign over the plight of the Nuba people, who occupy several villages in the Nuba Mountains in Southern Kordofan Province and were reported to have been reduced "to a subclass of displaced people" following a government campaign of ethnic cleansing. A message issued in 1997 by the Committee to Support Nuba Women and Children stated:

> Dear International community, individuals, organizations, and officials:
>   We are writing to alert you to the humanitarian tragedy of the people, especially women and children, of the Nuba Mountains of southwestern Sudan. In this remote and internationally isolated region of the Sudan, a long-running human rights disaster is precipitously worsening. Therefore, we urge you to demand your governments to act immediately, and with the requisite political will, to help put an end to this unfolding human tragedy—We call on the international community to acknowledge the state of genocide in the Nuba Mountains and therefore to take the appropriate actions required by the United Nations Convention on the Prevention and Punishment of the Crime of Genocide. (Discussion Group for Sudanese Concerns)

Another area where political engagement has been significant is activism against the operations of international oil companies in southern Sudan. The Canadian Talisman Energy Company was subject to migrant protest for working with the Sudanese government in this war-scorched region. The Sudanese associations of Manitoba, Calgary, Toronto, Vancouver, and Ottawa called for a rally to protest the Canadian government's decision not to call for a withdrawal of Talisman from the Sudan "in spite of the conclusions in the report by John Harker to foreign minister Axworthy stating that Talisman's business operations are contributing to the killing of innocent civilians" (Discussion Group for Sudanese Concerns). A statement released by southern exile groups protests:

> We, the Southern Sudanese community in Canada at large, think that this is the most unfortunate decision by Minister Axworthy. We want to express our

Displaced Nuba women in Khartoum at work. 1998.

profound dismay, anger and outrage. The government of Canada has missed
the opportunity to be a positive influence in Sudan. It has instead decided to
be a passive witness to the slaughter of innocent men, women and children.
We urge the Canadian government to:
1/ Apply sanctions on Talisman Energy Inc. as stated in the policy paper on
Sudan last October, now that it has been found that this company's activities
are contributing to human rights abuses.
2/ initiate an international effort to implement multilateral sanctions to be applied to Sudan's oil industry until there is a just and comprehensive agreement.
3/ publicly condemn the Khartoum regime for its recent bombing of children in
Upper Kaouda Holy Cross school in Sudan, which resulted in many tragic deaths.
4/ Ensure that the charges of chemical weapons violations in Sudan are inves-
tigated by the appropriate international authorities.
Put an end to killing: Stop Talisman.

Another event which provoked the protest of exiles against the Canadian
government was its invitation to the Sudanese Foreign Minister to attend a
conference on war-affected children in Winnipeg in 2000. The Federation
of Sudanese Canadians Association wrote:

Prime Minister Jean Chretien,
We have recently heard that Canada has invited the Sudanese Foreign Minister to attend the conference on war-affected children to be held in Winnipeg
next week.
Your Excellency, we are totally confused about this. How could the Canadian government invite one of the worst violators of human rights and killers
of children in the world to attend such a conference? Surely your government
cannot be ignorant of the atrocities committed almost on a daily basis by the
National Islamic Front (NIF) regime in Khartoum. We briefed you on these
terrible events, including slavery, many times. Is it the intention of your government to bring the Foreign Minister to Canada to let him proclaim his
propaganda to the Canadian people and thereby allow him to provide them
with false assurances regarding the nature of Canadian business activities
(which produce income for your government as well as military hardware for
the genocidal policies of the National Islamic Front).
Indeed we are shocked that your government, which claims to be concerned for the welfare of war-affected children, could do such a thing, especially when there are UN sanctions against Sudanese officials' travel in effect.
Yet, we are at a loss to understand any other logical explanation. Perhaps,
Canada has lost the moral ground which it claims to exhibit.
We want you to know that we regard this action as a serious affront, and a
provocative insult to the Sudanese people; regard it as a failure of your foreign
policy on Sudan and a confirmation of your government's economic interest in
the Sudan. We demand an immediate explanation, and demand that your government reverse its decision.

The frustration of Sudanese exiles reflects what they and others see as political rationalizations for neglect of Africa by the West. As anthropologist Johannes Fabian argues: "More and more parts of Africa are receding from western consciousness and taking their place in a vast realm of poverty, misery, and illness. They are being abandoned economically and politically because they are not interesting to this post–cold war global economy" (1998, 103).

Drawing Political Boundaries

Sudanese who identify themselves as political exiles spare no effort to protest and to distinguish themselves from other Sudanese who are sympathetic to, or work for, the government of the Sudan. A Sudanese diplomat at his country's American mission remarked cynically on the numerous demonstrations by the exile community: "Many who come to these demonstrations are people awaiting asylum decisions by the United States Government. To have their pictures taken in front of the Sudanese Mission to the United States, demonstrating and carrying antigovernment signs, is very beneficial for their cases." The ghorba community has a more nuanced interpretation, and they see political stances as a source of tension among Sudanese migrants. Hashim, forty-three years old and living in Washington, D.C., explained: "In this country, not everybody is opposed to the Islamist regime. Many defend the status quo under the false argument [that there is no alternative]. These migrants are here to make money, and sometimes they almost appear to be representatives of the government abroad. What is dangerous is that they try to penetrate our jalia association, and for that many of us do not want anything to do with them. These people gave us a hard time back home, they cannot do the same here in the U.S." Hashim's view was substantiated during a jalia meeting in Toronto at which tensions escalated as people demanded to know the political views of the elected leaders. In exasperation, Salima, a migrant residing in St. Catharines, Ontario, implored: "Brothers and sisters: please understand that the jalia's work is for our cultural and social life. People are volunteering their time to create a sense of community. Please remember that we did not come to Canada as kings and queens, we are refugees who need the moral support of each other. We are uprooted; our hearts are broken over the loss of our families and neighbors. God only knows when, or if ever, we will see them again. Let's clean up these problems and try just to be Sudanese." In Washington, D.C., Ali Sayyid told me: "There are certain Muslim brothers groups in this country who consider themselves representatives of the Sudan government. They seize every opportunity to control and manipulate our jalia. Now most people have started to boycott participation in the jalia because of the presence of this group." In 1996 I interviewed Amin, a fifty-seven-year-old former Sudanese diplomat living in Silver Springs, Maryland, who was opposed to the current government. He acknowledged the increasing politicization of Sudanese associations throughout North America: "We need to organize ourselves into a more influential jalia that does not concern itself with merely social events but also with political events, as well as to try to influence policies and urge the U.S. government to take strict measures toward human rights abuses in the Sudan. What we need to do is to be more effective through strong political associations, despite the existing differences among ourselves."

The Sudanese National Democratic Rally (SNDR) in New England is an overtly antigovernment exile organization. Its bylaws read:

> It is our belief that Sudanese people for long have chosen democracy based on a multi-party system of government, to protect their constitutional rights, and to preserve their basic human right and dignity with a view to establish a fundamental interrelation between citizens and the government. Therefore, in pursuit of Sudanese unity and the equality among them, regardless of any religious, traditional, lingual, ethnic differences and considering the fascist junta that took power in Sudan in June 30, 1989, which was backed by the National Islamic Front, and managed to interrupt the path to democracy, a Sudanese National Movement has been established in the New England region and committed itself to follow the SNDR, as agreed upon by all Sudanese political parties (excluding the National Islamic Front), trade unions, and professional groups.

Membership in the SNDR in New England is open to all Sudanese. Its stated objectives are to support the struggle for democracy at home against the current regime; to struggle for the achievement of democracy based on a multiparty system; and to support the 1989 Charter of the Defense of Democracy (*mithag el difaa an el democratia*).

Another exile political group, Darb El-Intifada, supported a Day of Protest on June 30, 1998, the ninth anniversary of the establishment of the El-Bashir regime. It announced:

> Today, the Sudanese in diaspora, individuals and organizations, have owed a great honor and respect by signing their names on an international unified memorandum which demands the National Islamic Front and the government of Sudan's illegitimate regime to step down and let the Sudanese people decide their own destiny! By starting the international campaign, the Sudanese in diaspora have in fact started to play a more positive and effective role in supporting the legitimate struggle of our people inside Sudan. We are very

glad that over 30 organizations around the world and over 800 Sudanese around the globe have decided to join their hands and efforts to support the Sudanese struggle for freedom and democracy. Today, we call upon all Sudanese around the globe to play their nationalistic role and support the International Campaign, which will start today and continue through the end of July 1998.

Another cornerstone of Sudanese exile political organization is its press. Sudanese ghorba newspapers and newsletters such as *El-Ray El-Akhar*, *El-Sahifia*, *El-Nilain*, and *Al-Khalas* (the latter published by the Sudan National Democratic Alliance in Washington, D.C.) furnish a forum in which political issues are defined and discussed. When *El-Ray El-Akhar*, published in Fort Worth, Texas, reported that Sudanese president Omer El-Bashir accused the United States of recruiting Sudanese migrants to work against their nation and stressed his intention to stop Sudanese migration to the United States, a migrant from Oklahoma responded: "President Omer El-Bashir has described Sudanese migrants in the U.S. as 'the modern slaves,' adding that he will prohibit the migration of Sudanese to the United States. We do not wish to equate this 'modern slavery' here with the fundamentalist slavery that our kind people in the Sudan are subjected to." On January 1, 1996, the fortieth anniversary of Sudanese independence, *El-Ray El-Akhar* published a special issue with interviews of political leaders in exile and members of the migrant community. The exiled newspapers also provide information about asylum lawyers, sending money home safely, cultural events, and births, deaths, and new arrivals in the migrant community all of which serves real daily needs of Sudanese migrants in North America.

Epilogue

Racialization and a Nation in Absentia

The exile knows that in a secular and contingent world, homes are always provisional. Borders and barriers which enclose us within the safety of familiar territory can also become prisons, and are often defended by reason or necessity. Exiles cross borders, break barriers of thought and experience.

Edward Said, 1990

Two phenomena identified over and again by Sudanese migrants and exiles in their experience in North America are a pronounced national homogenization as Sudanese and a racialization as Black people in a White-dominated society.

Sudanese society encompasses a myriad of ethnic identities within its borders, a diversity that is mirrored in its ghorba community in North America. However, in North America a pronounced de-ethnicization is replacing these carefully differentiated, age-old identities, and a fundamentally new one arises. Outside the Sudan, one is now transformed from being a Shaiqi, Nuer, Beja, or Rubatabi to being a Black person. Racialization of Sudanese in North America is leading people in the ghorba to revisit long-held notions of skin pigmentation, ethnicity, and national identity.

Two stories reveal the crux of the matter. A Sudanese migrant from the riverine village Gabal Umm Ali in northern Sudan returned home for a visit. The people of Gabal Umm Ali are known by neighboring groups for their ethnic pride in Arab ancestry, a pride not uncommon to other communities claiming mores and value-systems derived from their Islamic-Arab forebears. Upon his arrival, relatives and neighbors surrounded the returned migrant to welcome him and learn about life in America. He began to tell them that life in America is both good and bad. What can be bad about America? they asked. He proceeded to tell them about racial discrimination and how he himself was subject to incidents he felt to be demeaning and dehumanizing. Confounded by her son's story, his proud mother interrupted, "Didn't you tell them that you are a Shaiqi, from Gabal Umm Ali?" The son replied, "No, they only know that I am Black."

Another story concerns a typically dark-skinned southern Sudanese who visited New York and wanted to go to Harlem to see the Black Americans. When he arrived there and walked around with his friends, he asked, "Where are the Blacks? These people are northern Sudanese Arabs." What these stories illustrate is that Sudanese in North America must chart their way through a sometimes new, ambiguous world where their ethnicity, identity, and religion are subject to confusion or even hostility. This experience has prompted many to resist interaction with the new society. It also has led to the evolution of a new consciousness in North America. A similar observation is reported of Haitian immigrants in New York by Elizabeth McAlister: "Haitians are assigned by the dominant society to the African American proximal host niche, yet they do not understand themselves to be African American. Haitian Americans' identities are in tension as the immigrant population struggles to define itself on its own terms" (1998, 153; see also Waters 1990).

To put the predicament of the racialization of Sudanese in North America in its proper context, one must know that Sudanese conceptions of skin color are complex. These ideas cannot be articulated in terms of a simple Black/White dichotomy. Instead, Sudanese perceive shades of skin color that include *akhdar* (green), *asfar* (yellow), *asmar* (brown), *azrag* (blue), and *ahmar* (red) (see Al-Shahi 1972; Mohamed 1980). A common joke illuminates the racial predicament facing Sudanese abroad. A Sudanese gets separated from his friend in London during a short visit. The friend stops to ask a British policeman if he has seen a "green man" in the vicinity. The police officer responds in the negative, saying "I would have certainly noticed that."

In the Sudan, Arabs can be very dark-skinned and non-Arabs can be very light-skinned. There are "red persons" who are almost European in appearance, resembling Turks. Neither "yellow" nor "brown"—a shade darker than yellow—are recognized to be "African" but refer, stereotypically, to Sudanese Arabs. However, the Beja, an ethnic group in the eastern part of Sudan, are "brown" but are not Arab, nor are they "African." (In fact, they feel so distinct from other Sudanese that they are mounting their own nationalist movement.) The origin of the term "green" is unclear but is never questioned; it is used to describe certain "African" and "Arab" types. "Blue" is a very dark pigmentation, covering Shaigi and Rubatabi of Arab ancestry in the north as well as Nuer, an "African" group from the south.

In North America, Sudanese categorizations of color are eclipsed by the Black/White dichotomy, and self-conceptions are forced to undergo fundamental shifts. Can the discovery of shared "Sudanese-ness" and "blackness" in exile become a seed for a more unified Sudan? Can Sudanese discover in their exile the essence of nationhood? From my observations and conversations with people coping with life in the ghorba, one thing is clear: the Sudanese migrant community in North America has been becoming a nation in absentia. The New Webster's Dictionary defines a nation as "a body of people recognized as an entity by virtue of their historical, linguistic, or ethnic links; a body of people united under a particular political organization and usually occupying a defined territory" (cited in Khalid 1989). As Sudanese scholar Mansour Khalid (1989) argues, nations should not be too narrowly defined by geography or political structures: the definition needs to allow for other significant characteristics, such as national consciousness and the will to place loyalty to that entity over any competing loyalty. Overwhelmed by civil strife for decades, in the Sudan the sense of belonging to a nation-like whole is evanescent and often indiscernible. Loyalties are expressed rather in terms of ethnic identification. The dangers of this, as Francis Deng notes, occur when these loyalties move beyond the realm of mere self-perception to the political stage, where they affect the sharing of power and wealth and the defining of shared national values (1995, 4).

Regardless of one's ethnic affiliation and religious faith, Sudanese life in the ghorba reflects a "will to be Sudanese." Exile has made it possible for diverse Sudanese to pledge loyalty to the larger community as a national entity. The expansion of political life in exile provides numerous examples of this desire to reconsider nationhood and ultimately to become part of a whole. Exile has allowed Sudanese to debate identity, ethnicity, and religion by providing them the freedom of unfiltered communication. Exile shows the importance and possibility of becoming a nation by deconstructing hierarchies of power that otherwise divide the Sudanese polity.

Migration therefore has fundamentally altered how Sudanese interact with, identify, and connect to each other. It has provided a medium through which exiled Sudanese may be defining the geopolitics of the future Sudan. As Kamal, a refugee living in Los Angeles, states: "In this country there is no Arab or African or Nuba. We are Sudanese first and foremost." Except for the Bahhara, who came here under unique historical circumstances and managed to exist as a separate ethnic community, Sudanese are revisiting their homegrown "ethnicity." Their reinvention of Sudanese identity in the ghorba is a potentially liberating device for national politics in a postcolonial state and a crucial step in fulfilling the dream of becoming a nation. To the extent that migrants identify themselves above all else as Sudanese, national consciousness replaces the long-standing ethnic consciousnesses that have contributed to antagonisms and strife for decades. It remains to be seen whether these Sudanese can one day create a new, united Sudan upon their return.

Glossary

ahmar	red
akhdar	green
Allah yarood ghorbatu	may God reverse [a person's] alienation
angaraib	bed
asfar	yellow
asmar	brown
azrag	blue
agir	infertile
awlia amr	guardians
bahhara	seamen
baira	unmarried, unwanted commodity
baraka	blessings
dalooka	drum
dawa	invitation
darira	mixture of herbs and perfumes put on newlyweds' hair
Dongolawi	native of Dongola; plural, Danagla
Eid El Adha	Muslim feast following the pilgrimage to Mecca
Eid Elfitr	Muslim feast celebrated at the end of Ramadan
farda	woven cotton cloth
fatiha	The opening chapter of the Quran
fatwa	legal religious opinion
gana	bamboo sticks
ghorba	alienation/life away from home
ghuloof	uncircumcised people

gurba or garaba	proximity, kinship, nearness
guama	authority, protection, guardianship
hajj	pilgrimage
halal	allowed, or ritually clean
hasid	envious
hijab	veil, cover, Islamic dress, a charm
hudud	penal code of the sharia law
ightirab	living abroad
imam	religious leader
imamm	turbans
intifada	uprising
itkabasat	filled
jalia	immigrant group or civic association
jallabia	Sudanese long white robe-like outfit; plural jallalib
jamiiaa	group or union
jihad	holy war
jirtig	ritual of fertility
jumaa	Friday or Friday Prayer
kainoona	identity
kaizan	members of National Islamic Front
kashif	donor list
khabeez	cookies
khadadeem	hired help or servants
khalwa	religious school
leigeimat	fried dough
lilat el dukhla	night of entry in wedding ceremonies
maattam	mourning ritual
madih	religious praise
makhnooga	suffocated
mahia	salary
masakin	helpless, poor
masjid	mosque
matalig	free, unrestrained
moda	fad
mughtaribeen	those who work abroad
muhajjaba	veiled
mujawara	settlement in the Muslim holy city of Mecca
mushat	hair braiding
nadi el-khirijeen	graduates' club
nas el-khalij	term for Sudanese who work in the Persian Gulf states
oud	lute

sanbooksa	fried stuffed dough
sandug	rotating (box) credit association
shabab	youth
shagawa	hard life, struggle
shammasa	thugs, or market squatters
sharaka	joint ownership
sharia	Islamic law
simaya	naming ceremony
tahara	purification
tobe	Sudanese dress, similar to Indian sari; plural, tiab
twagi	skull-caps
wanasa	chat
wazirat elarous	maid of honor
zaffa	procession
zagharid	ululations
zikir	a Sufi remembrance ritual

References

Abdelrahim, Mohamed. 1952. *Alnidaa fi daff' eliftiraa* (Scuffling mendaciousness). Cairo: Albarlaman Press.

Abdel Nur, Adil. 1989. *Elmusharka Elsiasia lil alaqbat elsudaniyeen fi intikhabat 1986* (The political participation of Sudanese Copts in 1986 elections). Khartoum: published by the author.

Abdel Rahim, Mudathir. 1969. *Imperialism and Nationalism in the Sudan: A Study in Constitutional and Political Development, 1899–1956*. Oxford: Clarendon.

———. 1973. "Arabism, Africanism, and Self-Identification in the Sudan." In *The Southern Sudan: The Problem of National Integration*, ed. Dunstan Wai, 29–47. London: Frank Cass.

Abul Fadl, Mona. 1991. *Introducing Islam from Within*. Wiltshire: Cromwell Press Limited.

Abu Labban, Bahaa. 1969. "The Arab Canadian Community." In *Arab Americans: Studies in Assimilation*, ed. E. Hogopian and A. Paden, 18–37. Wilmeete, Ill.: The Medina University Press International.

Abusharaf, Rogaia Mustafa. 1997a. "The Making of a Professional Clergy in the New World: Changing Social and Religious Practices in a Congregation in Diaspora." Paper presented at Georgetown University.

———. 1997b. "Sudanese New World Migration: Socioeconomic Characteristics." *International Migration* 35 (4): 513, 537.

———. 1998a. "Unmasking Tradition: A Sudanese Anthropologist Confronts Female Circumcision." *The Sciences* 38 (2): 22–28.

———. 1998b. "Structural Adaptations in an Immigrant Muslim Congregation in New York." In *Gatherings in Diaspora: Religious Communities and the New Immigration*, ed. R. Stephen Warner and Judy Wittner, 235–36. Philadelphia: Temple University Press.

———. 1998c. "War, Politics, and Religion: An Exploration of the Determinants of

Southern Sudanese Migration to the United States and Canada." *Northeast African Studies* 5 (1): 31–47.

———. 2001. "Virtuous Cuts: Female Genital Excision in an African Ontology." *Differences: Journal for Feminist Cultural Studies* 12 (1): 112–40.

Abu Sin, Mohamed. 1995. "Environmental Causes and Implications of Population Displacement in Sudan." In *War and Drought in Sudan*, ed. E. Eltigani, 11–23. Gainesville: University of Press of Florida.

Adam, Sabah. 2001. "Northern Sudanese Customs Adopted by Southerners in Khartoum: Interviews with Pressla Joseph, Rose Pauolino, and Veronica Lewis" (in Arabic). *Alayam Newspaper* 6834 (August 21). Khartoum.

Adams, William. 1984. *Nubia: Corridor to Africa*. London: Allen Lane.

Addelton, J. 1991. "The Impact of the Gulf War on Migration and Remittances in Asia and the Middle East." *International Migration* 29 (4): 509–27.

Africa Watch. 1989. "Political Detainees in Sudan." New York: Human Rights Watch Publications Department 1 (20).

———. 1991. "Sudan: New Islamic Penal Code Violates Basic Human Rights." New York: Human Rights Watch Publications Department.

——— 1992a. "Sudan: Violations of Academic Freedom." *Human Rights Watch Publications* 4 (12).

——— 1992b. "Eradicating the Nuba." *Human Rights Watch Publications* 4 (10).

——— 1993. "Sudan: The Copts, Passive Survivors under Threat." *Human Rights Watch Publications* 5 (3).

Agger, Inger. 1992. *The Blue Room: Trauma and Testimony among Refugee Women*. London: Zed Books.

Ahmed, Mohamed Abdelhamid. 1978. *Islamic Preaching in America*. Khartoum: Ministry of Culture and Information.

———. 1995. *Sati Majid: Islamic Missionary in North America, 1904–1929*. Khartoum: Institute of Social Research.

Ahmed, Osman Hassan. 1983. *Sudan and Sudanese: A Bibliography of American and Canadian Dissertations and Theses on the Sudan*. Sudanese Embassy: Sudanese Publications Series.

Ali, Ali. 1985. *The Sudan Economy in Disarray*. Khartoum: Khartoum University Press.

Al-Shahi, Ahmed. 1972. "Proverbs and Social Values in a Northern Sudanese Village." In *Essays in Sudan Ethnography* (presented to Sir Edward Evans-Pritchard), ed. Ian Cunnison and Wendy James, 87–105. London: Hurst.

———. 1986. *Themes from Northern Sudan*. London: Ithaca Press.

Amin, Samir. 1974. *Modern Migrations in West Africa*. Oxford: Oxford University Press.

———. 1995. "Migrations in Contemporary Africa: A Retrospective View." In *The Migration Experience in Africa*, ed. T. Akin and J. Adam, 29–41. Uppsala, Sweden: Nordiska Africainsitutet.

Amin, Samira, and Mahgoub Mahmoud. 1991. "Hawl Moashirat Eltakhtit lil higra el Khargia fi el Sudan" (Planning for external migration in the Sudan). Paper presented at the Regional Conference for the Study of Migration in the Sudan. Khartoum.

Anderson, Benedict. 1991. *Imagined Communities: Reflections on the Origin and Spread of Nationalism*. London: Verso.

An-Na'im, Abudlahi. 1987. "Religious Minorities under Islamic Law and the Limits of Cultural Relativism." *Human Rights Quarterly* 9:1–18.

Annas, C. L. 1996. "Irreversible Error: The Power and Prejudice of Female Genital Mutilation." *Journal of Contemporary Health Law and Policy* 12:325–53.

Appleyard, Reginald. 1991. *International Migration: Challenge for the Nineties*. Geneva: International Organization of Migration.

Asad, Talal. 1970. *The Kababish Arabs: Power, Authority, and Consent in a Nomadic Tribe*. London: Hurst.

Atkinson, Paul. 1990. *The Ethnographic Imagination: Textual Constructions of Reality*. London and New York: Routledge.

Attia, A. 1979. *The Copts and Christian Civilization*. Salt Lake City: University of Utah Press.

Bales, Kevin. 1999. *Disposable People: New Slavery in the Global Economy*. Berkeley: University of California Press.

———. 2000. "The Expendable People: Slavery in the Age of Globalization." Paper presented at the University of Connecticut Distinguished Human Rights Lecture Series.

Balan, J. 1988. "Selectivity of Migration in International and Internal Flows." In *International Migration Today*, ed. C. Stahl. UNESCO: Center for Migration Studies.

Ballard, J. 1987. "The Political Economy of Migration in Pakistan, Britain, and the Middle East." In *Migrants, Workers, and the Social Order*, ed. J. Eade, 17–42. London: Tavistock Publications.

Bariagaber, Assefaw. 1995. "Linking Political Violence and Refugee Situations in the Horn of Africa: An Empirical Approach." *International Migration* 33 (2): 209–29.

Basch, Linda. 1987. "The Vincentians and Grenadians: The Role of Voluntary Associations in Immigrant Adaptation to New York City." In *New Immigrants in New York*, ed. Nancy Foner, 159–95. New York: Columbia University Press.

Bascom, Jonathan. 1995. "The New Nomads." In *The Migration Experience in Africa*, ed. T. Akin and J. Adam, 197–220. Uppsala, Sweden: Nordiska Africainsitutet.

Baya, Philister. 1999. "Seeking a Refuge or Being Displaced?" In *The Tragedy of Reality: Southern Sudanese Women Appeal for Peace*, ed. Magda El Sanosi, 58–67. Khartoum: Sudan Open Learning Organization.

Bechtold, Peter. 1992. "More Turbulence in Sudan: A New Politics This Time." In *Sudan: State and Society in Crisis*, ed. John Voll, 1–24. Washington, D.C.: Middle East Institute.

Berger, John. 1975. *A Seventh Man: Migrant Workers in Europe*. New York: Viking Press.

Beshir, Mohamed Omer. 1968. *The Southern Sudan: Background to Conflict*. New York: Frederick Praeger Publishers.

Birks, S., and C. Sinclair. 1980. *International Migration and Development in the Arab Region*. Geneva: International Labor Office.

Boddy, Janice. 1989. *Wombs and Alien Spirits: Men, Women, and the Zar Cult in Northern Sudan*. Madison, Wisc.: University of Wisconsin Press.

Bottomley, Gillian. 1992. *From Another Place*. Cambridge: Cambridge University Press.

Bouhdiba, Abedlwahab. 1974. "International Migration and Social Change." In *International Migration*, ed. G. Tapinos, 204–9. Buenos Aires: CICRED.

References

Canadian Immigration and Refugee Board, 1989–1994. *Annual Report*. Ottawa: La commission de l'immigration et du statut de refugie.

Castles, Stephen, and Godula Kosack. 1973. *Immigrant Workers and Class Structure in Western Europe*. London: Oxford University Press.

Chambers, Iain. 1994. *Migrancy, Culture, Identity*. London and New York: Routledge.

Chan, Sucheng. 1990. "European and Asian Immigration in the United States: A Comparative Perspective." In *Immigration Reconsidered*, ed. Virginia Yans-McLaughlin, 37–79. Oxford: Oxford University Press.

Chow, Rey. 1995. "The Politics of Admittance: Female Sexual Agency, Miscegenation, and the Formation of Community in Franz Fanon." *UTS Review* 1 (1): 5–29.

Comaroff, John. 1997. "Of Totemism and Ethnicity: Consciousness, Practice, and Signs of Inequality." In *Perspectives on Africa*, ed. R. Grinnker and C. Steiner, 69–87. Oxford: Blackwell.

Comitas, Lambros. 1992. Preface to *Towards a Transnational Perspective on Migration: Race, Class, Ethnicity, and Nationalism Reconsidered*, ed. Nina Schiller et al. New York: New York Academy of Sciences.

Cook, Richard, and Brian Morton. 1992. *The Penguin Guide to Jazz*. New York: Penguin Books.

Corbett, Sara. 2001. "From Hell to Fargo: The Lost Boys of Sudan Land in America." *New York Times Magazine* (April 1/section 6): 48–56.

Cunnison, Ian. 1966. *Baggara Arabs: Power and the Lineage in a Sudanese Nomad Tribe*. Oxford: Clarendon.

Dafaallah, H. 1975. *The Nubian Exodus*. London: Hurst.

Daughtry, Carla. 2001. "Ethnographic Notes on a Dinka Language Institute in Cairo." Paper presented at the Twentieth Anniversary of the Sudan Studies Association: The Sudan and Its Community of Scholars. East Lansing: Michigan State University.

Davis, A. J. 1973. "Coptic Christianity." In *Peoples and Cultures of Africa*, ed. Elliot Skinner, 678–89. New York: The American Museum of Natural History.

Deng, Francis. 1972. *The Dinka of the Sudan*. Prospect Heights, Ill.: Waveland Press.

———. 1978. *Africans of Two Worlds: The Dinka in Afro-Arab Sudan*. New Haven: Yale University Press.

———. 1986. *The Man Called Deng Majok: A Biography of Power, Polygyny, and Change*. New Haven: Yale University Press.

———. 1991. "War of Visions for the Nation." In *Sudan: State and Society in Crisis*, ed. John Voll, 24–43. Bloomington: Indiana University Press.

———. 1995. *War of Visions in the Sudan*. Washington, D.C.: Brookings Institution Press.

Dinnerstein, Leonard. 1996. *Natives and Strangers: A Multicultural History of Americans*. New York: Oxford University Press.

Drumtra, Jeff. 1999. Preface to *Sudan: Personal Stories of Sudan's Uprooted People*. Washington D.C.: U.S. Committee for Refugees.

Dudu, Christina. 1999. "Southern Sudanese Displaced Women: Losses and Gains."In *The Tragedy of Reality: Southern Sudanese Women Appeal for Peace*, ed. Magda El Sanosi, 48–58. Khartoum: Sudan Open Learning Organization.

DuToit, Brian. 1990. "People on the Move." *Human Organization* 49 (4): 305–17.

Eastmond, Maria. 1993. "Reconstructing Life: Chilean Refugee Women and the Dilemmas of Exile." In *Migrant Women*, ed. Gina Buijs, 35–55. Oxford: Berg.

Eissa, Garrout. 1986. "International Migration as a Channel for the Transfer of Productive Capacity between Rich and Poor Countries: The Case of the Sudan." Ph.D. diss., University of Pittsburgh.

Eissa, Suaad Ibrahim. 1996. *Masirat eltalim alali fi elsudan* (The path of higher education in the Sudan). Khartoum: Khartoum Publication and Distribution.

———. 2000. "Women and the Law of Public Order." Paper presented at Women's Initiative Group. Khartoum, El Shariqa Hall, April 11–16, 2000.

El Amin, Nafisa Ahmed, and Magda El Sanusi. 1994. "The Women's Movement, Displaced Women, and Rural Women in Sudan." In *Women and Politics Worldwide*, ed. B. Nelson and N. Chowdhury, 674–90. New Haven and London: Yale University Press.

El Dareer, Asma. 1982. *Woman, Why Do You Weep? Circumcision and Its Consequences*. London: Zed Books.

Elguindi, Fadwa. 1996. *El Soubu: Egyptian Celebration of Life*. Film Study Guide. Los Angeles, El Nil Research.

El Shazali, Salah El Din. 1995. "War Displacement: The Sociocultural Dimension." In *War and Drought in Sudan*, ed. Eltigani E. Elitigani, 35–47. Gainesville: University Press of Florida.

Eltayeb, Abdallah. 1955. "The Changing Customs of Reiverain Sudan." *Sudan Notes and Records* 35:146–58.

El Tayeb, Ahmed Abbashar. 1985. "The Sudan Skill Exodus." *African Administrative Studies* 26:87–106.

Eltayeb, Griselda. 1987. "Women's Dress in the Northern Sudan." In *The Sudanese Woman*, ed. Susan Kenyon, 8–40. Khartoum: Khartoum University Press.

Eltigani, Azza, and Mohamed Khaled. 1998. "State Violence against Women: A Current Perspective from the Sudan." *Resources for Feminist Research* 26 (3–4): 221–23.

Evans-Pritchard, E. 1940. *The Nuer*. Oxford: Oxford University Press.

———. 1956. *Nuer Religion*. Oxford: Clarendon.

———. 1974. *Man and Woman among the Azande*. New York: The Free Press.

———. 1976. *Witchcraft, Oracles, and Magic among the Azande*. Oxford: Clarendon.

Evanzz, Karl. 1999. *The Messenger: The Rise and Fall of Elijah Muhammad*. New York: Pantheon.

Fabian, Johannes. 1998. *Moments of Freedom: Anthropology and Popular Culture*. Charlottesville: University Press of Virginia.

Fakhouri, Hani. 1987. *Kafr El-Elow: Continuity and Change in an Egyptian Community*. 2d ed. Prospect Heights, Ill.: Waveland Press.

Faris, James. 1972. *Nuba Personal Art*. London: Duckworth.

———. 1989. *Southeast Nuba Social Relations*. Aachen, the Netherlands: Verlag.

Fauset, Arthur. 1944. *Black Gods of the Metropolis: Negro Religious Cults of the Urban North*. Philadelphia: University of Pennsylvania Press.

Feather, Leonard, and Ira Gitter. 1999. *The Biographical Encyclopedia of Jazz*. Oxford: Oxford University Press.

Fernea, Robert. 1961. *Nubian Ethnographies*. Prospect Heights, Ill.: Waveland Press.

Freeman, James. 1995. *Changing Identities: Vietnamese Americans, 1975–1995*. Boston: Allyn and Bacon.

Galal el Din, M. 1988. "Sudanese Migration to the Oil-Producing Countries." In *Econ-*

omy and Class in Sudan, ed. Nelson O'Niell and Jay O'Brien, 291–308. New York: Gower Publishing Company.

Geertz, Clifford. 1971. *Islam Observed.* Chicago: University of Chicago Press.

———. 1973. *The Interpretation of Cultures.* New York: Basic Books.

Geiser, Peter. 1973. "The Myth of the Dam." *American Anthropologist* 75 (1): 184–93.

———. 1986. *The Egyptian Nubians: A Study in Social Symbiosis.* Cairo: American University Press.

Gibran, Khalil. 1979. *The Prophet.* New York: A.A. Knopf.

Gold, Stephen. 1992. *Refugee Communities: A Comparative Field Study.* London: Sage Publications.

Guha, B. 1977. "Brain Drain Issues and Indicators on Brain Drain." *International Migration* 15 (1): 3–20.

Guinier, Lani. 1994. *The Tyranny of the Majority: Fundamental Fairness in Representative Democracy.* New York: The Free Press.

Hackett, Beatrice. 1996. *Pray God and Keep Walking: Stories of Women Refugees.* London: McFarland.

Haddad, Yvonne Yazbeck, and Adair Lummis. 1987. *Islamic Values in the United States.* New York: Oxford University Press.

Haddad, Yvonne Yazbeck, and Jane Smith. 1993. *Mission to America: Five Islamic Sectarian Communities in America.* Gainesville: University Press of Florida.

Hale, Sondra. 1996. *Gender Politics in Sudan: Islamism, Socialism, and the State.* Boulder, Colo.: Westview Press.

Halliday, Fred. 1984. "Labor Migration in the Arab World." *MERIP Reports,* no. 123.

Handlin, Oscar. 1959. *Immigration as a Factor in American History.* Englewood Cliffs, N.J.: Prentice Hall.

———. 1973. *The Uprooted.* New York: Atlantic Monthly Press.

Harvey, David. 1989. *The Urban Experience.* Baltimore: Johns Hopkins University Press.

Haykal, Mohamed Hassanain. 1983. *Autumn of Fury: The Assassination of Sadat.* New York: Random House.

Heisler, B. 1992. "The Future of Immigrant Incorporation: Which Concepts, Which Models?" *International Migration Review* 41 (2): 623–45.

Henderson, K.D. 1953. "Midweek Broadcast." London: The British Broadcasting Corporation (November 23). Durham, U.K.: Sudan Archive at Durham. File #478/3/32.

Heyden, H. 1991. "South-North Migration." *International Migration* 29 (2): 281–90.

Hill, Richard, and Peter Hogg. 1995. *Black Corps d'Élite: An Egyptian Sudanese Conscript Battalion with the French Army in Mexico, 1863–1867, and Its Survivors in Subsequent African History.* East Lansing: Michigan State University Press.

Hobsbawm, Eric. 1990. *Nations and Nationalism since 1780.* Cambridge: Cambridge University Press.

Holborn, Louise. 1975. *Refugees: A Problem of Our Time. The Work of the United Nations High Commissioner for Refugees, 1951–1971.* Metuchen, N.J.: Scarecrow Press.

Holt, Peter, and Martin Daly. 1988. *A History of the Sudan: From the Coming of Islam to the Present Day.* London and New York: Longman.

Holtzman, Jon. 2000. *Nuer Journeys, Nuer Lives: Sudanese Refugees in Minnesota.* Boston: Allyn and Bacon.

Holy, Ladislav. 1991. *Religion and Custom in a Muslim Society: The Berti of Sudan.* Cambridge: Cambridge University Press.

Hurreiz, Sayyid. 1989. "Ethnic, Cultural, and National Identity in the Sudan: An Overview." In *Ethnicity, Conflict, and National Integration in the Sudan,* ed. Sayyid Hurreiz and Elfatih Abdelsalam, 69–97. Khartoum: Institute of African and Asian Studies.

Ibrahim, Abdullahi. 1994. *Assaulting with Words: Popular Discourse and the Bridle of Shariah.* Evanston, Ill.: Northwestern University Press.

Ibrahim, Fatima Ahmed. 1994. "Arrow at Rest." In *Women in Exile,* ed. Mahnaz Atkhami, 191–208. Charlottesville: University Press of Virginia.

———. 1996. "Sudanese Women's Union: Strategies for Emancipation and the Counter Movements." *UFAHAMU: Journal of the African Activist Association* 24 (2–3): 3–20.

Immigration and Naturalization Service Report. 1991. Washington, D.C.: Government Printing Office.

Indra, Doreen, ed. 1999. *Engendering Forced Migration: Theory and Practice.* Oxford: Berghahn Books.

James, Wendy. 1979. *Kwanim Pa: The Making of the Uduk People.* Oxford: Clarendon.

Kaplan, Caren, et al., eds. 1999. *Between Woman and Nation: Nationalism, Transnational Feminisms, and the State.* Durham, N.C.: Duke University Press.

Kasinitz, Philip. 1992. *Caribbean New York: Black Immigrants and the Politics of Race.* Ithaca and London: Cornell University Press.

Kassindja, Fauziya. 1998. *Do They Hear You When You Cry?* New York: Dell Publishing.

Kennedy, John. 1970. "Circumcision and Excision in Egyptian Nubia." *Man* 5:175–91.

Kenyon, Susan. 1991. *Five Women of Sennar.* Oxford: Clarendon.

———. 1997. "Boxes and Networks of Obligation among Women in Central Sudan." Paper presented at the American Anthropological Association Annual Meeting, Washington D.C.

Khaleefa, Omer, et al. 1996. "Gender and Creativity in an Afro-Arab Islamic Culture: The Case of Sudan." *Journal of Creative Behavior* 30 (1): 52–60.

Khalid, Mansour. 1989. *The Government They Deserve: The Role of the Elite in Sudan's Political Evolution.* London and New York: Kegan Paul International.

Khan, Shahnaz. 1995. "The Veil as a Site of Struggle: The Hejab in Quebec." *Canadian Woman Studies/Les cahiers de la femme* 15 (2–3): 146–53.

Kramer, Robert. 1993. "Non-Muslims in an Islamic State: The Masalma of Omdurman." Paper presented at the Twelfth Annual Meeting of the Sudan Studies Association. Michigan State University.

Lado, Augustino. 1994. *Arab Slavery in Southern Sudan.* London: Pax Sudani Organization.

Laguerre, Michel. 1984. *American Odyssey: Haitians in New York City.* Ithaca and London: Cornell University Press.

Lange-Kubick, Cindy. 2000. "Lincoln Offers New Life for Boys from Sudan." *Lincoln Journal Star,* December 16.

Lee, E. 1966. "A Theory of Migration." *Demography* 3 (1): 47–57.

Lessinger, Johanna. 1995. *From the Ganges to the Hudson: Indian Immigrants in New York.* Boston: Allyn and Bacon.

References

Lienhardt, Godfrey. 1961. *Divinity and Experience: The Religion of the Dinka*. Oxford: Clarendon.
———. 1967. "Shilluk." *Encyclopedia Britannica*. 14th ed. Chicago: Encyclopedia Britannica, 338.
MacMichael, H. A. 1974 [1912]. *The Tribes of Northern and Central Kordofan*. Cambridge: Cambridge University Press.
Mahler, Sarah. 1995. *American Dreaming: Immigrant Life on the Margins*. Princeton: Princeton University Press.
Mahmoud, Mahgoub. 1983. *The Impact of Partial Modernization on the Emigration of the Sudanese Professionals and Skilled Workers*. Ph.D. diss., Brown University.
Malwal, Bona. 1993. "Sources of Conflict in Sudan." Paper presented at a Symposium on the Situation in the Sudan. Washington, D.C.: United States Institute of Peace.
Marable, Manning. 1995. "Beyond Racial Identity: Toward a Liberation Theory for Multicultural Democracy." In *Race, Class, and Gender: An Anthology*, ed. P. Collins and M. Anderson, Belmont, Calif.: Wadsworth.
Marcus, George. 1998. *Ethnography through Thick and Thin*. Princeton: Princeton University Press.
Margolis, Maxine. 1994. *Little Brazil: Ethnography of Brazilian Immigrants in New York*. Princeton: Princeton University Press.
——— 1998. *An Invisible Minority: Brazilians in New York City*. Boston: Allyn and Bacon.
Massey, Douglas. 1987. "The Ethnosurvey in Theory and Practice." *International Migration Review* 21 (4): 1498–1522.
Massey, Douglas, et al. 1987. *Return to Aztlan*. Berkeley: University of California Press.
Mazrui, Ali. 1973. "The Black Arabs in Comparative Perspective: The Political Sociology of Race Mixture." In *The Southern Sudan: The Problem of National Integration*, ed. D. Wai, 47–83. London: Frank Cass.
McAlister, Elizabeth. 1998. "The Madonna of 11th Street Revisited: Voodoo and Haitian Catholicism in the Age of Transnationalism." In *Gatherings in Diaspora*, ed. R. Stephen Warner and Judy Wittner, 123–60. Philadelphia: Temple University Press.
Meinardus, Otto. 1970. *Christian Egypt: Faith and Life*. Cairo: American University in Cairo Press.
Miller, Kerby. 1990. "Class, Culture, and Immigrant Group Identity in the United States: The Case of Irish-American Ethnicity." In *Immigration Reconsidered*, ed. Virginia Yans-McLaughlin, 96–130. Oxford: Oxford University Press.
Mohamed, Abbas A. 1980. *White Nile Arabs: Political Leadership and Economic Change*. London: London School of Economics Monographs on Social Anthropology, no. 53.
Morrison, Toni. 1992. *Playing in the Dark: Whiteness and the Literary Imagination*. Cambridge, Mass.: Harvard University Press.
Mullan, B. 1989. "The Impact of Social Networks on the Occupational Status of Migrants." *International Migration* 27 (1): 69–87.
Murphy, Joseph. 1994. *Working the Spirit: Ceremonies of the African Diaspora*. Boston: Beacon Press.
Nabti, Patricia. 1992. "Emigration from a Lebanese Village: A Case Study of Bishmizzine." In *The Lebanese in the World: A Century of Emigration*, ed. Albert Hourani, 41–65. London: Center for Lebanese Studies.

Nadel, S. 1947. *The Nuba.* London: Oxford University Press.

Nigem, E. 1986. "Arab Americans: Migration, Socioeconomic and Demographic Characteristics." *International Migration Review* 20 (3): 629–50.

Noivo, E. 1997. *Inside Ethnic Families: Three Generations of Portuguese-Canadians.* Montreal: McGill-Queens University Press.

Ogden, P. 1984. *Migration and Demographic Change.* Cambridge: Cambridge University Press.

Osman, Khalid Elkid, et al. 1996. "Sudanese Immigrants in Britain: New Routes for an Old Trek." Paper presented to the International Union for the Scientific Study of Population, Arab Regional Population Conference, Cairo.

Park, Kyeyoung. 1997. *The Korean American Dream: Immigrants and Small Business in New York.* Ithaca and London: Cornell University Press.

Pessar, Patricia. 1986. "The Role of Gender in Dominican Settlement in the U.S." In *Women and Change in Latin America,* ed. June Nash and Helen Safa, 273–93. South Hadley, Mass.: Bergin and Garvey.

Pohjola, A. 1991. "Social Networks—Help or Hindrance to the Migrant?" *International Migration* 29 (3): 435–45.

Poston, Larry. 1991. "Da'wa in the West." In *The Muslims of America,* ed. Yvonne Yazbeck Haddad, 125–36. New York: Oxford University Press.

Rahman, Anika, and Nahid Toubia. 2000. *Female Genital Mutilation: A Guide to Laws and Policies Worldwide.* London: Zed Books.

Refugee Board and Documentation Center. 1991. *A Report on the Persian Gulf: The Situation of Foreign Workers.* Ottawa: Immigration and Refugee Board.

Richey, P. 1976. "Explanations of Migration." *Annual Review of Sociology* 2:363–404.

Richmond. Anthony. 1974. "Migration, Ethnicity, and Race Relations." In *International Migration,* ed. G. Tapinos, Buenos Aires: CICRED.

———. 1988. "Socio-Cultural Adaptation of Immigrants." In *International Migration Today,* ed. C. Stahl. UNESCO: Center for Migration and Development Studies.

Rose El Youssif. 2000. "Migration to Egypt: Are Refugees Guests or Criminals." *Rose El Youssif* 3764:25–31.

Rouse, Roger. 1992. "Making Sense of Settlement: Class Transformation, Cultural Struggle, and Transnationalism among Mexican Migrants in the United States." In *Towards a Transnational Perspective on Migration,* ed. N. Schiller et al., 25–53. New York: New York Academy of the Sciences.

Roy, D. 1989. "Development Policy and Labor Migration in the Sudan." *Middle Eastern Studies* 25 (3): 300–322.

Rudnick, Edward. 1971. "The Immigration and Naturalization Service and the Administration of the Naturalization and Citizenship Laws." *International Migration Review* 4:420–36.

Ruiz, Hiram. 1998. "The Sudan: Cradle of Displacement." In *The Forsaken People,* ed. Roberta Cohen and Francis Deng, 139–75. Washington D.C.: Brookings Institution Press.

Russell, S. 1992. "International Migration and International Trade." Washington, D.C.: World Bank discussion paper.

Said, Edward. 1990. "Reflections on Exile." In *Out There: Marginalization and Contemporary Cultures,* ed. R. Ferguson, M. Gever, T. Mihn-ha, and C. West, 357–63. Cambridge, Mass.: MIT Press.

References

Saikinga, Ahmed. 2000. "Military Slavery and the Emergence of Southern Sudanese Diaspora in the Northern Sudan, 1884–1954." In *White Nile, Black Blood*, ed. Jay Spaulding and Stephanie Beswick, 23–39. Lawrenceville, N.J.: Red Sea Press.

Salih, Tayeb. 1979. *Season of Migration to the North*, trans. Denys Johnson-Davies. London: Heinemann.

Sanasarian, E. 1995. "State Dominance and Communal Perseverance: The Armenian Diaspora in the Islamic State of Iran, 1979–89." *Diaspora: Journal of Transnational Studies* 4 (3): 243–67.

Scott, David. 1991. "That Event, This Memory: Notes on the Anthropology of African Diasporas in the New World." *Diaspora: Journal of Transnational Studies* 1 (3): 261–85.

Scott, Joan. 1996. *Only Paradoxes to Offer: French Feminism and the Right of Man*. Cambridge, Mass.: Harvard University Press.

Seligman, C. G. 1932. *Pagan Tribes of the Niolitic Sudan*. London: Routledge.

Shah, Nasra. 2000. "Relative Success of the Male Workers in the Host Country, Kuwait: Do the Channels of Migration Matter?" *International Migration Review* 341 (1): 59–78.

Shakir, Evelyn. 1997. *Bint Arab: Arab and Arab American Women in the United States*. Westport, Conn.: Praeger.

Sidahmed, Abdel Salam. 1998. *Politics and Islam in Contemporary Sudan*. New York: St. Martin's Press.

Simmons, Ann. 2000. "Sudanese Teens Begin Journey to New Life: Resettlement in U.S. Poses Challenge for 'Lost Boys' of Country's Civil War." *Hartford Courant*, November 5, 2000, A12; reprinted from *Los Angeles Times*.

Simone, Abdou Maliqlim. 1994. *In Whose Image? Political Islam and Urban Practices in Sudan*. Chicago: University of Chicago Press.

Sowell, Thomas. 1996. *Migrations and Cultures*. San Francisco: Harper Collins.

Sudanet. Website for Discussion of Sudan's Concerns (http://www.sudanet.net).

Sudan Economic Survey. 1996. "El ard el Iqtissadi" (The economic survey). Khartoum: Ministry of Finance and Economic Planning.

Sudan Ministry of Labor. 1996. *Labor Force Survey*. Khartoum: Government Publications.

Teegardin, Carrie. 2000. "Life Better for Refugees, but Some Still Live in Squalor." *Atlanta Journal Constitution*, November 26.

Todaro, M. 1976. *Internal Migration in Developing Countries. A Review of Theory, Evidence, Methodology, and Research Priorities*. Geneva: International Labor Office.

Tölölyan, Khachig. 1996. "Rethinking Diaspora(s): Stateless Power in the Transnational Moment." *Diaspora: Journal of Transnational Studies* 5 (1): 3–36.

Toomey, Jeanne. 1951. "Arabs Find Welcome in Boro." *Brooklyn Eagle*. August 16, 1951, 10.

Turner, Richard. 1986. "Islam in New York in the 1920s: A New Quest in Afro-American Religion." Ph.D. diss., Princeton University.

———. 1997. *Islam in the African-American Experience*. Bloomington: Indiana University Press.

Ueda, Reed. 1994. *Postwar Immigrant America*. Boston: Bedford Books of St. Martin's Press.

United States Department of State. 1991. "Displaced Persons in the Middle East." *Fact Sheet*. United States Department of State Dispatch 2:199.

U.S. Copts Association Home Page. 2000–2001. (http://copts.com).

U.S. Committee for Refugees. 1999a. *Sudan: Personal Stories of Sudan's Uprooted People*. Washington, D.C.: U.S. Committee for Refugees.

——. 1999b. *Sudan Fact Sheet*. Washington, D.C.: U.S. Committee for Refugees.

U.S. Immigration and Naturalization Service. 1995. *INS Fact Book*. Washington D.C.: Government Printing Office.

——. 1999. *Statistical Yearbook of the Immigration and Naturalization Service*. Washington, D.C.: Government Printing Office.

Vatini, John. 1978. *Tarikh elmasihia fi elmamalik elnubia elgadima wa el Sudan elhadith* (History of Christianity in ancient Nubian kingdoms and modern Sudan). Khartoum: published by the author.

Voll, John. 1990. "Political Crisis in Sudan." *Current History* 89:153–56.

Voll, John,. ed. 1992. *Sudan: State and Society in Crisis*. Washington, D.C.: Middle East Institute.

Wai, Dunstan. 1973. "The Southern Sudan: The Country and the People." In *The Southern Sudan: The Problem of National Integration*, ed. Dunstan Wai. London: Frank Cass.

Wakin, Edward. 1963. *A Lonely Minority: The Modern Story of Egypt's Copts*. New York: Morrow.

Waller, John. 1988. *Gordon of Khartoum: The Saga of a Victorian Hero*. New York: Athenaeum.

Warburg, Gabriel. 1992. "The Sharia in Sudan: Implementation and Repercussions." In *Sudan: State and Society in Crisis*, ed. John Voll, 90–108. Washington, D.C.: Middle East Institute.

Warner, R. Stephen. 1993. "Work in Progress toward a New Paradigm for the Sociological Study of Religion in the United States." *American Journal of Sociology* 98:1044–93.

——. 1994. "The Place of the Congregation in the Contemporary American Religious Configuration." In *American Congregations*, vol. 2, ed. James P. Wind and James W. Lewis, 54–99. Chicago: University of Chicago Press.

Waters, Mary. 1990. *Ethnic Options: Choosing Identities in America*. Berkeley: University of California Press.

Waugh, Earle. 1991. "North America and the Adaptation of the Muslim Tradition: Religion, Ethnicity, and the Family." In *Muslim Families in North America*, ed. Earle Waugh et al., 68–101. Alberta: University of Alberta Press.

Weeks, Richard, ed. 1984. *Muslim Peoples: A World Ethnographic Survey*, 2d ed. Westport, Conn.: Greenwood Press.

White, Constance. 2000. "Alek Wek: Living a Model Life." *Essence* 31 (5): 160–224.

Williams, Raymond. 1989. *Resources of Hope: Culture, Democracy, and Socialism*. London: Verso.

Winter, Roger. 1999. Afterword to *Sudan: Personal Stories of Sudan's Uprooted People*. Washington D.C.: U.S. Committee on Refugees.

World Refugee Report. 1992. *A Report Submitted to the Congress as Part of the Consultations on FY 1993 Refugee Admissions to the U.S.* Washington, D.C.: Bureau for Refugee Programs.

References

Wright, Thomas, and Rody Onate. 1998. *Flight from Chile: Voices of Exile.* Albuquerque: University of New Mexico Press.

Yanney, Rudolph. 1989. "Aspects in the Life of the Copts and Their Church in the U.S." *Coptologia* 10:65–70.

Yans-McLaughlin, Virginia, ed. 1990. *Immigration Reconsidered: History, Sociology, and Politics.* Oxford: Oxford University Press.

Zarroug, Mohi el Din. 1991. "The Kingdom of Alwa." African Occasional Papers, no. 5. Calgary, Alberta: University of Calgary Press.

Zolberg, Aristide. 1989. *Escaping from Violence.* Oxford: Oxford University Press.

Index

Index

Cultural practices, 140–55
 borrowing, 55
 eids, 144–47
 female circumcision, 55, 149–53
 influence on North American society,
  153–55
 and Islam, 41–42, 147–49
 Mawlid Elnabawi, 147–48
 naming ceremonies, 143–44
 wedding ceremonies, 140–43
 See also Cultural resilience; Social networks
Cultural resilience
 bahhara, 33, 34, 38–39, 40
 Copts, 92
 and Nubian migration to Egypt, 19
 and religion, 41–42
 and southern Sudanese migration, 59, 60,
  63, 102
 See also Cultural practices

Darb El-Intifada, 157, 162–63
Deng, Francis, 49, 52
Desert Storm. *See* Post-Gulf War migration
Deskilling. *See* Downward mobility
Discrimination against migrants
 bahhara, 34–35
 and social networks, 139–40
 See also Racialization
Displacement. *See* Southern Sudanese inter-
  nal/African displacement
Diversity Visa Lottery Program, 10, 95,
  108–9, 119–20, 134–35
Downward mobility, 116–21
Drew Ali, Noble, 26–29
Drumtra, Jeff, 6–7
Dudu, Christina, 54

Economic adaptation, 115–27
 downward mobility, 116–21
 and globalization, 115–16
 and legal immigration status, 117, 120–21
 mutual support strategies, 121–22
 small businesses, 124–27
 women's roles in, 122–24, 125–27
Education, 9, 10, 43–44, 58
Egypt, migration to, 3, 6, 18–19, 92. *See also*
  Southern Sudanese internal/African dis-
  placement
Eid El Adha, 144–47
Eid Elfitr, 144–45
Eissa, Omer Salih, 129
El-Bashir, Omer, 67–68, 163. *See also*
  Political turmoil
Elmagherbi, Sammy, 140
Elmaraghi, Mustafa, 28–29, 30
El-Ray El-Akhar, 163
Eltigani, Azza, 94

Ethnic diversity, 50–51, 53
Evans-Pritchard, Edward, 2, 49
Evanzz, Karl, 25, 27

Fabian, Johannes, 161
Fadl, Mona Abul, 41–42
Family size, 108
Fanon, Franz, 49
Faris, James, 2
Fauset, Arthur, 27
Female circumcision, 55, 149–53
Feminization of migration. *See* Women
Fernea, Robert, 19
Folk art, 127

Garang, John, 132
Garvey, Marcus, 27
Geertz, Clifford, 21, 41
Geiser, Peter, 18
Ghorba, 128–29. *See also* Migrant adaptation
Globalization, 115–16
Green-card marriages, 10, 120
Gulf region migration, 72–74
 and female North American migration,
  77–78, 95, 104–8
 female schoolteachers, 94
 See also Post-Gulf War migration
Gulf War. *See* Post-Gulf War migration

Hajj, 5–6
Hale, Sondra, 99
Handlin, Oscar, 42
"Harvest for Sudan: Women's Peace
  Initiative" conference (1995), 104
Haykal, Mohamed Hasanain, 82
Henderson, K. D., 132–33
Henna tattooing, 127
Hijab, 89, 94
Hill, Richard, 2–3
Hobsbawm, Eric, 51
Hogg, Peter, 2–3
Holtzman, Jon, 67
Home ownership, 137–38
Hurreiz, Sayyid, 132

Ibrahim, Fatima Ahmed, 99, 103–4, 119,
  128, 157
Ightirab, 73–74
Illegal immigrants. *See* Legal immigration
  status
Internal displacement. *See* Southern
  Sudanese internal/African displacement
International oil companies, 158, 160
International refugee organizations. *See*
  Refugee resettlement organizations
Islam
 and migrant cultural practices, 41–42,
  147–49

Index

Political turmoil (*continued*)
 and southern secession, 61–63, 102–3
 and southern Sudanese migration, 7, 8–9,
  49–50, 57–58, 61, 101, 102–3
 See also Islamization; Migrant political life
Politics and Islam in Contemporary Sudan
 (Sidahmed), 52
Ports of entry, 9
Post-Gulf War migration, 72–80
 forced departure, 75–77
 and Gulf labor market restructuring,
  78–79, 80
 immigration policies, 79
 movements within, 77–78
 and Sudanese migration to Gulf region,
  72–74
 women, 77–78, 95, 104–8
Proletarianization. *See* Downward mobility

Qatar, 78–79

Racialization, 63–64, 164–66
Racism. *See* Racialization
Rahim, Mudathir Abdel, 5
Refugee resettlement organizations, 9, 58,
 59, 61, 70–71
Refugees. *See* Political turmoil; Refugee
 resettlement organizations; Southern
 Sudanese internal/African displacement;
 Southern Sudanese migration
Religious experience, 8, 92. *See also* Islam;
 Religious freedom
Religious freedom, 59, 62. *See also*
 Islamization
Research methods. *See* Methodological
 issues
Resettlement experience, 64–67
Residential distribution, 9, 137
Richmond, Anthony, 129–30
Rouse, Roger, 39
Ruiz, Hiram, 53

El-Sahifia, 163
Said, Edward, 164
Salih, Tayeb, 1
Sandug, 121
Saudi Arabia, 5–6, 78
Schilippe, Pierre de, 49
Seligman, Charles, 49
Sex ratios, 19
Shakir, Evelyn, 93
Shyam, Bhatia, 53
Sidahmed, Abdel Salam, 52
Simaya (naming ceremonies), 143–44
Simone, Abdou Maliqlim, 130
Simonse, Simon, 49
Slavery, 53, 68
Small businesses, 124–27

Social networks, 9, 133–38
 and chain migration, 134–37
 and discrimination, 139–40
 jalias, 138–40
 and southern Sudanese migration, 60
 and women, 100–101, 110–11
 See also Cultural practices
Southern Sudanese internal/African displacement
 acceptance of, 54
 extent of, 6, 7, 52
 living conditions, 56, 68–69
 and migrant political life, 158, 159
 and women, 54–55, 94–95
 See also Southern Sudanese migration
Southern Sudanese migration, 57–71
 and cultural resilience, 59, 60, 63, 102
 and ethnic diversity, 50–51
 impact on Sudanese communities, 54
 and Islamization, 57, 58, 60, 61
 and migrant political life, 64, 67–68, 158,
  159
 and political turmoil, 7, 8–9, 49–50, 57–58,
  61, 101, 102–3
 pull factors for, 59
 residential distribution, 137
 and southern secession, 61–63, 102–3
 unaccompanied children, 69–71
 women, 101–4
 See also Southern Sudanese
  internal/African displacement
Sowell, Thomas, 153
Sudanese American Society, 35, 37, 38
Sudanese Human Rights Organization,
 157
Sudanese migration
 diversity of, 3–4
 historical background, 2–3
Sudanese National Alliance, 157
Sudanese National Democratic Rally, 157,
 162
Sudanese People's Liberation Army, 132
Sudanese society, 4–7
 economy, 7, 44–45
Sudanese Victims of Torture Group, 157
Sudanese Women's Union, 103–4
Sudan Human Rights Organization, 157
Sudan Opposition Group, 157
Sudan's Women's Voice for Peace, 104
Support sources, 9

Terrorism, U.S. war on, 10
Tölölyan, Khachig, 13, 40
Turner, Richard, 24

UN High Commissioner for Refugees, 70
United States Committee for Refugees News,
 52

The Anthropology of Contemporary Issues
A series edited by Roger Sanjek

[191]

Lady Friends: Hawaiian Ways and the Ties That Define
by Karen L. Ito
Dismantling Apartheid: A South African Town in Transition
by Walton R. Johnson
Caribbean New York: Black Immigrants and the Politics of Race
by Philip Kasinitz
Antler on the Sea: The Yup'ik and Chukchi of the Russian Far East
by Anna M. Kerttula
The Solitude of Collectivism: Romanian Villagers to the Revolution and Beyond
by David A. Kideckel
Nuclear Summer: The Clash of Communities at the Seneca Women's Peace Encampment
by Louise Krasniewicz
Between Two Worlds: Ethnographic Essays on American Jewry edited by Jack Kugelmass
American Odyssey: Haitians in New York City
by Michel S. Laguerre
From Working Daughters to Working Mothers: Immigrant Women in a New England Industrial Community
by Louise Lamphere
Sunbelt Working Mothers: Reconciling Family and Factory
by Louise Lamphere, Patricia Zavella, Felipe Gonzales, and Peter B. Evans
Creativity/Anthropology
edited by Smadar Lavie, Kirin Narayan, and Renato Rosaldo
Cities, Classes, and the Social Order
by Anthony Leeds
Lesbian Mothers: Accounts of Gender in American Culture
by Ellen Lewin
Civilized Women: Gender and Prestige in Southeastern Liberia
by Mary H. Moran
Blood, Sweat, and Mahjong: Family and Enterprise in an Overseas Chinese Community
by Ellen Oxfeld
The Magic City: Unemployment in a Working-Class Community
by Gregory Pappas
The Korean American Dream: Immigrants and Small Business in New York City
by Kyeyoung Park
Inside the Revolution: Everyday Life in Socialist Cuba
by Mona Rosendahl
State and Family in Singapore: Restructuring an Industrial Society
by Janet W. Salaff
The Future of Us All: Race and Neighborhood Politics in New York City
by Roger Sanjek
Medicalizing Ethnicity: The Construction of Latino Identity in a Psychiatric Setting
by Vilma Santiago-Irizarry
Diamond Stories: Enduring Change on 47th Street
by Renée Rose Shield

115 end → geography

11 - gd quote on observer, observed

23 - imagined community

13 - diaspora